I0066599

INC 2014

Plymouth University, UK
8-9 July 2014

Proceedings of the
10th International Network Conference

Editors

Paul S Dowland
Steven M Furnell
Bogdan V Ghita

ISBN: 978-1-84102-373-1

Preface

This book presents the proceedings of the Tenth International Network Conference (INC 2014), hosted by Plymouth University, UK, from 8th to 9th July 2014.

A continuing aim of the INC series is to provide an opportunity for those involved in the design, development and use of network systems and applications to meet, share their ideas and exchange opinions. The 2014 event again succeeds in this aim by bringing together leading specialists from academia and industry, and enabling the presentation and discussion of the latest advances in research.

These proceedings contain a total of 16 papers (including three papers drawn from the 9th International Workshop on Digital Forensics and Incident Analysis). The papers cover many aspects of modern networking, including web technologies, network protocols and performance, security and privacy, mobile and wireless systems, and the applications and impacts of network technology. As such, it is hoped that all readers will find a variety of material of interest. Each paper was subjected to double-blind review by at least two members of the International Programme Committee. We would like to thank all of the reviewers for their efforts, as well as the authors for their willingness to share their ideas and findings.

The conference team is also most grateful to our keynotes speakers for accepting our invitation to share their expertise in the keynote lectures.

We hope that all of our delegates enjoy the conference, and that other readers of these proceedings will be able to join us on a future occasion.

Prof. Steven Furnell & Dr Bogdan Ghita
Conference Co-Chairs, INC 2014

Dr Nathan Clarke & Dr John Haggerty
Conference Co-chairs, WDFIA 2014

Plymouth, July 2014

About the Centre for Security, Communications and Network Research

The INC conference series is organised by the Centre for Security, Communications and Network Research (CSCAN) at Plymouth University, UK.

CSCAN is a specialist technology and networking research facility at Plymouth University. Originally established in 1984 (under the original name of the Network Research Group), the Centre conducts research in the areas of IT Security, Internet & WWW technologies and Mobility, and has a proven pedigree including projects conducted for, and in collaboration with, commercial companies, as well as participation in European research initiatives. Over the years, our research activities have led to numerous successful projects, along with associated publications and patents.

At the time of writing, the Centre has fifteen affiliated full-time academic staff and over sixty research degree projects (at PhD and MPhil levels). The Centre also supports Masters programmes in Communication Engineering and Signal Processing, Computer and Information Security, Computer Science and Network Systems Engineering, and hosts a significant number of research-related projects from these programmes.

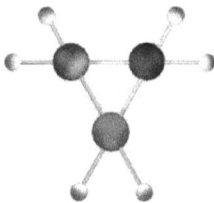

Address	Centre for Security, Communications and Network Research Plymouth University Drake Circus Plymouth PL4 8AA United Kingdom
Telephone	+44 (0) 1752 586 234
Fax	+44 (0) 1752 586 300
Email	info@cscan.org
URL	www.cscan.org

INC 2014 Committees

International Programme Committee

Nikos Antonopoulos	University of Derby	UK
Dominig ar Foll	Intel Open Source	Brittany-France
Harald Baier	Center for Advanced Security Research Darmstadt (CASED)	Germany
Frank Ball	Frank Ball Consulting	UK
Udo Bleimann	University of Applied Sciences Darmstadt	Germany
Eugen Borcoci	University POLITEHNICA of Bucharest	Romania
Reinhardt Botha	Nelson Mandela Metropolitan University	South Africa
Aurelian Bria	Ericsson	Sweden
Arslan Brömme	GI BIOSIG	Germany
Phil Brooke	Teesside University	UK
Nathan Clarke	Plymouth University	UK
Jeff Crume	IBM	USA
Mark Culverhouse	Cisco	UK
Paul Dowland	Plymouth University	UK
Mariki Eloff	University of South Africa	South Africa
Christophe Feltus	Public Research Centre Henri Tudor	Luxembourg
Klaus-Peter Fischer-Hellmann	Digamma Communications Consulting GmbH	Germany
Ulrich Flegel	HFT Stuttgart, University of Applied Sciences	Germany
Woldemar Fuhrmann	University of Applied Sciences, Darmstadt	Germany
Steven Furnell	Plymouth University	UK
Bogdan Ghita	Plymouth University	UK
Martin Gonzalez Rodriguez	University of Oviedo	Spain
Carsten Griwodz	Simula Research	Norway
Vic Grout	Glyndwr University, Wales	UK
Holger Hofmann	Cooperative State University Baden-Wurttemberg Mannheim	Germany
Vasilios Katos	Democritus University of Thrace	Greece
Sokratis Katsikas	University of Piraeus	Greece
Raj Kettimuthu	Argonne National Laboratory and The University of Chicago	USA
Martin Knahl	Furtwangen University	Germany
George Magklaras	University of Oslo	Norway
Dwight Makaroff	University of Saskatchewan	Canada
Jacques Ophoff	University of Cape Town	South Africa
Vassillis Prevelakis	Technische Universität Braunschweig	Germany
Shukor Razak	Universiti Teknologi Malaysia	Malaysia
Andreas Rinkel	University of Applied Sciences Rapperswill	Switzerland
Miguel Rio	University College London	UK
Angelos Rouskas	University of Piraeus	Greece
David Schwartz	Bar-Ilan University	Israel
Ingo Stengel	Plymouth University	UK
Kerry-Lynn Thomson	Nelson Mandela Metropolitan University	South Africa
Ulrich Trick	University of Applied Sciences Frankfurt/M.	Germany
Dimitrios D. Vergados	University of Piraeus	Greece
Merrill Warkentin	Mississippi State University	USA

Organising Committee

Paul Dowland, Steven Furnell, Bogdan Ghita

Keynote Speakers

Doug Williams
BT Research

Doug Williams works for BT research. He has a PHD in the design and fabrication of optical fibre devices; in more recent years his research has focused on understanding the applications and services that will fill the apparently limitless capacity of optical fibres.

David Emm
Kaspersky Lab

David Emm holds the position of Senior Security Researcher at Kaspersky Lab, a provider of security and threat management solutions. He has been with Kaspersky Lab since 2004 and worked in the antivirus industry since 1990 in a variety of roles, including that of Senior Technology Consultant with Dr. Solomon's and Systems Engineer and Product Manager at Network Associates.

David has a strong interest in malware, ID theft and the security industry in general and developed the company's Malware Defence Workshop. He is a knowledgeable advisor on all aspects of online security, and a regular presenter at exhibitions and events, frequently providing comment to both broadcast and print media on the latest security threats and how users can stay safe online.

Contents

Chapter 2: WDFIA Papers

Chapter 1

INC Papers

A Taxonomy of Defence Mechanisms to Mitigate DoS Attacks in MANETs

A.F.Alsumayt and J.Haggerty

School of Science and Technology, Nottingham Trent University, Clifton Campus, Clifton Lane, Nottingham, NG11 8NS, United Kingdom
e-mail: Albandari.Alsumayt2013@my.ntu.ac.uk; john.haggerty@ntu.ac.uk

Abstract

In recent years MANETs (Mobile ad hoc Network) have had a large prevalence in many sectors. Due to their nature, MANETs have faced some challenges, especially with regard to security;- dynamic topology, power and bandwidth constraints and the absence of central administration make MANETs vulnerable to many attacks. DoS (Denial of Service) attacks are a major problem for the network. These attacks deplete resources and greatly degrade network performance. In this paper, a taxonomy of the defence mechanisms is identified and their advantages and disadvantages are discussed. As posited in this paper, this taxonomy provides the basis for the development of an approach to detect DoS attacks in MANETs.

Keywords

MANET, Denial of Service, Intrusion detection

1. Introduction

It is notable that MANETs (Mobile *ad hoc* network) have received tremendous attention over the last few years with the rapid growth of the interconnected network technologies. When there is a pressing need to communicate between devices, MANETs help to set up a connection without any fixed infrastructure. It is a type of wireless network and includes the contents of a group or collection of nodes that communicate with each other without any central form of administration such as access points. Each node in MANET is considered to be a router and a host for forwarding and receiving packets. The use of MANETs have been proposed for emergency and disaster situations and may be utilised in other environments such as conferences, meeting rooms, the military arena and airports. There are other advantages of MANETs such as high level of convenience, small size, support for many different devices (laptops, smart phones, iPads, etc) as well as the low costs of setting the network up and high mobility. There are also some disadvantages such as power constraints, link failures and a lack of security. Indeed, as there is little or no central management in MANETs, security awareness is critical.

In the MANET environment there are many problems that need to be tackled such as quality of service (QoS), optimization, scalability and security issues. The main interest here is security; in particular, the mitigation of DoS (Denial of Service) attacks. As discussed above, the continuous changing topology of MANETs, its dynamic nature, and the fact that it has no central administration makes it vulnerable to many attacks. Applying security to MANETs is a complex task. Many security parameters need to be applied for a MANET to be considered secure: confidentiality, integrity, availability, non-repudiation and authentication. As such, many challenges to security in MANETs remain. First, as mentioned above, the power and resource constraints on nodes limit cryptographic measures which are used to apply a secure connection in other environments. In addition, bandwidth constraints can prevent nodes from communicating with other nodes which are not in the network domain. Second, static configuration is not generally effective in a MANET environment. For example, any node can pretend to be a legitimate node and provide incorrect information. Third, nodes without a central management and with dynamic topologies may lead to compromise and the ability to launch some attacks, such as DoS.

A DoS attack paralyses and degrades the performance of the network resulting in the unavailability of key network nodes. This kind of disruptive attack affects and causes harm in many ways such as financial losses, time wasting, and wasting of resources. If one popular and successful website such as Amazon is affected by such an attack even for an hour, the financial losses can be huge. There is not always a clear reason for the attackers to perpetrate such an attack and range from personal reasons such as the desire for revenge against certain organisations, gain prestige or the respect of the hacker community or for political reasons. Thus MANET is vulnerable to DoS attack. This is due to a number of contributory factors; their open nature, lack of authentication, heterogeneity of devices, no central control beyond network tasks such as IP address configuration and allocation, and lack of computing resources for security countermeasures. There are many types of DoS attack and each attack has a different mechanism requiring a specific algorithm to detect it.

The novelty of this paper is that existing taxonomies have been posited for DoS attack in general but not specifically aimed at MANETs. The aim of this paper is to examine approaches to DoS attacks in other network environments to determine the requirements for a novel approach to detect such attacks in MANETs. This paper therefore posits a taxonomy of such approaches.

The rest of the paper is organized as follows. Section 2 illustrates related work. Section 3 presents the taxonomy of different approaches to handle DoS attacks on MANETs and a discussion of this taxonomy and its applicability to MANETs. Finally, section 4 concludes the paper and proposes future work.

2. Related work

This section outlines related work in MANET and DoS attack mitigation, beginning with the common or traditional methods such as firewalls. Different approaches are also illustrated with regard to preventing DoS attacks.

Madhurya et al. (2014) identify the advantages and limitations of MANETs. In addition, a novel cryptographic algorithm named Disturbance Detection System (DDS) has been proposed in order to detect attacks on MANET. Garg et al. (2009) also specify the challenges to MANET such as dynamic topology, bandwidth and power constraints. The MANET architecture is shown below in Figure 1.

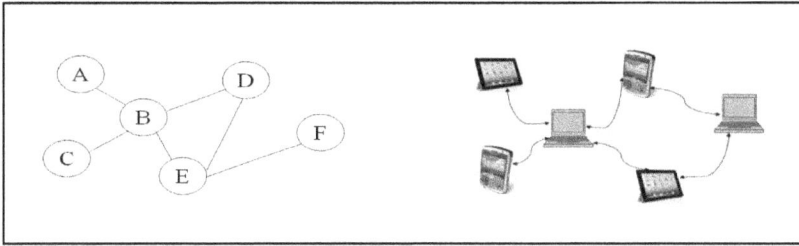

Figure 1: The MANET architecture

Khan and Vasta (2011) present a novel mechanism to detect DDoS (Distributed Denial of Service) attacks on MANETs based on reputation. The architecture of both DoS and DDoS attacks are shown below in Figure 2.

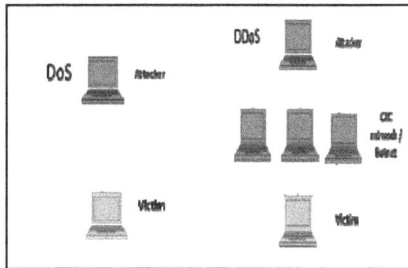

Figure 2: The architecture of DoS and DDoS attacks

Many defence mechanisms have been used to mitigate DoS attacks on MANET. Gupta et al. (2012) posits some common defence approaches against DoS attacks such as firewalls. A firewall is a system that is set up in order to monitor and control traffic between two networks. Unfortunately, the traditional firewall is considered to be unreliable because firewalls cannot distinguish between normal traffic and DoS attack traffic. Moreover, firewalls are susceptible to this type of attack as they act as a chokepoint between internal and external networks. Firewalls have simple and basic rules, such as allowing or denying some ports or IP addresses. In addition, most people do not keep their firewall up to date, which raises the level of vulnerability. Thus, distributed firewalls work efficiently in MANETs to prevent DoS attack. . In addition, many small devices do not have the computational power to employ such countermeasures or provide only limited security functions.

Akram et al. (2009) point out that distributed firewalls use a central policy framework which defines inbound and outbound movements, and seek to define what is permitted and appropriate connectivity. The distributed firewalls are designed to be reconfigurable so it can be considered that they are used in filtering in MANETs.

Filtering is another technique to mitigate DoS attacks. Filtering could be local or global. Local filtering means that filtering is implemented on the victim's side or the local network. This method is considered a short-time solution, and involves installing a filter on the local router to stop the infiltrating IP packets. DoS attack exploits the deficiencies of the internet and sometimes local filtering is unable to solve the problem. Global filtering is better to mitigate DoS attacks from the logical standpoint. In global or coordinated filtering, the idea is based on preventing any

5

accumulation of malicious packets in an appropriate time frame. Filters are installed throughout the internet, thereby helping victims to disseminate information about the detected attacks. As a result, the malicious packets will be stopped early. This method is effective, even though the intruder succeeds in seizing many botnets to launch the attack. Tyagi et al. (2013) assume that this technique cannot be considered reliable as sometimes the packets can overwhelm the router and cause a DoS attack.

Tan et al. (2005) propose the statistical filtering concept. This is considered to be a reactive method of detecting DDoS attacks in MANETs by using traffic profiling for the purpose of filtering and detection. The main advantage of using this mechanism is that the packet delivery ratio is raised, whereas the average end-to-end delay is clearly decreased. The major limitation of using this method is the cluster-based routing protocol filtering mechanism.

An IDS (Intrusion Detection System) is another common approach to mitigate DoS attack. Shrestha et al. (2010) propose a novel intrusion detection system to detect malicious nodes that perform DoS attacks. By exploiting the information which is available this protocol helps to improve the detection process drastically. Sahu et al. (2013) classify the different attacks and methods which are used for IDS and specify some challenges and limitations of IDS such as resource usage problem, reliability problems, and fidelity problems.

Another method of detecting DoS attacks is Watchdog, as proposed by Marti et al. (2000). This method shows how it is possible to increase the throughput of the network despite the presence of malicious nodes. The aim of this method is to detect nodes that are misbehaving. Watchdog is set in this node when forwarding a packet to ensure that the next node will also forward the packet in the same path. Watchdog performs this task by listening to all nodes within the transmission range in the network. The node will be tagged as a misbehaving node if it fails to forward the packet to the next node. The limitations of the Watchdog scheme fail to detect malicious nodes in some situations as posited by Buddha (2013). For instance, Watchdog cannot detect malicious nodes in the presence of receiver collisions, limited power for transmission or false misbehaviour reports. These limitations mean the Watchdog method is not an ideal method of detecting DoS attack. According to the easy implantation and the effectiveness of the Watchdog mechanism, many methods, such as Pathrater, use it as a base. With the Pathrater method, each node uses the information which is obtained from Watchdog to rate its neighbours. Neighbour nodes can be classified as members, fresh, unstable or malicious.

Jin et al. (2006) propose ZSBT traceback which is another method of detecting denial of service. Traceback is a useful method which helps identify the source of an attacker. Belenky et al. (2003) assume that manual traceback schemes have many disadvantages, such as management cost, inaccuracy of results and slow tracking speeds.

Ioannidis et al. (2002) posit a pushback approach to detect DDoS attacks. In a pushback mechanism, routers are enabled to identify the high bandwidth aggregates that contributes to the congestion rate and helps to limit it.

Khan and Vasta (2011) propose another scheme to detect DoS attacks in MANET based on using a reputation-based incentive mechanism. In order to perform reputation data management in distributed states, the authors suggest a clustering architecture. It might be possible to compromise a DoS attack via the information exchange and via collaborative monitoring.

A related method which is used to avoid DoS attack in MANET is trust between nodes. The first research into trust management for network security was carried out by Blaze et al.(1996).

DiDDeM (**Di**stributed **Do**S **De**tection **M**echanism) is another method for the early detection of DoS attack, which is described by Haggerty et al. (2005). The strength and effectiveness of this scheme stem from the early detection of DoS which enable a quick response in order to block the attack on the attack source side rather than on the intended victim's side.

This paper aims to find a new method of detecting DoS attacks on MANET, taking into consideration the existing methods of detecting DoS attacks. In the next section, a taxonomy is outlined which can help to develop a new approach to detecting DoS attacks in the MANET environment. The main contribution of this study is to: Determine the features and limitations of the existing defence approaches, and use these results to develop a novel approach to mitigate DoS attacks on MANETs.

3. A Taxonomy of DoS attack in MANET

The term 'taxonomy' refers to an order or classification of things according to specific conditions. In this paper, a taxonomy of defence approaches to detect DoS attacks on MANET is discussed. General detection methods to detect DoS attack, with their advantages and limitations are explained. As suggested in Section 1, there are many challenges to MANET security and it can become vulnerable to severe attacks, such as DoS attacks. There is a pressing need to mitigate such attacks in order to maintain security in the network. The victims of this attack could be a whole network, resources, or users. This Section presents taxonomy based on identifying the advantages and disadvantages of existing defences against DoS attack.

The taxonomy of common detection methods to detect DoS attack with their advantages and limitations are shown in Table 1.

Detection method	Advantages	Disadvantages
Firewalls and proxies	Has simple rules and easy to perform commands. (Gupta et al, 2012)	Firewalls cannot prevent DoS attack because it is hard to it to distinguish between legitimate and malicious traffic. (Gupta et al, 2012)
Ingress/ egress filtering	Success in thwarting DoS attacks before they are launched. (Jain et al,2011)	Unreliable in compromised machines – difficult to deploy this method universally. (Tupakula et al,2003)
Monitor process based on Bloom filter technique	Success in detecting attacks such as SYN flooding attack. (Geneiatakis et al, 2009)	Resource consumption such as CPU time, bandwidth, and memory during detection. (Geneiatakis et al, 2009)
Using statistical tests. Determining the threshold value of the normal traffic flow and checking it against incoming threshold. Comparing income traffic with normal traffic is the main method used here, in order to detect attacks.	This method gives an impression of the packet flow. (Chen ,2009)	It is difficult to model and even estimate the network traffic. (Chen ,2009)
Abnormal statistical method based on correlation analysis. The main idea of this method is based on extracting the anomalies from the network traffic	This method is intended to detect this attack compared with other methods by monitoring the derivation in co-relation analysis of the network traffic. (Li et al,2008)	The efficacy of this method could be unreliable if the attacker perpetrates a DoS attack using a low rate. (Li et al,2008)
An AIDS (Agent Intrusion Detection System) based on Chi-Square statistical method	It is necessary to analyse the variation and the amount of the packet which is sent by the sender. (Leo and Pai ,2009)	As this method is based on statistical analysis, it does not reflect the behaviour of AIDS. There are limitations of the communication performance (latency). (Leo and Pai ,2009)
Using detection method and a prevention algorithm based on a data mining concept	This technique can do a quick identification to determine if the traffic is normal or not. Moreover, this method can detect a DoS attack at an early stage. (Garg and Chawla ,2011)	Overhead in resource consumption such as CPU time and memory. (Garg and Chawla ,2011)
Hybrid IDS (Intrusion Detection System) based on an artificial neural network	Qualitative and quantative analysis has been applied in this method. This approach has a roughly 90% detection rate. (Jirapummin et al,2002)	This method fails to detect modern and current DoS and DDoS attacks. (Jirapummin et al,2002)
Uses fuzzy logic method	This method attains good results in detecting DoS attack. (Tuncer and Tatar ,2008)	It is difficult to model network traffic before and after an attack due to the packet flow characteristics. (Tuncer and Tatar ,2008)
Trust management / reputation	The effectiveness of trust management is that it is possible without any previous interactions so the nodes in the network can participate with an acceptable average of trust relationships of nodes. (Li et al,2012)	It is not based on an entirely decentralised concept, just localised trust management which is essential for policy information. (Li et al,2012)
Using machine learning algorithm	This method success to detect many types of DoS attacks such as ICMP flood and SYN flood attacks. (Suresh and Anitha ,2011)	This method increases the overhead of the network and cannot be integrated with the new types of attacks. Equally important is the redundant alert which is annoying as the attack. (Suresh and Anitha ,2011)

Table 1: the taxonomy of the existing detection methods against DoS attack

Related to Table 1, it can be seen that an optimal approach to mitigating DoS attacks without any flaws is rare. Common approaches such as firewalls, filtering, IDS,

Traceback, and Pushback which help to mitigate attacks are used on both the victim server and source server sides and even between them. Obviously, the nature of a MANET makes it hard to manage an attack. For example, filtering is unreliable for the detection of anomalies in MANET according to the continuous changing topology. Moreover, a firewall cannot prevent malicious nodes in when performing a DoS attack in a MANET according to its architecture. A distributed firewall is designed especially for MANET (Akram et al., 2009) which can protect network bandwidth and also end-host resources. The only problem with a distributed firewall is the need to use cryptographic operations which apply overhead to the network and cause latency.

There are some common disadvantages of the existing approaches such as latency in detection, resource consumption, difficulties in universal deployment, unreliability and difficulty in distinguishing between legitimate and malicious traffic. These flaws mean that the use of these approaches is not completely secure in the MANET environment. For example, monitor process is based on the Bloom filter technique, using a detection method and a prevention algorithm based on a data mining concept, and using a machine learning algorithm containing some of the common limitations.

Abnormal statistical method based on correlation analysis is another method to detect anomalies. The efficiency of this method is better than others to detect attacks like DoS attacks, but not if the attack rate is low. Therefore, identifying an attack in this situation is described as unreliable. In AIDS, there is a need to decrease the latency in detecting malicious nodes, which will be optimal for detecting DoS attacks in the early stages. Using a detection method and a prevention algorithm based on a data mining concept is efficient for the detection of DoS attacks in the early stages. The only drawback of this method is the resource consumption on the network and again that not capable with the energy constrained in MANET. Besides, the hybrid IDS, which is based on an artificial neural network, succeeds in detecting 90% of both DoS and DDoS attacks, respectively. However, this type of intrusion detection system is considered an old method and fails to detect new algorithms or types of DoS and DDoS attacks.

Using the fuzzy logic method gains excellent results for detecting DoS attacks, but it is difficult to deploy it in a MANET, as with a dynamic topology, it is hard to model the packet flow before and after the attack.

One of the modern methods to mitigate DoS attacks is based on trust management and reputation. Vasta (2011) posited the scheme to detect DoS attacks based on reputation between nodes by information exchange. In addition, trust management is considered a separate component of security services within the network. The effectiveness of trust management is that it is possible that the nodes in the network can participate, without any previous interaction, with an acceptable average of trust relationships. The main objectives of this framework are to support localised control and relationships by binding public keys to allow the access control process without complex security authentication procedures. The only limitation of this method is that it is not based on an entirely decentralised concept, just the localised trust management, which is not appropriate in MANET (Blaze et al., 1996).

Furthermore, considering a node as being always malicious or trusted can affect network communication. There is a pressing need to design a novel method to detect a DoS attack on MANET and to consider the limitations of the existing methods, along with the following four factors. First, any node should have an ID number, which establishes its identity. Second, each node should be subject to regular monitoring, so that its state as either normal or malicious can be established. Third, it is crucial to find a way to distinguish between legitimate and malicious traffic which will help in detecting this attack at an early stage and avoiding false alarms. Fourth, time and resource consumption should be considered in developing the new approach. The novel approach should try to correct the weaknesses of some approaches which help to mitigate DoS attacks as much as possible.

This section discusses the results of Section3 and also briefly analyses the elements of the taxonomy.

4. Conclusion and future work

MANETs have risen in prominence in recent years due to the requirement for heterogeneous devices to be networked together seamlessly. However, there are many challenges to this network environment such as power constraints and lack of computational resources available for security functions. This ensures that this environment is vulnerable to many attacks such as DoS. Such attacks can withstand some common defence mechanisms like firewalls. In this paper, a taxonomy of approaches to DoS in larger networks with more computational resources available has been conducted in order to identify the requirements of DoS attack mitigation in MANETs. This taxonomy takes into account the approaches to detection and response to DoS attacks. Future work aims to develop new and novel methods of detecting DoS attacks in MANETs. It will also be necessary to account for the results of these taxonomies, the location of the detectors and the flaws in the existing defence methods in order to mitigate the DoS attack in a better way.

5. References

Akram, S., Zubair, I. & Islam, M. H. (2009, July). Fully distributed dynamically configurable firewall to resist DOS attacks in MANET. In *Networked Digital Technologies, 2009. NDT'09. First International Conference on* (pp. 547-549). IEEE.

Belenky, A. & Ansari, N. (2003). IP traceback with deterministic packet marking. *Communications Letters, IEEE, 7*(4), pp. 162-164.

Blaze, M., Feigenbaum, J. & Lacy, J. (1996, May). Decentralized trust management. In Security and Privacy, 1996. *Proceedings., 1996 IEEE Symposium on (pp. 164-173). IEEE.*

Buddha, G. (2013). Improved watchdog intrusion detection systems In MANET. *International Journal of Engineering, 2* (3).

Chen, C. L. (2009). A New Detection Method for Distributed Denial-of-Service Attack Traffic based on Statistical Test. *J. UCS, 15*(2), 488-504.

Garg, K., & Chawla, R. (2011). Detection of DDOS attacks using data mining.*International Journal of Computing and Business Research (IJCBR), 2*(1).

Garg, N., & Mahapatra, R. P. (2009). MANET Security issues. *International Journal of Computer Science and Network Security, 9*(8), 241.

Geneiatakis, D., Vrakas, N., & Lambrinoudakis, C. (2009). Utilizing bloom filters for detecting flooding attacks against SIP based services. *computers & security, 28*(7), 578-591.

Gupta, B. B., Joshi, R. C. & Misra, M. (2012). Distributed Denial of Service Prevention Techniques. *arXiv preprint arXiv:1208.3557.*

Haggerty, J., Shi, Q., & Merabti, M. (2005). Early detection and prevention of denial-of-service attacks: a novel mechanism with propagated traced-back attack blocking. *Selected Areas in Communications, IEEE Journal on, 23(*10), 1994-2002.

Ioannidis, J. & Bellovin, S. M. (2002). Implementing pushback: Router-based defense against DDoS attacks.

Jain, P., Jain, J., & Gupta, Z. (2011). Mitigation of Denial of Service (DoS) Attack.*International Journal of Computational Engineering & Management IJCEM, 11.*

Jin, X., Zhang, Y., Pan, Y. & Zhou, Y. (2006). ZSBT: A novel algorithm for tracing DoS attackers in MANETs. *EURASIP Journal on Wireless Communications and Networking,* 2006(2), pp. 82-82.

Jirapummin, C., Wattanapongsakorn, N., & Kanthamanon, P. (2002). Hybrid neural networks for intrusion detection system. In *ITC-CSCC: International Technical Conference on Circuits Systems, Computers and Communications* (pp. 929-932).

Khan, R., & Vatsa, A. K. (2011). Detection and control of DDOS attacks over reputation and score based MANET. *J Emerg Trends Comput Inf Sci, 2*(11), 646-655.

Leu, F. Y., & Pai, C. C. (2009, August). Detecting DoS and DDoS Attacks using Chi-Square. In *Information Assurance and Security, 2009. IAS'09. Fifth International Conference on* (Vol. 2, pp. 255-258). IEEE.

Li, W., Parker, J. & Joshi, A. (2012). Security through collaboration and trust in manets. *Mobile Networks and Applications, 17*(3), pp. 342-352.

Li, Z. L., Hu, G. M., & Yang, D. (2008, July). Global abnormal correlation analysis for DDoS attack detection. In *Computers and Communications, 2008. ISCC 2008. IEEE Symposium on* (pp. 310-315). IEEE.

Madhurya, M., Krishna, B. A., & Subhashini, T. (2014). Implementation of Enhanced Security Algorithms in Mobile Ad hoc Networks. *International Journal of Computer Network & Information Security, 6* (2).

Marti, S., Giuli, T. J., Lai, K. & Baker, M. (2000, August). Mitigating routing misbehaviour in mobile ad hoc networks. In *International Conference on Mobile Computing and Networking: Proceedings of the 6th annual international conference on Mobile computing and networking* (Vol. 6, No. 11, pp. 255-265).

Sahu, L. & Sinha, C. (2013). A cooperative Approach to understanding the behaviour of intrusion detection systems in mobile ad hoc networks. *International Journal Of Computer Science, 1*(1)

Shrestha, R., Han, K. H., Choi, D. Y., & Han, S. J. (2010, April). A novel cross layer intrusion detection system in MANET. In *Advanced Information Networking and Applications (AINA), 2010 24th IEEE International Conference on* (pp. 647-654). IEEE.

Suresh, M., & Anitha, R. (2011). Evaluating Machine Learning Algorithms for Detecting DDoS Attacks. *In Advances in Network Security and Applications* (pp. 441-452). Springer Berlin Heidelberg.

Tan, H. X. & Seah, W. K. (2005, December). Framework for statistical filtering against DDoS attacks on MANETs. In *Embedded Software and Systems, 2005. Second International Conference on* (pp. 8-pp). IEEE.

Tuncer, T., & Tatar, Y. (2008, April). Detection SYN flooding attacks using fuzzy logic. In *Information Security and Assurance, 2008. ISA 2008. International Conference on* (pp. 321-325). IEEE.

Tupakula, U. K. & Varadharajan, V. (2003, February). A practical method to counteract denial of service attacks. In *Proceedings of the 26th Australasian computer science conference-Volume 16* (pp. 275-284). Australian Computer Society, Inc.

Tyagi, S. S. (2013). Analysis of techniques for mitigating DOS attacks on MANET. *International Journal of Engineering, 2* (4).

Smart Grid Communications:
A Renewed Challenge to Multiservice Networking

F.Ball[1], K.Basu[2], A.Maqousi[3] and T.Balikhina[3]

[1]Frank Ball Consulting, Oxford, UK.
[2]Oxford Brookes University, Oxford, UK.
[3] University of Petra, Amman, Jordan.
e-mail: Frank_ball@ntlworld.com; kbasu@brookes.ac.uk;
{amaqousi|tbalikhina}@uop.edu.jo

Abstract

This paper focuses on the multiservice aspects of the Smart Grid communications system with particular emphasis on the real time requirements of its control system. A general outline of the Smart Grid is presented and its general communications requirements are identified. The stringent real-time requirements of substation and transmission line control are discussed in greater detail. An overview of previous and current research into multiservice networking is given with the aim of identifying areas that need to be revisited, and extended, in order to meet the real time needs of the Smart Grid. The paper then presents proposals for future research into number of specific areas relevant to meeting these requirements.

Keywords

Smart Grid communications; Multiservice Networking; Network Control Systems.

1. Introduction

The Smart Grid concept is motivated by the desire to make greater use of renewable energy sources and the need for a more efficient utilisation of existing energy supplies. The realization of the Smart Grid involves the amalgamation of a power distribution network and a communications system so that together they become a single more powerful system

Communication systems have played an important role in the management of power grids for many years, supporting both data acquisition for systems monitoring, and control functions. Existing power grids are mainly concerned with bulk generation of power, and its transmission and distribution to the consumers, who generally play a passive role in the process. However, in the Smart Grid, not only will there be a greater variety of power generation sources to manage, including many based on renewable energy, there will also be the need for more efficient control over existing resources. Furthermore the consumer's role will no longer be passive. The introduction of smart metering, demand response, real time pricing and other interactive services will enable consumers to have greater control over their energy consumption. Consumers will also have the opportunity to implement the monitoring and control of smart devices within their own domain through the deployment of home area networks (HANs) that will be connected to, and thereby becoming part of, the Smart Grid communications system. Furthermore, the most significant paradigm shift is that consumers can also become suppliers, generally via renewable energy sources, e.g. solar, wind or water power. In addition to providing services for the monitoring, control and management of the technological infrastructure of the Smart Grid its communication system will be expected to provide services for a wide range of commercial and organizational activities, example of which include smart meter reading, automatic billing, real-time pricing, marketing etc. Many of these applications will have requirements very similar to those of applications being served by the current Internet, including the need for wide area, and possibly global, interconnectivity. Therefore, it is generally agreed that IP networks will form the basic transport mechanism for Smart Grid communications. However, many Smart Grid control functions have real-time requirements, some of which are both time critical and stringent. Therefore, the Smart Grid communication system will need to be a fully multiservice network. This paper presents an outline of the Smart Grid to identify its general characteristics and discusses its communications requirements with particular focus on its real-time needs. It then reviews the current state of research into multiservice networking, identifying what requirements can be met by existing facilities and those that will need additional support to be developed. The paper then presents some proposals for future research aimed at meeting the real-time requirements of the Smart Grid.

The remainder of this paper is structured as follows: section 2 introduces the Smart Grid and indentifies its communication requirements; section 3 discusses previous works into multiservice networking, indentifies the current state of the Internet's multiservice capabilities, and reviews more recent developments that could contribute to Smart Grid communications; section 4 presents some proposals for further research aimed at meeting the real-time requirements of Smart Grid communication; and finally section 5 concludes.

2. The Smart Grid

Over the past few year researchers have been addressing the problems of evolving and extending grid communications into a greater and more heterogeneous system that can support, and will help bring into being, the Smart Grid. This body of work has focused largely on the overall physical systems architecture of the smart grid, considering general infrastructure, the interoperation and integration of heterogeneous technologies and the relationship between different participants in the Smart Grid (Bouhafs 2012, Budka 2010, Fan 2010). It has resulted in the generalization of a Smart Grid system, a simplified topology of which is shown in Fig. 1. It has also addressed the challenge of Smart Grid communications and the Quality of Service (QoS) requirements of Smart Grid applications and services, including management, control and security (Budka 2010, Fan 2010). Collectively, this body of work presents a general picture of the Smart Grid system and its basic requirements that generally can be summarized by the following points.

- The Smart Grid will have a hierarchical structure
- It will comprise multiple domains of ownership that do not necessarily have a one-to-one correspondence with the hierarchical structure.
- It will involve bi-directional flow of both power and information.
- The Smart Grid will be built using heterogeneous technology.

- Its communication infrastructure will need to provide appropriate QoS for a number of different classes of communications traffic some of which will have stringent timing requirements
- Both power distribution and communications will need to be secure and robust.
- Because of the need for wide area connectivity, it is generally expected that IP networks will provide the basic transport mechanism for Smart Grid communications.

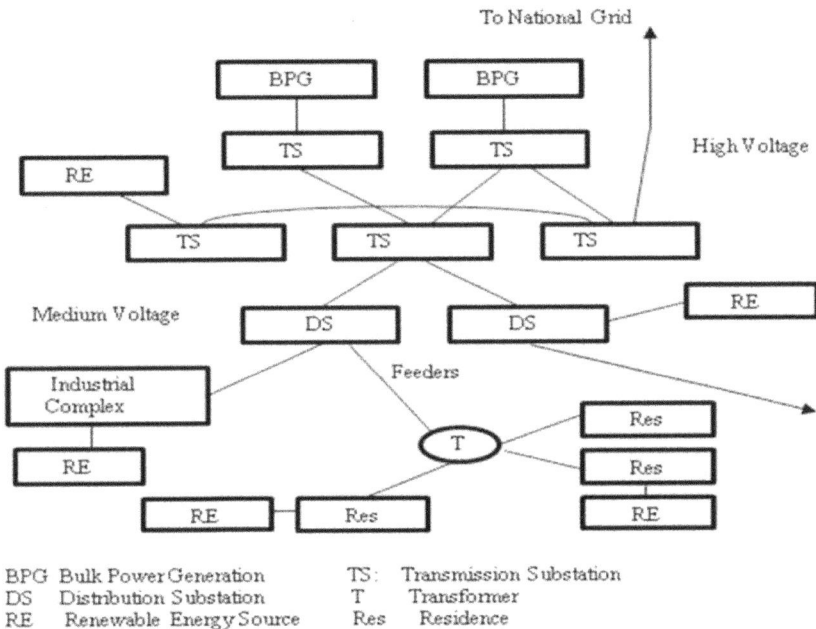

BPG Bulk Power Generation   TS: Transmission Substation
DS   Distribution Substation   T   Transformer
RE   Renewable Energy Source   Res   Residence

Figure 1: A Simple Example of a Smart Grid Topology

2.1. Heterogeneity and Diversity in the Smart Grid

The Smart Grid will comprise a wide range of heterogeneous equipment and technologies in both its power distribution network and it communications system. There will be a wide diversity of stakeholders and multiple domains of ownership. To compound this, these domains of ownership may not always correspond directly to the power distribution hierarchy. Furthermore, Smart Grid consumers can play a more active role in the control of their consumption (Bouhafs 2012, Budka 2010, Jeon 2011) and will also have the opportunity to become consumer-suppliers. In some cases the consumer-supplier could be a relative large scale industrial complex, in which case it could well have its own networked control system interconnect to the Smart Grid communications system. Although not as yet widely discussed, there is also the potential for communities of consumer-suppliers to form their own mini-grids of renewable energy resources and thereby sharing surplus generation between themselves before taking from, or putting into, the main grid. Because of this diversity the problem of building the Smart Grid will need to be addressed at multiple levels of abstraction, and to consider numerous different perspectives, e.g. scientific, technical, commercial, economic, political and social etc.

2.2. Smart Grid Communications Requirements

Wang and Khanna (Wang 2011) present a thorough and comprehensive discussion on the requirements for Smart Grid communications. In this section we highlight those elements which are most relevant to the objective of this paper. Firstly, the Smart Grid communication system will have many requirements in common with the global Internet and other networks, i.e. it will need to be reliable, secure and resilient (Sterbenz 2020). One difference being, that certain Smart Grid applications require a reliability of better than 99.999%, which translates to an average downtime of 5.3 minutes/year (Budka 2010). Also, many of the applications relating to its commercial activities such a marketing, customer relations, financial transaction etc. will have requirements identical to this type of application currently being served by the Internet.

The most significant difference arises due to the requirements of Smart Grid control applications, in particular substation control and transmission line monitoring. Both require real-time bidirectional communications and for certain of their activities, e.g. teleprotection, the real-time requirements are quite stringent. These are also the applications that have the highest reliability requirements. Furthermore, it is almost certain that meeting these requirements will be enforced by regulation. Failure of teleprotection applications may result in outages, destruction of grid infrastructure, and in the worst case, potential loss of life (Budka 2010). Exchange of protection information has the shortest delay requirements: 10ms for messages conveying control and monitoring information; and 3ms for urgent fault reporting messages (Wang 2011). Delay is defined as the end-to-end delay, including both processing latency and network delays. Response messages have identical delay requirements. This class of traffic will require high transmission rates, but will produce a relatively low volume of traffic. Teleprotection devices produce continuous data streams with typical rates of between 60 and 100 messages per second for control and monitoring, and individual asynchronous messages for fault reporting. Also, in the case of substation control the domain of operation is within a relatively small geographical area as shown below in Figure 2.

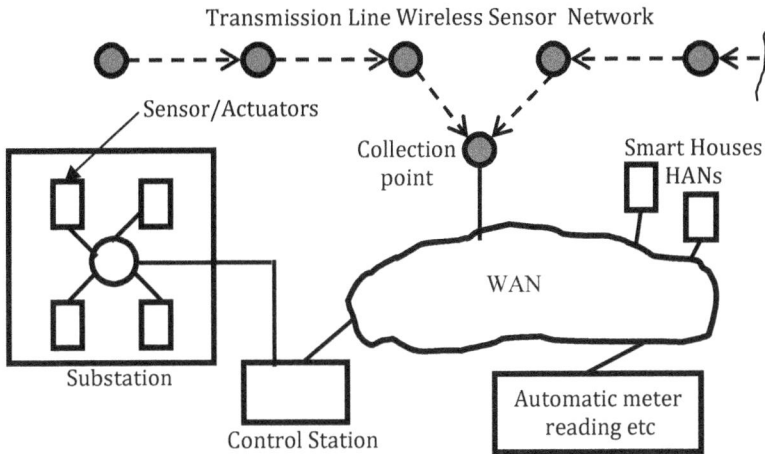

Figure 2: Substation and Transmission Control Domain

However, as shown in figure 2, protection information for transmission line monitoring may need to pass through a wide area network. Furthermore, for reasons of economy it is generally expected that wireless sensor networks will be used to collect real-time status information. Therefore, meeting the real time requirements of transmission line monitoring may be more problematic than meeting those of substation control. Substation control and transmission line monitoring are both examples of a Networked Control System (NCS) (Gupta 2010), i.e. a control system that operates over an open network that is shared with other classes of traffic. Designers of NCSs face two challenges: maintaining the appropriate QoS in the networks; and ensuring that the required Quality of Control (QoC) is provided. Therefore research into NCSs focuses on two objectives: Control of the network, to ensure a suitable QoS; and control over the network, that seeks to minimise adverse conditions in the network. The possibility that NCSs methodologies could achieve some relaxation of the more strident timing requirements is worthy of further investigation. Other Smart Grid applications that have less stringent real-time requirements are: voice communication, whose requirements are identical to those of VoIP; and video streaming for surveillance, the requirement of which are not as yet defined.

Finally, due to the complexity of the Smart Grid and diversity of its requirement a significant number of researchers support the need for a new reference model for Smart Grid communications (Bouhafs 2012, Budka 2010, Fan 2010, Jeon 201, Maqousi 2013).

3. Multiservice for Smart Grid Communications

Research into multiservice networking began more than two decades ago and early work clearly demonstrated that in order to meet QoS requirements of different classes of data traffic, continuous media traffic (real-time audio and video) and other real-time traffic within the same network three basic functions must be provided within that network (Campbell 1997): Bandwidth Partitioning or Class isolation; Admission Control; and Access Control. Also, the general philosophy at this time was that meeting QoS was the primary objective, and efficient utilization of bandwidth was a secondary goal. This early research activity focused on bandwidth partitioning mechanisms leading to the development of WQF, CBQ and their many variants. Hybrid CBQ-WFQ approach based on non-preemptive priority queuing were shown to fully meet the QoS requirements of both date and real-time traffic in IP networks (Ball 1999) and it also shown they could operate in conjunction measurement based admission control mechanisms (Maqousi 2002) to further improve the efficiency of bandwidth allocation.

However, at some point in the late 1990s, the increasing popularity of the Internet and consequential increase in demand for the fast transfer of bulk data led to a change in priorities. Research into multiservice networking and QoS began to focus more on the higher layer and in meeting the requirements of adaptive applications. This change also reversed the earlier philosophy and placed a greater importance on maximizing throughput. Research that continued in the network layer focused mainly on active queue management e.g WRED etc, Diffserve, MPLS and QoS routing.

In general, today's Internet has become optimized for the rapid transfer of high volume data traffic. Service differentiation is offered but generally limited to a small number of classes with different levels of throughput assurance. Expedited Forwarding is available but is not guaranteed to be respected on a global basis. Real-time continuous media traffic is accommodated, but only with loose guarantees. In general, these services reflect the current commercial and economic demands of the Internet's users and providers.

Some Smart Grid applications such as automated meter reading, real time pricing, marketing etc., have very similar requirements to current Internet applications, and therefore could be served adequately by the current Internet. However, it is clear that, without significant changes, the current Internet is not capable of meeting all the requirements for Smart Grid communication. However, from the point of view of cost effectiveness, making as much use of existing infrastructure would be beneficial, although new infrastructure will need to be developed to meet the new requirements where necessary.

Fortunately, concepts such as virtualisation, and overlay networks provide the means to integrate exiting and new infrastructure into one generalised communication system. Fan et al (Fan 2010) consider the use of self-organizing overlay networks over the wide range of existing infrastructure to be the best way forward for developing Smart Grid communications. However, it is emphasised that in order to meet delivery guarantees the real-time requirements of certain Smart Grid applications, appropriate support mechanisms will also need to be deployed within the lower layers of the network. Without this support in the lower layers, overlay approaches would be unable to request guaranteed communication channels. Therefore the requirements of Smart Grid Communication are renewing the old challenge of fully supporting the QoS requirement for all classes of traffic within the lower levels of the network.

Recently, researchers have begun to revisit the problem of multiservice at the network level in line with the requirements of Smart Grid communications (Alishahi 2013, Sadeghi 2012). Proposing the combination of non-preemptive priority based scheduling, CBQ/WFQ and AQM mechanisms within the network layer to provide the necessary degree of class isolation. They indentify that the current Diffserve framework has an insufficient number of classes to meet the needs of Smart Grid traffic, and that more classes will need to added. Apart from the specific focus on Smart Grid requirements, this work mainly confirms the findings of much earlier research.

However, there have been many changes during interceding years that can influence performance within the substrate. In particular, robust security is an essential requirement, resulting in security measures being almost universally applied throughout all levels of the communications process. Davies et al (Davies 2011) demonstrated by measurement and experimentation that security measures, in particular the processing of Access Control Lists (ACLs), can add significantly to packet forwarding delay. Producing a general increase in the order of 100%, and even greater in certain cases. Furthermore, they discovered that the magnitude of these delays was such that packet forwarding, and not link speed, could becoming the limiting factor for throughput, thereby invalidating a general assumption used in many performance evaluation scenarios. This work clearly demonstrates the importance of understanding the performance characteristics of specific network equipment, and the effects of certain configurations, when carrying out performance evaluations. This is particularly important if these evaluations are to be used in the design of networks that are expected to meet real-time requirements.

Fortunately, there have also been potentially beneficial developments. Cross-layer Architectures (Kliazvich 2011) have been proposed as a solution to the problem of providing interaction and exchange of information between non-adjacent layers in the protocol stack. Software Defined Networking (SDN) paradigm, of which OpenFlow is a particular example (Egilmez 2012), separates packet forwarding from network control and allows complex functions e.g. route management, dynamic QoS routing, dynamic resource allocation etc, to be executed in the higher layers of the network. It also provides for the dynamic reconfiguration of network equipment itself, i.e. routers and switches. Egilmez et al (Egilmez 2012) have shown that QOS-routing implemented in a SDN framework can provide an improvement in QoS for video streams without the need for resource allocation, however, the improvements shown relate only to the image quality and the effects on temporal quality are not discussed. Meeting strict real-time requirements will most probably need class isolation to be provided in the routers. Both cross-layering and SDN will inevitably generate some form of control traffic, however, to some degree this may be predictable from the type of control functions being used. SDN is based on a central controller for the network or for large networks, a domain. Domain controllers can be connected together via a higher level controller to form hierarchies in the network. Network equipment and traffic control mechanisms can be configured to suit the individual requirements within the domain. The SDN paradigm supports the dynamic reconfiguration of network equipment, and the provisioning of resources on a domain by domain basis, therefore making it a suitable framework within which to develop a Smart Grid communications system. The potential reliability problem associated with central controllers may need to be addressed, however, substation control and transmission line monitoring are already based on a single control centre.

4. Addressing the Real Time Requirements of the Smart Grid

The real-time requirements for certain Smart Grid functions are quite stringent and must be met or these functions will fail to work correctly. Failure could have serious consequences; therefore, meeting these requirements must be the primary objective, with efficient utilization of resources as a secondary goal. Fortunately, the most stringent requirements will, in general, only need to be met within particular domains (e.g. within substations), and along certain paths through other domains. There is also a possibility that these requirements may be mandated by some regulatory body, or through standards. Therefore, whatever solution is deployed to meet these requirements, its ability to meet them must be known *a priori* to deployment. Therefore, some form of pre-deployment evaluation or compliance testing may be required. With these points in mind we offer the following proposals for future research into meeting Smart Grid real-time requirements.

We believe there is the need for a number of performance evaluation studies to be carried out within the context of a network domain and using relative detailed modeling of network equipment. One focus for study is the case of strong class isolation through multi-level priority queuing and resource allocation for the priority based classes being implemented within the lower layers. Results from such studies would be aimed at supporting the design, and deployment of future networking equipment. Another focus would be based on the deployment of existing networking equipment and the use of over provisioning in an attempt to meet these requirements. These two focuses represent the two extremes of the available options; therefore other studies could consider the evaluation of some examples of DiffServe implementations. Results obtained from the different focuses could be used for comparative evaluations of the various options, and the models developed during these investigations could serve as tools for network design. It is also possibly that these evaluations could identify a baseline, below which certain options could be eliminated as suitable candidates.

A significant problem faced when attempting a detailed performance evaluation of existing equipment is the lack of detailed information regarding its internal operations. Such information is not generally available from vendors for reasons of commercial confidentiality. However, if the required information could be provided in the form of some generic model, or abstraction that would meet the needs for performance evaluation without disclosing sensitive information, this could be a solution to the hidden-detail problem. The Queuing Network Model (QNM) is one potential abstraction that might serve this purpose. QNMs are generic to any system of flow involve discrete entities, of which a communication network is a prime example. Although very often difficult to solve analytically, with some experience forming the model itself is not too difficult, and once formed it can be evaluated via simulation. We have used QMN successfully in our previous work and would recommend them as a potential candidate for the proposed evaluation studies presented above. Their potential as a possible solution to the hidden-detail problem could be investigated as a related side issue.

There also the need for performance evaluation studies of the combined operation of the SDN control system and the substrate, since both will influence the overall performance within the domain. At this level evaluation will need to consider the influence and effectiveness of dynamic reconfiguration, QoS routing, dynamic resource allocation, security and reliability and the influence of different protocols. Models that have been developed for evaluation at substrate level could be incorporated into this high level study possibly leading to a layered evaluation model. Furthermore, given that functionally, control and communication are effectively one system, co-evaluation may also be required. Co-design and co-simulation is considered the way forward by the NCSs community for respectively developing and evaluating NCSs. Therefore, a structured evaluation methodology developed in conjunction with the initial evaluation studies, and based on the experience gained, could make a useful contribution to the design of future Smart Grid networks.

5. Conclusions and Future Work

This paper has outlined the Smart Grid concept and discussed the requirements of its communication system. It has reviewed the current state of multiservice networking research and practice, recognising that certain Smart Grid communication requirements that cannot be supported by existing networks in general. The paper then considered how results of earlier work could be revisited and extended to provide the appropriate level of support for these new multiservice requirements. Finally, the paper offered some proposals for further research that could contribute to the development of a fully multiservice Smart Grid communications system. In future work the authors will be pursing research in line with the proposals presented in this paper, and are interested in discussion and collaboration with others involved in related work.

6. References

Alishahi, M. (2013), *22nd International Conference on Electricity Distribution*. Stockholm, 10-13 June, ISBN 978-1-84919-628-4 , ISSN 2032-9628

Ball, F. and Callinan, P.(1999), "Supporting Guaranteed Services in Packet Switched Networks: a study of Two alternative methods", *Proceeding of the International Conference on Parallel and Distributed Processing Techniques Applications PDPTA '99*, vol 5, pp 2450-2456, H.R. Arabnia (Ed), ISBN 1-892512-13-0

Bouhafs, F., Mackay, M. & Merapti, M.(2012), "Links to the Future", *IEEE Power & Energy Magazine*, January/February 2012, pp. 25-32.

Budka, K..C., Deshpande, J.G., Doumi, T.L. Maddan, M. Mew, T. (2010), *"Communication Netwrok Architecture and Design Principles for Smart Grids"*, *Bell Labs Technical Journal*, vol. 15 No. 2, , pp 205-228.

Campbell, A. and Coulson, G. (1997),"A QoS adaptive multimedia transportsystem: design, implementation and experiences", *Distrib. Syst. Engng* , Vol 4, p 48–58.

Davies, J.N, Comerford, P. and Grout, V. (2011) "Optimization of delays experienced by packets due to ACLs within a domain", The 4th International Conference on Internet Technologies and Applications, Glyndwr University , 6-9th September, 2011, pp. 277-284.

Egilmez, H. E., Dane, S. T., Bagci, K. T. and Teklap, A. M. (2012) "OpenQoS: An OpenFlow Controller Design for Multimedia Delivery with End-to-End Quality of Service over Software-Defined Networks", *Proc. Signal & Information Processing Association Annual Summit and Conference (APSIPA ASC 2012)*, Dec. 2012, pp. 1-8.

Fan, Z., Kalogridis, G.,C. Efthymiou, M. Soorrriyabandara, M. Serizawa, and J McGeehan (2010), " The New Frontier of Communications Research: Smart Grid and Smart Metering", *e-Energy 10*, April 13-15, 2010, Passau Germany.

Gupta, R.A. and Chow, M-Y. (2010), "Networked control system: Overview and research trends", *IEEE Trans. Ind. Electron.*, vol. 57, no. 7, pp. 2527–2535.

Jeon, Y. H.(2011),"QoS Requirements for the Smart Grid Communications Systems", *IJCSNS International Journal of Computer Science and Network sercurity*, Vol. 11 No. 3, pp 86-94.

Kliazovich, D. & Granelli, F. (2011) "Why Cross-layer? its Advantages and Disadvantages", In Zorba,N., Skianis, C. and Verikoukis, C (Eds), *Cross Layer Designs in WLAN Systems*, Troubador Publishing 2011 ISBN:1848768109 9781848768109

Maqousi, A., & Ball, F. (2002) "The Development and Evaluation of a monitoring Technique for M-FAC", *International Journal of Simulation, Systems, Science & Technology*, Vol. 3 No 1-2, pp 101-110, ISBN: 1473-8031

Maqousi, A., Balikhina, T., Basu, K. and Ball, F.(2013), "Towards an Open Architecture for Smart Grid Communications: Possible Pointers from Multiservice Network Research" , *Proceedings of the 1ˢᵗ International Conference on the Application of Information Technology in Developing Renewable Energy Processes & Systems (IT-DREPS '13)*, Petra University, Amman, Jordan–April 9-11, 2013.

Sadeghi, S. Yaghmaee Moghddam, M.H.;Bahekmat, M.; Heydari Yazdi, A.S.(2012), "Modeling of Smart Grid traffics using non-preemptive priority queues". *In: Smart Grids (ICSG), 2012*. IEEE, 2012. pp. 1-4.

Sterbenz, J., Hutchison,D., Cetinkaya, E., Jabbar, A., Rohrer, J., Scholler, M., Smith, P. (2012) "Resilience and survivability in communication networks": Strategies, principles, and survey of disciplines", *Elsevier Computer Networks*, June 2010.

Assay of White Space Technology Standards for Vehicular Cognitive Access

M.Dawood[1, 2], W.Fuhrmann[1, 2] and B.V.Ghita[2]

[1]Faculty of Computer Science, University of Applied Sciences Darmstadt, Germany
[2]Centre for Security, Communications and Network Research,
Plymouth University, Plymouth, United Kingdom
e-mail: {muhammad.dawood|bogdan.ghita}@plymouth.ac.uk;
woldemar.fuhrmann@h-da.de

Abstract

The provisioning of innovative connections between vehicles and backend information systems will enable new ways of vehicle management, traffic safety and efficiency. In this article we present Vehicular Cognitive Access, the concept of using TV white space access technology to support and facilitate end-to-end connectivity for certain types of automotive applications. We defined common requirements that an optimized radio system is expected to fulfill. An overview of different TV white space access standards is presented; motivations and open challenges of these standards as enabling technologies for vehicular communications are analyzed. It also provides an evaluation of the overall suitability of TV white space access for these applications and discusses research directions. TV white space access standards do show significant potential for vehicular cognitive access. However, some issues such as seamless handover schemes for high speed vehicles and the capability to support applications that have strict timeline and reliability requirements need to be further optimized before its full potential can be realized.

Keywords

White space standards, vehicular communications, automotive applications

1. Introduction

Intelligent Transportation Systems (ITS) need reliable and capable wireless connectivity supporting, infotainment (information and entertainment), road safety and traffic efficiency through vehicle-to-vehicle (V2V) and vehicle-to-infrastructure (V2I) communications. It is anticipated that the level of automotive information exchanges enabled by wireless communications will significantly increase in the near future due to a growing number of wireless-enabled vehicles (Al-Hazmi et al. 2013). In addition vehicular communications have some unique features, in terms of generation patterns, delivery requirements, communication primitives, and spatial scope.

Current and upcoming wireless communication systems have been trying to exploit many techniques to provide seamless access solutions for automotive applications. Dedicated Short Range Communications (DSRC) is a type of wireless communications specially designed for vehicles. Standard IEEE 802.11p WAVE (Wireless access in Vehicular environments) was proposed to exchange data between high speed vehicles and between the vehicles and the roadside infrastructure (IEEE 2010). IEEE 802.11p supports vehicular applications in vehicular ad hoc networks. Easy deployment, low cost, mature technology, and the facility to natively support V2V communications in ad hoc mode are among its advantages. However this technology suffers from scalability issues, unbounded delays and lack of deterministic quality of service guarantee. Without a pervasive roadside communication infrastructure, it can only offer intermittent and short-lived V2I connectivity (Amadeo et al. 2012).

Among cellular systems Long Term Evolution (LTE) (3GPP 2010) is the most promising current wireless broadband technology that provides high data rate and low latency to mobile users. Like all cellular systems, it can benefit from a large coverage area, high penetration rate, and high-speed terminal support. Indeed, LTE particularly fits the high-bandwidth demands and QoS-sensitive requirements of a category of vehicular applications known as infotainment, which includes traditional and emerging Internet applications (e.g. content download, media streaming, VoIP, web browsing, social networking, blog uploading, gaming, cloud access). In any case, its capability to support applications specifically conceived for the vehicular environment to provide road safety and traffic efficiency services is still an open issue. The main concern comes from the centralized LTE architecture: even for localized V2V data exchange, communications always have to cross infrastructure nodes, with negative consequences on message latency for safety-critical applications (Araniti et al. 2013).

In addition, in dense traffic areas, the heavy load generated by periodic message transmissions from several vehicles strongly challenges current radio systems capacity and potentially penalizes the delivery of traditional applications. Furthermore due to growing demand of wireless communications for wide range of purposes, current radio systems may come to practical limits of frequency spectrum bands. To overcome bandwidth scarcity issue global interest in new solution is being fuelled. Use of the vacant frequencies at a given time in a given geographical area not being used by licensed services has been identified as an important spectrum resource. This spectrum has been termed as *white space*. The unused spectrum in UHF TV broadcast band (470-790 MHz) is one of these vacant frequencies and is referred as *TV white space*, providing excellent propagation characteristics and appears to be a relatively large amount of white space. In response to these observations, in this article we intend to make the following contributions:

- We present Vehicular Cognitive Access, the concept of using TV white space access technology to support and facilitate end-to-end connectivity for certain types of automotive applications.

- Realizing the future automotive environment: We defined common requirements that an optimized radio system is expected to fulfill in order to be aligned with vehicular cognitive access described in the present document.

- By analyzing three different TV WS access standards; we evaluate the overall suitability of TV WS access for vehicular communications and identify the research directions.

The rest of this article is organized as follows. In Section 2, we identify automotive communication scenarios and define common requirements for vehicular cognitive access. Key characteristics of different TV WS access standards and important aspects of their suitability in vehicular environment are discussed in section 3. We evaluate the overall applicability of TV WS technology standards for the purpose and discuss research directions. We conclude the article in Section 4.

2. Communication Aspects of Centralized ITS Applications

2.1. Floating Car Data

In this paper, applications based on a floating car data (FCD) service are considered. The FCD requires periodic collection of information by vehicles, from internal and external sensors (e.g. CAN bus, in-vehicle camera, environmental monitoring sensors) and transmission of this information to a centralized backend information system on the network side. The backend system collects data from vehicles for further processing and analysis. This real-time data is combined with other existing quality traffic information sources such as traffic management centers, Automated Vehicle Location systems, mobile devices, and Connected Vehicle equipments, resulting in the most complete and reliable traffic information and provided back to vehicles. Based on the underlying application this system could be further connected with service delivery platforms, enterprise applications or service providers. Figure 1 shows a conceptual view of end to end wireless communications and innovative ITS applications of FCD class considered in this contribution.

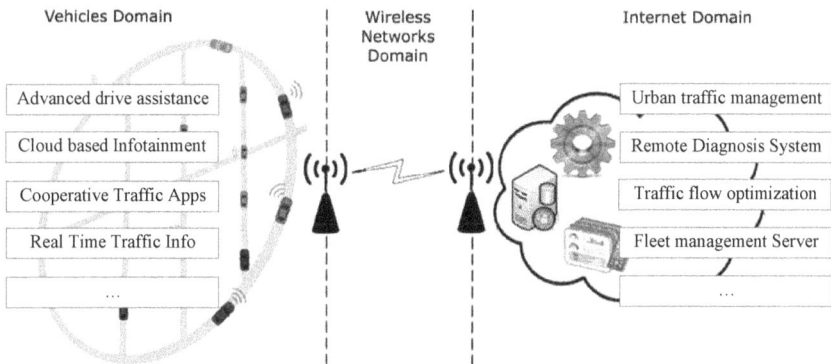

Figure 1: conceptual view of wireless communications for ITS applications

2.2. Vehicular Cognitive Access

Vehicular communication for Intelligent Transportation Systems (ITS) based on short-range wireless communications (IEEE 802.11p/ITS G5), ad hoc networking and cellular mobile networks has been extensively studied and for road safety application is being tested in major field trials. An opinion is raised that cognitive radio technology should be involved as a building block when designing a general purpose wireless communication system for future vehicles. In this paper the acronym VCA is used for vehicular connectivity using TV white space wireless technologies that should fulfill following functional requirements:

- Ability to obtain knowledge of its current geographical and operational radio environment (available resources, target applications, number of vehicles), established policies and its internal state.
- Dynamically and autonomously adjust its operational parameters and protocols
- Operate in an uncertain environment where the frequency availability is not guaranteed and may change from location to location and time to time.
- Operate in an unlicensed environment where the interference caused by other unlicensed terminals cannot be predicted and must be avoided or overcome.
- Cause no interference to licensed users or causing unnecessary interference or blocking.

Following is a summary of the performance requirements for considered applications that an optimized radio system is expected to fulfill, in order to be aligned with vehicular cognitive access described in the present document:

Support of large number of vehicles: With growing number of connected vehicles it is anticipated that a single cell may need to serve very large number of connected vehicles (Boswarthick et al. 2012). Therefore appropriate network should provide a mechanism to reduce peaks in signalling and the data traffic resulting from large numbers of vehicles, almost simultaneously attempting data and/or signalling interactions. When the network is in overload, it should be capable to provide a mechanism to restrict downlink data and signalling as well as access towards a specific access point name (APN).

Extended coverage: Since vehicles have to travel across different regions and thus given applications require widespread coverage.

Reliable: One essential requirement is that the message or data delivery must be reliable.

Secure: With the growing threat of hacking and unauthorized compromising of systems, security is an issue high on the agenda of many users.

Broadcast message capability: There could be instances where broadcast messages may be needed. The system must be able to accommodate this type of message

Small data bursts: As many vehicles would send amounts of data at a time, the system must be able to efficiently handle packets of around 50 bytes

Mobility Support: Automotive applications are those that need to communicate wherever they are and as vehicles move around different regions. This requires mechanisms to provide mobility support for roaming scenarios and efficient seamless handoff schemes to enhance Quality of Service (QoS) and provide flawless mobility. There must be an optimized frequency of mobility management procedures.

3. Wireless Standards for TV White Space

Three standards are considered that provide the ability for exchanging data using radio transmissions in unoccupied TV transmission channel. Their key characteristics are summarized in Table 1 and their suitability for ITS applications is discussed in the next sections.

Feature	802.22	802.11af	Weightless
Frequency bands	54-862 MHz	300-710 MHz	470-790 MHz
Channel width	6, 7 or 8 MHz	6, 7 or 8 MHz	6 or 8 MHz
Max data rate	22.69 Mb/s	54 Mb/s	16 Mb/s
Range	Up to 100Km	Up to 5Km	Up to 5Km
Capacity	Potentially high	Medium	High (M2M)
multicast support / MIMO	No	Yes	Yes
Modulation Method	QPSK, 16-QAM & 64-QAM	BPSK, QPSK & 16-QAM	16-QAM, pi/4 QPSK, pi/2 BPSK
PHY Transport (Multiple Access Method)	OFDMA	CSMA/CA & TDMA	TDMA

Table 1: System parameters of TV WS access Standards

3.1. IEEE 802.22

The standard IEEE 802.22 belongs to the class of wireless regional area networks (WRAN). It defines cellular topology with control system composed of a base station (BS) and zero or more customer premises equipment (CPEs) associated to a cell. The coverage area of the cell extends up to the point where the signal received from the BS is sufficient to allow CPEs to associate and maintain communication with the BS.

The reference architecture for IEEE 802.22 systems as shown in figure 2 incorporates all communication related components as well as the interactions between the individual entities. The reference architecture indicates PHY and MAC levels and the interface between station management entity (SME) through PHY and MAC layer management entities (MLMEs). The higher layers such as IP layer, PHY and MAC levels interact with each other through the service access points (SAPs), which give modularity to the system. A spectrum management entity (SME) in its turn communicates with PHY level by the PHY layer management entity (PLME) and its SAPs (Stevenson 2009).

On the PHY level, there are three particularly important features: the main data communications, the spectrum sensing function (SSF), and the geolocation function. PHY communications specification is based on orthogonal frequency division multiple access (OFDMA) for both Upstream (US) and Downstream (DS). The standard optionally employs the duo-binary Convolutional Turbo Code (CTC), low density parity check codes (LDPC) and shortened block turbo codes (SBTC) coding. On MAC layer the 802.22 standard uses Time Division Multiplex (TDM) based access. The MAC also uses a synchronous timing structure, where frames are grouped into a superframe structure.

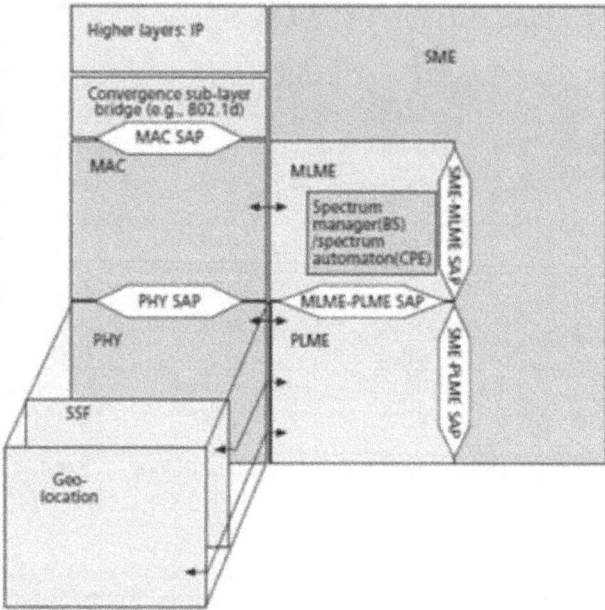

Figure 2: Reference architecture of IEEE 802.22 (Stevenson 2009)

3.2 Weightless Standard

Weightless is a standard designed specifically for machine-type communications within white space. The Weightless core network consists of service providers that communicate with base station networks. A base station networks operates one or more base stations. A base station is the grouping of a base station controller and a base station modem. The base station is intended to be kept as simple as possible to reflect the light-weight nature of the protocols used within the standard and to maximize the flexibility that arises from making key scheduling and assignment decisions in a central location. All of the MAC layer processing takes place within the base station controller within the network (Weightless SIG 2012), thus as far as possible the base station is sent complete frames of information which it passes to the physical layer. Hence, the message flow on the base station to network (BSN) interface is relatively limited.

The Weightless air interface has the flexibility to use either phase shift keying or quadrature amplitude modulation together with a scheme of Whitening to spread the signal and make it look more like white noise to reduce any levels of interference that may be caused. In addition to this the system uses time division duplex, TDD to enable both uplink and downlink transmissions to use the same channel. Physical layer design facilitate wide range of trade-offs between data throughput and available signal to noise ratio (SNR). The Weightless physical layer use frequency hopping, applied at the frame rate to mitigate interference as well as for propagation characteristics where some frequencies may experience deep fades as a result of multiple transmission paths. Whitening and interleaving is applied to the uplink and downlink transmissions in an identical manner. Continuous phase modulation (CPM) mode is supported for the uplink. There are two modes of downlink support, a high rate mode and a standard rate mode. Both modes are single carrier and are based on the same underlying signal bandwidth, pulse shaping and multiple access method. The spectral characteristics of the transmissions are the same for the high rate and standard rate modes, and the single carrier nature of the transmissions ensures low peak to average power ratio.

Weightless uses trade off data rate against range, this technology involves spreading the data to be transmitted. Spreading multiplies the data by a pre-defined codeword so that one bit of transmitted data becomes multiple bits of codeword. The receiver can then use correlation to recover the codeword at lower signal levels than would otherwise be possible. Spreading allows an extra gain on the link budget. Variable spreading factors are a core part of the Weightless specification, ensuring deep coverage. In cases where limited white space is available then Weightless can operate a mix of licensed and unlicensed Weightless technology using a few channels in the 900MHz (Weightless 2013).

3.2. IEEE 802.11af

The standard 802.11af is also called Super Wi-Fi or White-Fi because of its cognitive properties. The requirements specification of 802.11af system is formed, the standardization process is not yet finished and expected date of completion this work is Mar 2014 (IEEE 2014).

The 802.11af system is composed of three different station (STA) types: fixed, enabling, and dependent STA. Figure 3 shows two infrastructure BSSs where AP1 and AP2 are enabling STAs and the other STAs are dependent STAs. Fixed and enabling STAs are registered station that broadcast its registered location. The enabling STA is permitted to enable operation of unregistered STAs, i.e. dependent STAs. The enabling STA gets the available channel information from the TV WS database and transmits the contact verification signal (CVS). The CVS is used to determine that the dependent STAs are still within the range of enabling STAs, as well as for checking the list of available channels.

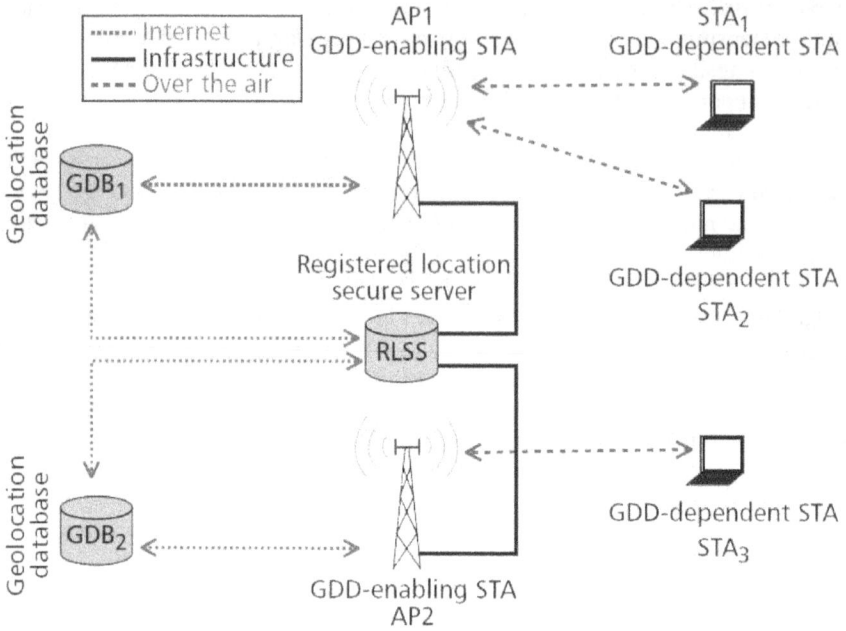

Figure 3: IEEE 802.11af Network Infrastructure (IEEE 2013)

The standards use the Orthogonal Frequency Division Multiplexing (OFDM) technology and Binary Phase-Shift Keying (BPSK), Quadrature Phase-Shift Keying (QPSK), 16-QAM (Quadrature Amplitude Modulation), 64-QAM payload modulations schemes at PHY layer. The standardization is ongoing in IEEE 802.11 TG (Task Group) as a major enhancement IEEE 802.11af (D5.0) introduced multi-channel support MIMO (Multiple-Input Multiple-Output) with aggregation (contiguous and non-contiguous mode) up to 4 channels to increase transmission data rate.

4.   Analysis of TV WS standards for vehicular access

The important aspects for TV white space applicability in vehicular environments are discussed in the following.

Architecture: The network *architectures* of these standards are relatively simple. In Weightless standard unlike cellular systems there are no defined interfaces within the network. All MAC layer processing takes place within the base station controller within the network and base station is sent complete frames of information which it passes to the physical layer. Since nearly all automotive applications of our interest follow a client-server paradigm so making key scheduling and assignment decision in a central location maximize the flexibility and suitability for V2I communications.

The IEEE 802.11af standard provides a common architecture, a communication scheme, and a control structure that adapts to the different operating parameters and regulatory domains around the world.

Capacity and date rate: IEEE 802.22 standard offers moderate uplink and downlink capacity, the maximum available data rate of 22.69 MB/s is calculated with quadrature amplitude modulation and at the coding rate of ¾ (Lekomtcev and Marsalek 2012). The Weightless provide up to 16 Mb/s downlink and 500 Kb/s uplink which is configurable to meet requirements. Weightless MAC enables Multicast with ability to handle large numbers of vehicles connected to a single base station. The weightless system provides mechanisms to efficiently maintain connectivity for a large number of vehicles by reducing peaks in the data and signalling traffic and restrict access towards a specific APN when the network is overloaded. It also supports multiple vehicles to transmit simultaneously, using FDMA, which increases uplink system capacity. The Weightless specification defines various RF parameters that minimum level must be to ensure that the capacity of the network is not degraded. IEEE 802.11af standard uses MIMO and channel aggregation mechanisms to meet the demand for ever-higher data rates, and offers up to 54 Mb/s download rate which are good enough for considered automotive applications.

Quality of Service and Security: The IEEE 802.22 QoS service model includes Service flow QoS scheduling: A service flow is a unidirectional flow of packets provided a particular QoS support level, which is specified by a set of QoS parameters such as latency, jitter, and throughput guarantees. Weightless scheduling techniques specifically accommodate the requirements of machine-type communications also applicable to vehicular applications. In weightless to protect integrity of payload, data is transferred to the service layers with no data loss (in acknowledged mode), unless the link is lost irrecoverably during data transfer. Data transported using unacknowledged mode is transferred to the service layers, but may be subject to drop-outs with error indication. Encryption and integrity protection of Control messages using keys provided by Higher Layer Network Management or Security entities. Encryption and integrity protection of User and Network Management messages using keys provided by Higher Layer Network Management or Security entities. IEEE 802.11af packet schedulers satisfy the objectives of high spectrum efficiency, throughput, and fairness.

Coverage and Mobility: TV white space bands are towards lower frequency, propagate long way and achieve greater distances, their infrastructure require around one third as many base stations as a traditional cellular network to offer ubiquitous wireless connectivity to vehicles in near future. In IEEE 802.22 standard the coverage area of a cell is generally 17–100 km and typically every CPE is considered as fixed user device that allows portability (nomadic use). For this reason, this standard is not suitable for adapting to mobile user devices. The Weightless standard support mobility, it deals with stationary and moving devices differently. As PHY transport is based on TDMA that is less expensive and much suitable for implementation of soft handovers, Moving terminals log onto a new cell as in WiFi, There are parameters to prevent excessive log-ons for fast moving terminals. To gain additional range the spreading process within the Weightless physical layer multiplies the data by a code-word to create a longer data sequence. It is used where there is insufficient signal level to support communications via an un-spread signal. IEEE 802.11af is designed for both mobile and fixed terminals with ~5 km outdoor radio range.

The evaluation of TV white space access for vehicular communications especially the coexistence with other wireless networks in mobility scenario is difficult to realize in feasibility study. Moderate coverage and capacity makes these standards adequate for considered vehicular scenarios. But as vehicles operating environment is highly mobile, supported mobility can encounter bad channel condition, high connection drop rate, signaling congestion and excessive power consumption with longer latency than cellular systems. These standards are initially designed for applications that are assumed not to require seamless handovers (i.e. a short break in transmission while a terminal moves to a different cell is acceptable). They are trying to tackle the problem with ability to reduce the frequency of mobility management procedures but support for special mobility pattern, the varying vehicle density, and interference with other types of networks need to be optimized. The standardization is ongoing, as a major enhancement of IEEE 802.11af in terms of bit rate, capacity, and spectral efficiency through the support of MIMO techniques. With IEEE 802.11af still in an early stage, the focus of the related work reported in this article is on Weightless standard, but IEEE 802.11af potentialities are discussed.

5.   Conclusions

In this article we presented an assay of TV white space access technology in the view of assessing its suitability to automotive applications. The conducted analysis qualitatively describes the main features, strengths, and open challenges of TV white space access standards and solutions under development. We conclude that TV white space technology could be involved in designing a general-purpose (in contrast to traffic efficiency applications) wireless communication system for future vehicles.

Discussed standards strikes a balance between coverage and capacity and can potentially support several thousand vehicles per cell. In the initial deployment phase of vehicular networks, with widespread transmission range TV white space access can particularly helpful to extend vehicular connectivity in those scenarios where DSRC ad hoc networks suffers from limited radio range and pervasive roadside communication infrastructure. In addition TV white space access expected to play a critical role in overcoming situations where cellular communications cannot be supported due to challenging propagation conditions (e.g., corner effect due to building obstructions at road intersections). These standards meet many of the common communication requirements of our target applications however some issues are still open such as seamless handover schemes for high speed vehicles. the capability to support natively V2I communications and QoS for application that have timeliness and reliability as the major requirements.

Since TV white space technology infrastructure exploitation also represent a viable solution to maximize the use of bandwidth resources, Studies should not only analyze the capacity of white space access in supporting vehicular applications, but also their potential impact on overall need for more spectrum to satisfy the growing demand. The introduction of TV white space as an additional candidate access technology would require some changes in the specification of automotive use cases, some amendments are necessary to the current standard documents and architectures. For example, TV white space access technology role in ITS reference architecture

6. References

3GPP (2010), TS 36.300 "Evolved Universal Terrestrial Radio Access (E-UTRA) and Evolved Universal Terrestrial Radio Access Network (E-UTRAN)" Rel. 8, April 2010.

Al-Hazmi, A., Campowsky, K. (2013), "M2M Communication Evolution" *Proceedings of 4th Fokus Fuseco Forum Berlin,* 28 November 2013, pp. 4-5.

Amadeo, M., Campolo, C., and Molinaro, A. (2012) "Enhancing IEEE 802.11p to Provide Infotainment Applications in VANETs" *Elsevier Ad Hoc Networks* vol. 10, no. 2, March 2012, pp. 253.

Araniti, G., Campolo, C., and Molinaro, A. (2013) "LTE for Vehicular Networking: A Survey" *IEEE Communications Magazine,* May 2013, pp. 148-157.

Boswarthick, D., Elloumi, O., Hersent, O. (2012) "M2M Communications: A System Approach" Edition 1, May 2012, pp. 313.

IEEE (2010), IEEE 802.11p "Amendment 6: Wireless Access in Vehicular Environments IEEE Std 802.11p WAVE".

IEEE (2013) "IEEE 802.11af Draft 5.0, Amendment 5: TV White Spaces Operation" June 2013.

IEEE (2014) "Official IEEE802.11 Working Group Project Timelines" Available at http://www.ieee802.org/11/Reports/802.11_Timelines.htm (Accessed: 03 January 2014).

Lekomtcev, D., and Marsalek, R. (2012) "Comparison of 802.11af and 802.22 standards " *Elektrorevue Magazine,* Vol. 3, No. 2, June 2012, pp. 12-18.

Stevenson, C. R. (2009) "IEEE 802.22: The First Cognitive Radio Wireless Regional Area Network Standard" *IEEE Communications Magazine,* January 2009, pp. 130-138.

Weightless SIG (2012) "Weightless System Specification Version 0.9" November 2012.

Weightless SIG (2013) "Weightless Core Specification Version 1.0" April 2013.

A M2M-based Automotive Service Delivery Platform for Distributed Vehicular Applications

M.Glaab[1,2], W.Fuhrmann[1], J.Wietzke[1] and B.V.Ghita[2]

[1]In-Car Multimedia Labs, Faculty of Computer Science,
University of Applied Sciences Darmstadt, Darmstadt, Germany
[2]Centre for Security, Communications and Network Research,
Plymouth University, Plymouth, United Kingdom
e-mail: markus.glaab@h-da.de

Abstract

Modern vehicles are connected with the Internet through a range of wireless cellular network technologies. This provides the basis for many novel applications and use-cases towards intelligent vehicles, offering enhanced vehicle safety, traffic management, and driver and passenger convenience capabilities. The connectivity further enables new distributed software architectures that can provide solutions to existing challenges in the field of automotive software engineering. This paper introduces the approach of an Automotive Service Delivery Platform, based on the Machine-to-Machine Communication Service Architecture. Experiences and findings are presented, gained by implementing core elements of the proposed architecture prototypically. This implementation makes apparent the range and capabilities of current Machine-to-Machine Service Architecture and describes remaining challenges to facilitate efficient distributed automotive services.

Keywords

Machine-to-Machine Communication, Automotive Software Engineering, Resource-Oriented Architecture, Service Delivery Platform, Data Opaqueness

1. Introduction

Driven by the recent progress of Consumer Electronics (CE) devices like smartphones and tablets, the customers' demands for functionality, customisability, and connectivity of their In-Car Multimedia (ICM) system is continually growing. Besides, in the context of Intelligent Transportation Systems (ITS), governments, standards development organisations (SDO), and engineers have been spending lots of research to enhance the traffic safety and efficiency for many years.

Connecting vehicles with the Internet is the foundation for these visions, and the number of cars, equipped with GPRS, UMTS, and LTE hardware, already increases. Although further advancements within wireless cellular network technologies, network protocols, and automotive embedded hardware are necessary, adequate automotive software (SW) architectures and platforms are the key to let vehicles become an integrated part of the Internet and to make them *intelligent* or *smart*. Use-cases and applications of former non-automotive domains must be integrated and formed into a homogenous overall system (Bauer, 2010). But the automotive industry, and e.g. the consumer electronics and communication industry have different performance or safety requirements, as well as lifespan and innovation cycles. For instance, vehicle models are usually produced seven to eight years and they have to be maintainable for at least 15 years after the purchase. In contrast, the lifecycle of hardware, e.g. CPUs, is less than five years (Broy et al., 2007). More frequently, and even during the production phase, OEMs may want to integrate new software features (e.g. of other vehicle series). This might already be influenced by the innovation cycle of CE-software, but the latter is even shorter (Shimizu, 2004). Many social network smartphone-applications, such as Facebook and Spotify, are updated within days to a few weeks. In contrast, the software of the vehicle is only updated during service in a garage. Although the general mechanisms do exist to perform Over-The-Air (OTA) updates, the current automotive software architectures are not adequate to implement this securely with respect to possible side-effects and compatibility (Pretschner et al. 2007). This is intensified by the huge number of possible variants of a vehicle, not only regarding HW and SW revisions, but also with respect to configuration possibilities for car equipment. The issues of today's automotive SW engineering is also emphasised by this fact: While the functionality from one vehicle generation to the next in many sub-domains only differs by 10% due to enhancements and changes, more than 90% of the software is rewritten (Broy, 2006). This is caused by low level, hardware specific code that is hard to change or port (Broy, 2006). Even though the software-related challenges can be largely solved, hardware limitations continue to exist. Due to the harsh environment of the automotive domain, with wide temperature and humidity ranges, and special requirements on shock resistance, specialised embedded hardware has to be used. They are usually less powerful, compared to CE, and usually more expensive. However, it can be assumed, that the implementation of new applications during lifetime into a "traditionally designed headunit", where all functionality is truly installed, will be limited by hardware constraints – similar to todays' CE, hardware upgrades or replacements must be taken into account.

Facing these challenges, a new architecture paradigm, including a substantial proportion of automotive applications implemented outside the vehicle as services residing on OEM servers (Glaab et al., 2010) might be valuable and constitutes the basis for the presented architecture. It is introduced in Section 2 in more detail, concluded with the motivation of an Automotive Service Delivery Platform (ASDP). Section 3 discusses architecture fundamentals, if such ASDP should be realised based on the M2M Service Architecture. Finally, the applicability of M2M is evaluated within section 4 by discussing results and experiences, gained during prototypical implementation of core elements at the ICM lab. Section 5 briefly summarises the findings of the paper and provides an outlook on future work.

2. Towards an Automotive Embedded Internet

As indicated, offloading of automotive functionalities ("intelligence") to servers is a promising approach for the next generation of automotive software architectures. Figure 1 shows the general architecture, and involved components/domains: The OEM headunit is the central component of the vehicle, functionally connecting the displays, sensors, actuators, etc. The headunit is connected via wireless cellular networks with an OEM server, located within the Internet domain ("Cloud"). This in turn might connect to 3rd party servers. Accordingly, "the clash" of different domains, with quite heterogeneous requirements, lifecycles, etc., should occur at the OEM server, where it is anticipated that they can be mitigated more easily.

This is expected to reduce the hardware requirements for the headunit. Furthermore customising and adding of new functions during the lifetime of the vehicle does not raise the hardware requirements of the headunit as much, as integrated approaches. But, not every automotive application is suitable to be transformed to a web service in the same way. Criteria are needed for profound decision whether functions should (still) be realised within the vehicle, or if it is advantageous to transfer them as a service on a web server (Glaab et al., 2011). In particular resulting requirements against the wireless access networks have to be considered, because they can be treated as the bottleneck of this approach. Finally, it has to be reflected that vehicles can transit areas with no coverage. Consequently the remaining functionality during connectivity-loss has to be well-considered. However, since many of the aforementioned future automotive functionalities need data connectivity anyway, it can be expected that the number of suitable applications for cloud-based realisation increase above average.

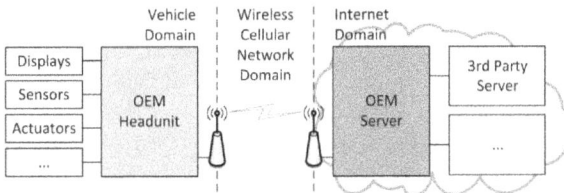

Figure 1: General architecture of distributed automotive software platform

Automotive software engineers need an end-to-end (E2E) solution, which extends their design space for the implementation of applications from the vehicle to the OEM server. We name this architecture an Automotive Service Delivery Platform (ASDP). According to our approach it should meet the following requirements: It shall offer appropriate open and standardised interfaces, and a modular design to enable re-use of common functions, following a Service-Oriented-Architecture (SOA). Resulting communication capabilities shall offer appropriate mechanisms for designing and controlling of data flows, and to prevent network-misalignments with respect to functional split and scalability. It shall offer capabilities for mediation and adaption of services. Since future vehicles, as part of an ASDP, will consume and also expose services, they should not only be treated as connected, but as an integrated part of the Internet towards an (automotive) Embedded Internet (Wu et al., 2011).

3. An Automotive Service Delivery Platform based on the M2M Service Architecture

Machine-to-Machine Communication (M2M), also known as Machine-Type-Communication (MTC), has been selected as the technology for realising an ASDP, while meeting the above listed requirements. There is no complete M2M architecture defined at the moment, as the preferred route has been to define M2M as a collection of functionality blocks, developed by different research institutes, companies and SDOs in particular European Telecommunications Standards Institute (ETSI) (ETSI, 2013a), 3rd Generation Partnership Project (3GPP) (3GPP, 2013) and Open Mobile Alliance (OMA) (OMA, 2013). The main standardisation activities have been bundled in oneM2M (oneM2M, 2013) for global harmonisation since July 2012.

3.1. Functional Architecture

The current ETSI M2M Service Architecture (ETSI, 2013b) specifies three types of components: *M2M Device* (D), *M2M Gateway* (G), and *M2M Network* (N). D and G are located inside the *M2M Device (and Gateway) Domain* and are connected by using wireless access networks to the *Network Domain*, where N is located. This allows hierarchical structures, where several D connect to one G and several G connect to one N, which emphasises the need for scalability in the context of millions of devices. With respect to an ASDP, the D is the vehicle and N is the OEM Server. A Gateway is currently not part of the considerations, as the vehicle has been decided to be M2M-compliant and it hence is able to connect directly to N.

In contrast to the currently widespread silos of vertically integrated applications, which are caused by the strive for the ultimate "killer application" (Wu et al., 2011), M2M has been developed as an open, horizontal, and hence more universal, integration platform. Thus, the *Service Capability Layer* (SCL), including the *Service Capabilities* (SCs), has been introduced within every M2M component, in order to encapsulate functions that are to be shared by many *M2M applications* (xA), which thus should only contain the business logic. Currently 11 SCs are proposed (ETSI, 2013b): *Application Enablement* (xAE), *Generic communication* (xGC), *Reachability, Addressing, and Repository* (xRAR), *Communication Selection* (xCS), *Remote entity management* (xREM), *SECurity* (xSEC), *History and data retention* (xHDR), *Transaction management* (xTM), *Compensation broker* (xCB), *Interworking proxy* (xIP), and *Telco operator exposure* (xTOE). The x is a placeholder for the component, in which SCL the SC is implemented. If the xAE, for example, is located on the D, it is called DAE, a xGC within the Network is called NGC, etc.

ETSI has defined four reference points (interfaces): *dIa* (vertical between DSCL and DA), *mIa* (vertical between NSCL and NA), *mId* (horizontal between D and N), and *mIm* (horizontal between N and N). Figure 2 depicts the compounded functional architecture, instantiated according to our proposed M2M-based ASDP.

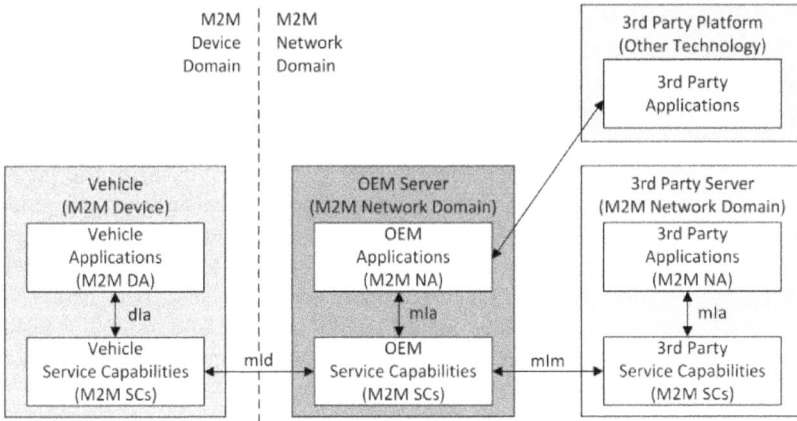

Figure 2: Compound functional Architecture of an M2M-based ASDP Resource Organisation and Management

Intrinsic to the M2M Service Architecture are that the resource organisation and related management procedures are following the RESTful architectural style, as defined in Fielding (2000). This style is particularly suitable for M2M communications (Pautasso et al., 2008).

A generic, hierarchical structured, *Resource Tree* is located inside each SCL for collaboration and exchange of applications, data, and SCs on the D, G, and N. It "describe[s] how the different resources relate to each other [, and it is introduced to] improve the overall system performance through the use of minimal structured data." (Boswarthick et al., 2012, p.127). The subtree within Figure 3 indicates the general structure of the *Resource Tree*. Several resources, e.g. data *containers* recur on different levels of the *Resource Tree*, which is used to model their scope.

The *Resource Tree* is mapped to Uniform Resource Identifiers (URIs) and manipulated via the RESTful reference points *dIa*, *mIa*, *mId*, and *mIm* by the four basic CRUD methods, the so-called "verbs": *CREATE, RETRIEVE, UPDATE, DELETE* and might be extended through *NOTIFY* and *EXECUTE* (ETSI TS 102 690 2013). These methods can be mapped to the RESTful application layer protocols, most likely HTTP (Hyper Text Transfer Protocol). Recently the Constraint Application Protocol (CoAP) was developed, which is especially designed for the RESTful communication of very limited electronics devices (Shelby et al., 2013; Bormann et al., 2012), but it might also be valuable for an ASDP.

4. Evaluation and Discussion

Core elements of an M2M-based ASDP have been prototypically implemented. To evaluate the capabilities of the current ETSI M2M Service Architecture and its applicability to an ASDP, as envisaged within our research, exemplary use-cases have been mapped according to the basic architecture presented above. Three of them are briefly presented below, but for the ease of understanding, the further evaluation and discussion is basically continued with the first use-case.

1. Floating Car Data (FCD) / Extended Floating Car Data (XFCD)

FCD describes vehicles that are used as driving sensors, periodically reporting at least their current location together with the timestamp to the OEM server. The trigger for the reporting might be time-related, distance-related, or a combination of both. The OEM server aggregates and analyses the data from all vehicles. Appropriate traffic algorithms and models enable the detection of traffic jams and average travelling times, which in turn can be used for enhanced route guidance purposes. XFCD may transmit additional data to the OEM server, such as rain sensor values, light sensor and hazard lights status, outside temperature, or vehicle dynamics data gained from active driver assistance systems. This data enables advanced inference of traffic safety and efficiency on a specific route. For instance, icy roads, heavy rain, or emergency braking can be determined and propagated to other vehicles that are approaching the relevant area.

2. Vehicle Maintenance

Modern vehicles have variable service intervals, depending on their usage, which is monitored over time, to estimate when thresholds are exceeded and service is necessary. Besides, various sensors and check routines may detect individual component failures. These are currently only locally stored using a fault recorder and manually readout at the car service station. M2M should enable use-cases, where relevant data can be submitted to the OEM server periodically, or event-/failure-/based. The gathered data may be subsequently used to initiate a separate business process of contacting the vehicle owner, discuss necessary service amounts, and arrange workshop dates, etc. Furthermore, it might be used for quality management and product improvements.

3. Enhanced Navigation, Social Driving, Intelligent Vehicles

Assuming the addition of an online navigation system, which calculates the routes on the OEM server, to the ASDP. In such a scenario, the server knows the destination, the route, and maybe even upcoming trips (through access to an online calendar). Additionally with XFCD and vehicle maintenance, the system also has information about the current tank level, remaining distance, and average economy. Based on these data, combined with statistical analysis of historical gas price data regarding cities, day, time, it can provide optimal suggestions for intermediate refuelling stops. The importance of such use-cases increases especially regarding electro mobility, where charging stops may require more comprehensive planning, with respect to minimised range, charging time, power plant capabilities etc.. Enhancing the calculation with these additional constraints requires only service advancements on the OEM server and no vehicular software updates, or considerable improved wireless access network capabilities. Equally, a car-pooling service can be added just by connecting it to the OEM server, since the necessary data (e.g. driving destination, route, and current position) is already available, because of a basic application like the navigation service.

4.1. Evaluation

The M2M Service Architecture in general facilitates the transparent transport of data between a D (vehicle) and an N (OEM server). DA and NA never exchange data directly, but via their local SCLs. With the "Announcement" and "Subscription" mechanisms of the ETSI M2M Service Architecture it is possible to fully or selectively transfer data from D to N and vice versa through the *Resource Tree*, SC(L)s, and RESTful communication. As a result a somehow vehicle' ("vehicle stub") arises within the NSCL, and an OEM server' ("OEM server stub") within the DSCL. Therefore local applications (lA) can consume data out of their local SCL (lSCL), originally generated by a remote application (rA), which spans the design space for data exchange, distribution, storage, wireless access network requirements, and connectivity handling.

Since vehicular sensor data is the foundation for many automotive-related applications, it should be made available to DAs and NAs within the ASDP. Accordingly, a DA "Vehicle Data Provider" has been introduced, to make location data (e.g. latitude, longitude, height, heading, speed) and sensor data (e.g. water temperature, oil temperature, service status, tank level, average economy) available in the local resource tree through tailored data containers such as XML. For this reason, the application may gets the vehicle data e.g. from an external source (such as a Controller Area Network fieldbus (CAN-bus)), and processes it accordingly. Besides, a NA "Floating Car Data" is introduced, to implement the FCD business logic. Figure 3 provides an architectural view of the resource structure and data flow.

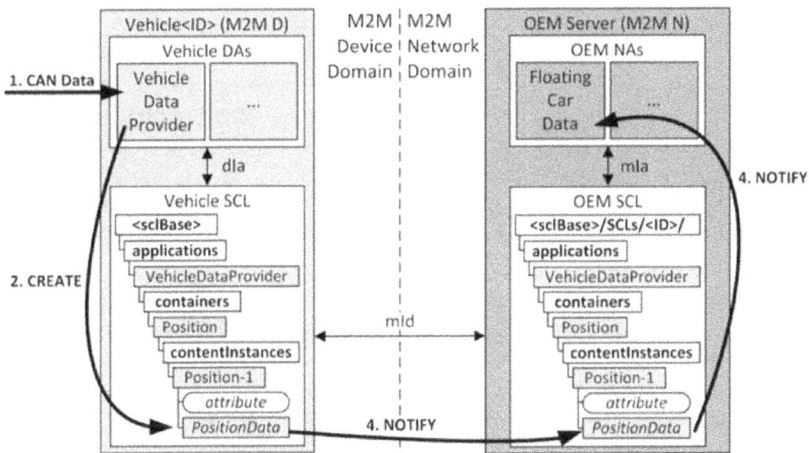

Figure 3: VehicleDataProvider-DA to FloatingCarData-NA Data-Flow Example

It is assumed, that all bootstrap and registration procedures of DA, DSCL, NSCL, and NA are successfully completed. Further, it is assumed, that necessary subscriptions from NA to NSCL, and NSCL to DSCL, are successfully created. Accordingly, the basic steps of a *VehicleDataProvider-DA* to *FloatingCarData-NA* data-flow are:

1. The *VehicleDataProvider-DA* reads the vehicle data (position) by use of its CAN-bus interface.

2. The position data is added to the resource tree, using a CREATE call of an appropriate *contentInstance: Position-1*.

3. Because of the existing NSCL-DSCL subscription, a NOTIFY from the DSCL to the issuing NSCL resource is sent, which contains the actual representation of the *contentInstances* resource.

4. Because of the existing NA-NSCL subscription, a NOTIFY from the NSCL to the issuing *FloatingCarData-NA* resource is sent, which contains the actual representation of the *contentInstances* resource.

The *FloatingCarData-NA* can process the vehicle's *PositionData* sample together with prior samples of this vehicle, and other samples of other vehicles, considering the respective positions and timestamps to fulfil the objectives of the FCD use-case.

4.2. Discussion

Modern vehicles produce several hundred megabyte of sensor data per second: For instance, location data, changes with 1-4 Hz, but frequency can go as high as 20 Hz in the case of speed, due to device capabilities, system design, or statutory provisions. Considering the presented use-cases, often only few, but maybe particular, data samples are needed. Accordingly, in theory, only few values must be transferred between D and N, what even enables some use-cases with respect to wireless cellular networks constraints and thousands of vehicles. But, in its current release, ETSI has been decided that the information, passed between M2M applications (e.g. DAs and NAs), is a black box – opaque – to the M2M platform (ETSI, 2013b). Currently, the *contentInstance* resource shall contain the attributes *contentSize*, *creationTime*, *lastModifiedTime*, and the *content* itself. The latter additionally can be described by the attribute *contentType*, according to MIME-Type definitions (Freed and Borenstein, 1996a; Freed and Borenstein, 1996b), where appropriate. But these attributes are only meta data and do not change that the actual content is not transparent to the M2M platform. Accordingly the *filterCriteria* resource, which indicates that e.g. the *SUBSCRIPE/NOTIFY* can be filtered in more detail, can only address meta data of the *contentInstance*. For example time-related criteria like *ifModifiedSince*, *ifUnmodifiedSince*, *createdAfter*, and *createdBefore* or content-size-related attributes like *sizeFrom*, *sizeUntil* can be used. Besides descriptive attributes like *searchString* are available (ETSI, 2013c). On one hand this seems to be a reasonable, central design decision to build a horizontal service platform and prevent building another vertical silo solution, and it might be sufficient and tolerable if e.g. only a very limited temperature sensor, providing one sample per minute, is connected. But on the other hand, this leaves tedious tasks ahead if a very complex device like a vehicle should be integrated, which offers a vast amount of complex data that might chance several times per second. Advantageous automotive data *subscriptions/filterCriteria* like

- "Provide speed, current position, and timestamp of the car every 100 m"
- "Send notification if water temperature is above 90 °C"
- "Provide speed, position, outside-temperature, rain sensor value, timestamp in case of an ABS or ESP control intervention"

are not feasible according to the current M2M release. Hence, to realise specific use-cases, vehicle data filtering can/must already be performed within the M2M application layer. Thus, as a workaround, data might be provided not common, but specific, e.g. within an appropriately filled data container *FloatingCarData*, on which the existing meta data *filterCriteria* are sufficient. Since it can be expected that the data acquisition rules are not fixed and may change often during runtime, depending on running applications, current driving region, traffic status, wireless access network utilisation, etc., extensions for dynamic configuration might be valueable. However, this again causes vertically integrated and isolated silo solutions on top of the common M2M Service Architecture.

M2M Service Architecture specifies values like *delayTolerance*, and *minimalTimeBetweenNotifications*, which indicate that timing-constraints can be defined for notification and data transmission. This should facilitate some network optimisations with respect to the number of packets and the reduction of overhead in case of aggregation of several packets (Lo et al., 2013). In the context of complex M2M-devices, like vehicles, which potentially offer a vast amount of information, semantics support – data-awareness – for *SUBSCRIPTION/NOTIFY* below the M2M application layer, promises an important bandwidth-reduction, while retaining most flexibility. This could also facilitate data-mediation functions on D and N, which prevent the multiple transmission of the same information, caused by independent, disjoint applications.

5. Conclusions

Connectivity and appropriate distributed automotive software platforms are the foundation for future vehicles to facilitate an additional level of inference, prediction, and responsiveness, to be perceived as *intelligence*. Such intelligent vehicles will offer enhanced user experience and evolve the activities associated with driving towards an Intelligent Transportation System, with increased traffic safety and efficiency. To enable this vision, this paper proposes an M2M-based Automotive Service Delivery Platform, facilitating many automotive applications implemented headunit-external on OEM servers. The ETSI M2M Service Architecture has been selected, because it specifies a horizontal service platform, with common Service Capabilities, interfaces, and resource-based, RESTful, communication on Resource Trees and it has been designed to offer an end-to-end integration solution for many different domains, including automotive. We presented experiences, gained during prototypical implementation of core elements according to the current M2M release, and evaluated the capabilities on the basis of representative use-cases, in particular Extended Floating Car Data. We noticed that by now, the M2M layer only helps to unify communication with and management of devices, to achieve decoupling between applications and devices, and to handle heterogeneous access network technologies. But, as discussed, ETSI M2M Service Architecture is currently not very efficient for complex devices, offering many information at a high rate, like vehicles. In order to support this, enhancements that make data understandable (transparent) to the M2M platform are necessary and will be subject of further research.

6. References

3GPP (2013), 3rd Generation Partnership Project (3GPP), http://www.3gpp.org/. (Accessed 10 April 2013)

Bauer, S. (2010), "Das vernetzte Fahrzeug – Herausforderungen für die IT", *Informatik-Spektrum*, Vol. 34, No. 1, pp. 38–41.

Bormann, C., Castellani, A.P. and Shelby, Z. (2012), "CoAP: An Application Protocol for Billions of Tiny Internet Nodes", *Internet Computing*, Vol. 16, No. 2, pp. 62–67.

Boswarthick, D., Elloumi, O. and Hersent, O. (2012), "M2M Communications: A Systems Approach", John Wiley & Sons, ISBN: 978-1-119-99475-6

Broy, M. (2006), "Challenges in Automotive Software Engineering", *Proceedings of the 28th International Conference on Software Engineering (ICSE)*, Shanghai, China, pp. 33–42.

Broy, M., Krüger, I.H., Pretschner A. and Salzmann C. (2007), "Engineering Automotive Software", *Proceedings of the IEEE*, Vol. 95, No. 2, pp. 356–373.

ETSI (2013a), "ETSI - M2M", http://www.etsi.org/index.php/technologies-clusters/technologies/m2m. (Accessed 10 April 2013)

ETSI (2013b), "Machine-to-Machine communications (M2M); Functional Architecture", *European Telecommunications Standards Institute*, TS 102 690, V.2.1.1.

ETSI (2013c), "Machine-to-Machine communications (M2M); mIa, dIa and mId interfaces", *European Telecommunications Standards Institute*, TS 102 921, V.2.1.1.

Fielding, R.T. (2000), "Architectural Styles and the Design of Network-based Software Architectures", *Doctoral dissertation*, University of California.

Freed, N. and Borenstein, N. (1996a), "Multipurpose Internet Mail Extensions (MIME) Part One: Format of Internet Message Bodies", IETF.

Freed, N. and Borenstein, N. (1996b), "Multipurpose Internet Mail Extensions (MIME) Part Two: Media Types", IETF.

Glaab, M., Fuhrmann W., Wietzke J. and Ghita B.V. (2010), "A New Architectural-Approach for Next Generation Automotive Applications", *Proceedings of the Sixth Collaborative Research Symposium on Security, E-Learning, Internet and Networking (SEIN2010)*, Plymouth, United Kingdom, pp. 11–18.

Glaab, M., Fuhrmann, W. and Wietzke, J. (2011), "Entscheidungskriterien für die Verteilung zukünftiger automotiver Anwendungen im Kontext vernetzter Fahrzeuge", *Mobilkommunikation 2011 - Technologien und Anwendungen - 16. ITG-Fachtagung*, pp. 149-154.

Lo, A., Law, Y. and Jacobsson, M. (2013), "A cellular-centric service architecture for machine-to-machine (M2M) communications", *Wireless Communications, IEEE*, Vol. 20, No. 5, pp. 143–151.

OMA (2013), "Open Mobile Alliance", http://openmobilealliance.org/. (Accessed 11 April 2013.

oneM2M (2013), "oneM2M", http://onem2m.org. (Accessed 16 April 2013)

Pautasso, C., Zimmermann, O. and Leymann, F. (2008), "Restful web services vs. 'big' web services: making the right architectural decision", *Proceeding of the 17th international conference on World Wide Web (WWW2008)*, ACM, pp. 805-814.

Pretschner, A., Broy, M., Kruger, I.H. and Stauner, T. (2007), "Software engineering for automotive systems: A roadmap", *Future of Software Engineering (FOSE'07)*, pp. 55–71.

Shelby, Z., Hartke, K., and Bormann, C. (2013), "Constrained Application Protocol (CoAP)", *CoRE Working Group*, IETF.

Shimizu, N. (2004), "Analysis of Automotive Telematics Industry in Japan", *Doctoral dissertation*, Massachusetts Institute of Technology.

Wu, G., Talwar, S., Johnsson, K., Himayat, N. and Johnson, K.D. (2011), "M2M: From Mobile to Embedded Internet", *Communications Magazine, IEEE*, Vol. 49, No. 4, pp. 36–43.

Load Balance & Congestion Avoidance in EIGRP Networks by using the Characteristics of the OpenFlow Protocol

H.Hasan and J.Cosmas

Electronic & Computer Engineering Department
School of Engineering and Design, Brunel University, London, United Kingdom
e-mail: {eepghah|john.cosmas}@brunel.ac.uk

This research is sponsored by the Higher Committee for Education Development in Iraq, The Office of the Prime Minister, The Green Zone, Baghdad/ Iraq

Abstract

In this paper, Enhanced Interior Gateway Routing Protocol (EIGRP) algorithm inside routers will be applied along with simple smart load distribution algorithm inside a controller which results a network that has the characteristics of the OpenFlow protocol.

OpenFlow protocol is a powerful method to deal with changing of traffic volumes across the links and it involves using a Controller that manages traffic across the network.

The aims of this project is to design an algorithm that combines the characteristics of both the traditional routing protocol (EIGRP) and the OpenFlow protocol, the flows from the sources to the destinations will be distributed across the network according to the mentioned algorithm which gives better load balance and avoiding channel congestion as much as possible. Both of the Routers and the Controller will share the responsibility of managing the traffic across the network.

1. Introduction and related work

Load balance has been considered as one of the most important issues in the development of network applications. Load balance can only be achieved in Dynamic Routing by comparing the links' cost of the different routes to the destination. However, this method is limited because the available bandwidth (link cost) over the links may change from time to time as many sources share parts of those links to communicate different destinations, which leads to changing of traffic loads during its active working time.

In dynamic routing networks, there are three types of routing protocols:

- Distance-vector, which finds the best path to the destination by using hop counts, for example: Routing Information Protocol (RIP).
- Link state, also called shortest-path-first protocols, which finds the best path to the destination by using bandwidth, for example: Open Shortest Path First (OSPF).
- Hybrid, which uses aspects of both the distance vector and link state, for example: Enhanced Interior Gateway Routing Protocol (EIGRP).

EIGRP routing protocol is CISCO proprietary routing protocol (Lammle, 2007, p 418).

EIGRP routing algorithm will be used in our project networks and according to this algorithm finding the best route to a specific destination, the following equation is used:

$$Metric = (\frac{10^7}{Bandwidth} + Delay) * 256 \qquad (1)$$

Bandwidth: represents is the least bandwidth of all outgoing links on the path to the destination (bits/seconds).

Delay: represents the sum of the delays configured on the interfaces, links and hops on the path to the destination (seconds).

The route that has the least *Metric* value is called the Successor, which is considered the best route to the destination (the Successor has the highest bandwidth and the lowest delay) (CISCO Web site, 2013).

The other discovered routes to the destination, which have the higher metric values, are called Feasible Successors.

Theoretically, for every destination there is only one successor and there are up to six Feasible Successors (Lammle, 2007, p 420).

Smart distribution of load among the Successor and Feasible Successors leads to better, even usage of all available links. In such load balance, the traffic will be distributed as much as possible among all the available paths, which results in less congestion, more efficiency, better usage of bandwidth and finally better performance (higher throughput) (Long et al., 2013).

Destination route map can be defined as a graphical representation of all the hops (routers) of the network path to a specific destination.

In Software-Defined Networking (SDN), the network's control plane is separated from the data forwarding plane.

This is represented in OpenFlow protocol where the flow tables are used by devices (routers or switches) rather than routing tables or MAC address tables (Klein and Jarschel, 2013) & (OpenFlow org Web Site 2013).

The OpenFlow system should contain at least one Controller, and a secure channel connects between devices (Routers/Switches) and the Controller. This secure channel requires very small bandwidth compared with the other channels of the network that connect routers (McKeown et al., 2008).

The Controller adds or deletes flow entries to the flow tables (Klein and Jarschel, 2013) & (OpenFlow org Web Site 2013).

Our project differs from the Openflow in one point that the discovery of the paths (routes) to the destination is the responsibility of the Router not the Controller, but the controller helps to manage the traffic across the network to provide better possible efficiency.

The reason is that if the controller fails (or the channel between the controller and any of the routers breaks down), the network will still work on with less efficiency, so this creates more reliable network. The load balance along with Openflow is discussed by several research papers. In (Long et al., 2013), Hui Long, suggests LABERIO (LoAd-BalancEd Routing wIth OpenFlow). LABERIO is designed to find alternative links for the busy ones. Part of our work will depend on the LABERIO idea.

2. Simulation software, Models and Methods used

To make a simpler simulation, the Internet Protocol address (IP address) has not been used in our simulation, however it can be added later on in further work and this does not contradict with the concept of our work.

2.1. Simulation software

Our project consists of a very general network, and can be implemented with Ethernet, fibre or wireless connections.

OMNeT++ simulation is the network modelling software that is used to build our project. OMNeT++ is an object oriented simulation that depends on both C++ and Network Description (NED) languages.

2.2. Models of the simulation network

The project consists of two networks, and each network has 16 Routers, 6 Hosts and multiple data rate channels connecting Routers and Hosts with each other. The first network is as shown in figure1.

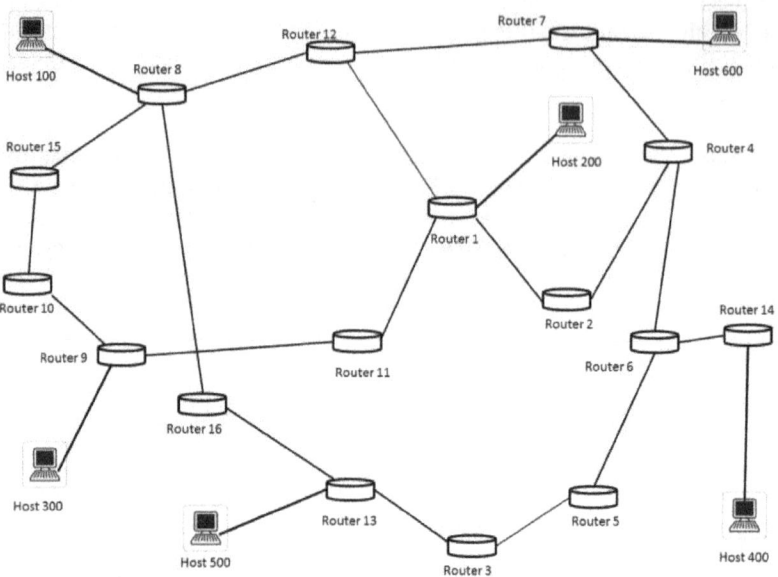

Figure1: Network without controller (the first simulation)

The second network, as shown in figure 2, is similar to the first network. The only difference is that there is a Controller device connected to each Router through very small bandwidth channels.

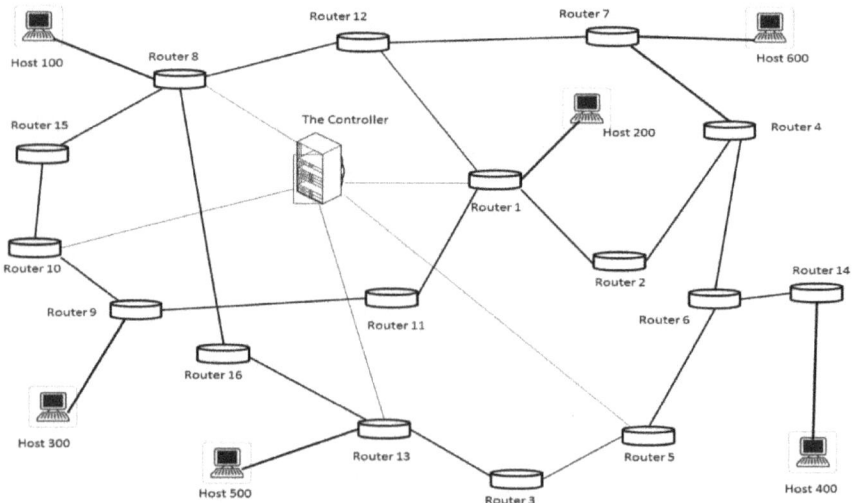

Figure2: Network with controller (the second simulation)

2.3. Methods used

EIGRP routing protocol algorithm has been built inside each router.

On the start of the simulation, all the devices identify themselves to their neighbours and the amounts of bandwidth of each of the connected channels (links) are recorded inside each router.

In the second simulation (figure 2), in addition to what has previously been mentioned, all Routers identify themselves to the Controller and the amounts of bandwidth of all the channels that connect routers are recorded in the Controller as well.

After neighbours' identification operation, the routers start exchanging information with each other and sending update packets to calculate the least *Metric* values to each destination (Host) through equation (1).

Routing loops problem may occur, and to overcome this problem *split horizon* is the best solution. In split horizon, the routing updates are not sent to the destination from which they came (Lammle, 2007, p 382).

The information that is exchanged by routers comprises the bandwidth and the delay of the connecting channels. By comparing the *Metric* different values, both of Successor and Feasible Successors are allocated, and in this operation the maps of each discovered path (Successor and Feasible Successor) to all destinations are drawn.

Note: In our simulation, One Successor and one or two Feasible Successors have been allocated.

In the first part of simulation figure 1, after exchanging of information and comparison operations are completed, the routing tables inside each router are completely built and routers are ready for routing. Hosts start sending Data flow packets to each other across the network and the routers connected to the hosts start receiving those data flow packets as the first step to forward them later to their destinations.

In our simulation, the routing table inside each router is built by using C++ map container method.

In the first simulation (figure 1) and after receiving data flow packets, each router starts the look up operation inside its routing table, then forwards each data flow packet through a specific out port. This operation is repeated in every router where the data flow packet has arrived, until those data flow packets reach their last destination.

Sometimes it is necessary for the router to send much more packets than the allowed rate through one port, because this amount of information is larger than the availability of the connected channel to bear. The Queue of the router's port will drop the extra packets which results in loss of information. This problem can be solved through smart load balancing.

In the second simulation (figure 2), after the exchange of update information and comparison operation is completed, routing tables inside each router are completely built. Then all routers send all the information they have (routing tables of Successor and Feasible Successor paths and their maps) to the Controller to be recorded there and then be dealt with later.

As a result of this mentioned operation, the controller obtains full knowledge about the topology and the components of the network as well as the successor and feasible successor routes from all routers to all destinations and their detailed paths, hops they pass through and bandwidths.

Through this knowledge, the controller will be able to manage the traffic across the network more efficiently by applying smart load balancing among routers and through channels.

3.   Practical Work

3.1. Flows applied

According to our simulation, the traffic flows applied on the network will be as shown below subsequently:

- Host 100 start sending data flow of size equal to 30Mbps to Host 400.
- Host 300 start sending data flow of size equal to 30Mbps to Host 500.
- Host 200 start sending data flow of size equal to 30Mbps to Host 600.
- Then after a small period of time, two other flows will be added:
- Host 100 start sending data flow of size equal to 30Mbps to Host 300.
- Host 500 start sending data flow of size equal to 30Mbps to Host 100.
- Each of Host 100, Host 200, Host 300 and Host 500 sends 30 packets.
- Host 400 and Host 600 do not send any packets.

The map of path (route map) from each router (for successor path and first and second feasible successor paths) to all destination hosts has been drawn and stored as two dimensional arrays in every router as well as inside the controller as shown in table 1.

For example, the map of paths (successor paths) that is calculated in router 1 to all the destination hosts is as shown in Table 1 below.

Destination Host	Hop1	Hop2	Hop3	Hop4
200	0			
500	3	13		
100	11	8		
600	11	8	12	7
300	11	9		
400	2	4	6	14

Table 1: Successor map paths of router 1

The map of paths (first feasible successor paths) that calculated in router 1 to all the destination hosts is as shown in Table 2 below.

Destination Host	Hop1	Hop2	Hop3	Hop4
500	13			
100	13	16	8	
600	2	4	7	
300	12	8	11	9
400	3	5	6	14

Table 2: First feasible successor map paths of router 1

For Table1, *0* means that the destination host is directly connected to the router and such destination has only a Successor (no feasible successors). The numbers below the Hop column represent the numbers of the routers along the discovered path. In some routers, it can be noticed that the first (or the second) feasible successor paths have not been discovered in our simulation, which means that there is only the successor path that leads to those destinations.

In the first simulation, where there is no controller (figure 1), each router uses the EIGRP traditional routing table to forward packets on Successor routes through the appropriate port to the next hop. In some of the hops, congestion on links occurs and several packets are dropped due to this congestion. This drop of packets has been managed by a queue put on each output port of each router. The queue is programmed to drop extra packets if it contains more than 5 packets at any moment and the data rate of the flow is more than the band width of the connected channel.

Forwarding operation is repeated on each hop (router) until packet reaches to its destination or dropped on the way because of congestion.

In the second simulation, where the controller exists (figure 2), when the routers connected to the hosts receive flow packets from hosts, they obtain the flow definition from the header of the first packet of the flow that they receive and then they create router to controller packet (flow request packet) and send it to the controller. This packet contains the details of the flow (source, destination, data rate and priority), the controller examines the situation of the links (the available and the used bandwidths as well as the data rate of the links of all paths that may be used by the flow) then it takes one of the following decisions:

- For the successor path, if there is no congestion across the network then the decision of the controller is ordering the router (where the flow request packet came from) to send the flow through the successor path.
- If there is a congestion that may occur (at any link) because of the flow across the network, then the first step is to process the new flow (or the existing changed date rate flow) with the other existing flows through the routing algorithm.

3.2. The routing algorithm

Inside the controller, the following tests are applied on the new started flow to find which test results in no congestion.

- Send the flow through the first feasible successor route (**Controller decision = 0**).
- Send the flow through the second feasible successor route (**Controller decision = 1**).
- Drop the Flow (**Controller decision = 2**).
- Send the flow through the third feasible successor route (**Controller decision = 3**).
- Distribute the flow equally (1:1 rate) or not equally (1:2 rate) among the successor and the first feasible successor routes (**Controller decision = 4**).
- Distribute the flow not equally (1:2 rate) among the successor and the first feasible successor routes (**Controller decision = 5**).
- Distribute the flow not equally (2:1 rate) among the successor and the first feasible successor routes (**Controller decision = 6**).

After the above tests, the test that gives no congestion will be the decision of the controller on how to deal with the flow. The flow **Bit Rate** represents the maximum constant number of bits sent by source host and inserted inside flow data packets.

The controller's decision is represented by a controller to router response packet (decision packet) and this packet will be sent to the router where the flow request packet came from (first router that flow packets start routing). The router receives the decision packet from the controller, matches the decision with its flow table and forwards (redirect) the next flow data packets according to the controller decision through the appropriate gates to their destinations.

The decisions of the controller in our second simulation (figure 2) will result in flows that will be redistributed across the network as shown in Table 3:

Flow				Controller
Flow No.	Source Host	Destination Host	Bit Rate	Decision
1	100	400	30Mbps	0
2	300	500	30Mbps	0
3	200	600	26Mbps	4
4	100	300	30Mbps	1
5	500	100	30Mbps	1

Table 3: Decisions of the controller for each started Flow

Then the bit rate of some of the flows will change gradually after some time(values either increase or decrease), and the decision of the controller for each change of flow bit rate may change or not change according to the situation that gives the best result as shown below:

The first change of bit rate will occur in flow No. 1 & flow No. 2

Flow			Controller		
Flow No.	Old Bit Rate	New Bit Rate	Old Decision	New Decision	changed
1	30Mbps	25Mbps	0	0	No
2	30Mbps	32Mbps	0	0	No

Table 4: Decisions of the controller for change of bit rate of flow No. 1 & flow No. 2

Then another flow bit rate changes

Flow			Controller		
Flow No.	Old Bit Rate	New Bit Rate	Old Decision	New Decision	changed
5	30Mbps	32Mbps	1	6	Yes
4	30Mbps	10 Mbps	1	1	No

Table 5: Decisions of the controller for change of bit rate of flow No. 5

Then bit rate of other flows change

Flow			Controller		
Flow No.	Old Bit Rate	New Bit Rate	Old Decision	New Decision	changed
3	26Mbps	28Mbps	4	4	No
5	32Mbps	34Mbps	6	6	No

Table 6: Decisions of the controller for change of bit rate of flow No. 3 & flow No. 5

Then bit rate of other flows change

Flow			Controller		
Flow No.	Old Bit Rate	New Bit Rate	Old Decision	New Decision	changed
2	32 Mbps	34 Mbps	0	0	No
1	25 Mbps	40 Mbps	0	5	Yes

Table 7: Decisions of the controller for change of bit rate of flow No. 2 & flow No. 1

Then bit rate of other flows change

Flow			Controller		
Flow No.	Old Bit Rate	New Bit Rate	Old Decision	New Decision	changed
3	28Mbps	30Mbps	4	4	No
2	34Mbps	35Mbps	5	5	No

Table 8: Decisions of the controller for change of bit rate of flow No. 3 & flow No. 2

Then bit rate of other flows change

Flow			Controller		
Flow No.	Old Bit rate	New Bit Rate	Old Decision	New Decision	changed
3	30Mbps	34Mbps	4	6	Yes

Table 9: Decisions of the controller for change of bit rate of flow No. 3

It can be noticed that in some cases the controller sends new decisions while in other cases the decision of the controller is the same as the previous decision, this depends on the availability of band width across the links and the conditions of the network at the time of decision.

Note each router sends regular flows updates to the controller every 30 seconds and the controller will modify the distribution of the load according to these updates.

3.3. Results

After running both of our simulations, the results are shown below:

- The number of packets that are dropped in the second network (Figure 2 with controller) during the simulation are 0 packets (there is neither congestion and nor packets' drop), while the number of packets that are dropped in the first simulation network (Figure 1 without controller) during simulation are 3 packets.
- The results of both first and second simulations are represented in figures 3 & 4 respectively. For both of Figure 3 & Figure 4, the X axis represents the distribution of the routers over the network while the Y axis represents the number of data flow packets that passed through each router during simulation time. However, in the first network, Figure 3, the load distribution is less efficient, since there are only 11 routers that forward packets and 5 disabled routers (router2, router5, router10, router15 and router16 are disabled), while in the second network, Figure 4, all routers in the network are used to forward packets which means that there is better flow of packets across the network (better use of bandwidth and network resources).

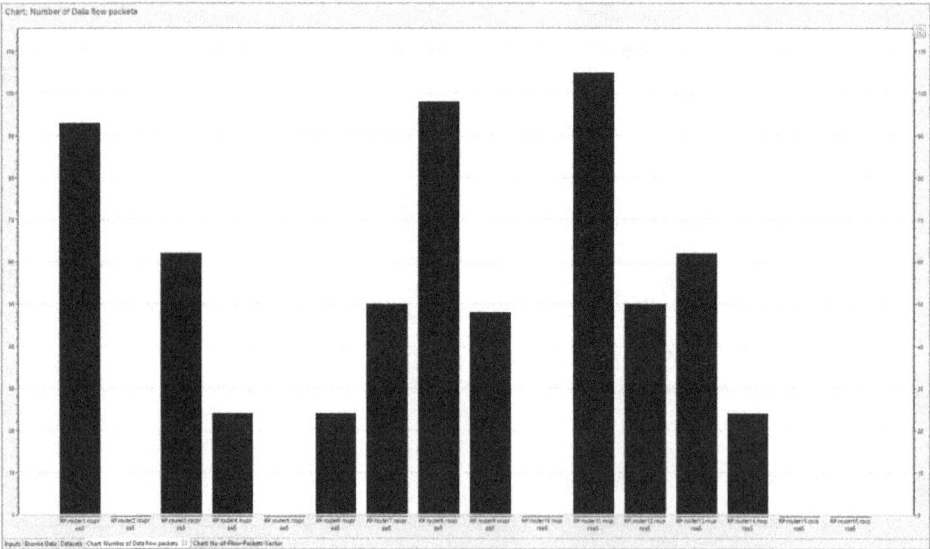

Figure 3: Load distribution (Data flow packets distribution) among routers in the first simulation without using controller

It also can be noticed in Figure 3 that the maximum load in some routers is much higher than that of their counterparts in Figure 4 which means that the load has not evenly distributed in the first simulation (without controller) as represented in Figure 3.

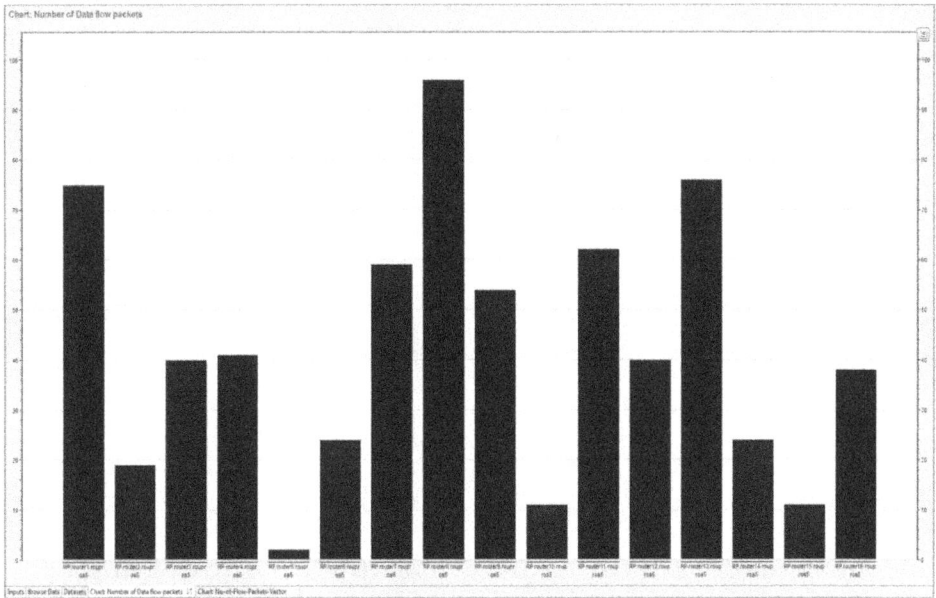

Figure 4: Load distribution (Data flow packets distribution) among routers in the second simulation by using controller (smart load balance)

4.   Conclusions & Future work

The performance of the network has been improved by using more of the available network resources and better load balance.

The duty of the controller now is to manage the traffic according to the routing tables that were discovered by the routers and the available bandwidth of the links.

If the available routing tables are not sufficient to fulfil the requirements of the flows, then the controller will take the responsibility to find alternative temporary path to the destinations, creating temporary flow tables and the new discovered paths may be called the **Temporary Successors.**

5.   References

CISCO web site (2013), 'Enhanced Interior Gateway Routing Protocol'. Available at: http://www.cisco.com/en/US/tech/tk365/technologies_white_paper09186a0080094cb7.shtml, (Accessed: December 2013).

Klein, D., and Jarschel, M., (2013) '*An OpenFlow Extension for the OMNeT++ INET Framework*' Available at: http://www3.informatik.uni-wuerzburg.de/research/ngn/ ofomnet/paper-acm_with_font.pdf (Accessed: January 2014).

Lammle, T. (2007) *CCNA Cisco Certified Network Associate Study Guide.* 6th edn. ISBN: 978-0-470-11008-9/ Wiley Publishing.

Long, H., Shen, Y., Guo, M., and Tang, F., (2013) '*LABERIO: Dynamic load-balanced routing in OpenFlow-enabled networks*', IEEE 27th International Conference on Advanced Information Networking and Applications, pp. 290 - 297.

McKeown, N., Anderson, T., Balakrishnan , H., Parulkar, G., Peterson, L., Rexford, J., Shenker, S., and Turner, J.,(2008) '*OpenFlow: Enabling Innovation in Campus Networks*', OpenFlow based Publications.

OpenFlow org Web Site (2013) Available at: http://archive.openflow.org/wp/learnmore/, (Accessed: December 2013).

A Self-Learning Network Anomaly Detection System using Majority Voting

D.Hock and M.Kappes

Department of Computer Science and Engineering, University of Applied Sciences, Frankfurt am Main, Germany
e-mail: {dehock|kappes}@fb2.fh-frankfurt.de

Abstract

Network traffic is constantly changing. However, many current Intrusion Detection Systems require somewhat static conditions in order to work properly. In this paper, we propose ongoing training and updating procedures and introduce a self-learning Anomaly Detection System based on majority voting that can adapt to network changes by steadily exchanging small parts of training data. We evaluate the performance of different replacement strategies for this process. Of the evaluated replacement strategies, the replace oldest strategy archived the best results.

Keywords

Anomaly Detection, Self-Learning, Majority Voting, Replacement Strategies

1. Introduction

As shown in recent surveys, the number of threats has continuously increased, along with their sophistication (Richardson 2011). The prevention of network intrusions and attacks is an increasingly important issue as more and more critical processes and sensitive data depend on network security. One way to detect attacks early on are Intrusion Detection Systems (IDS). Krügel et al. (2005) specified intrusion detection as "the process of identifying and responding to malicious activities targeted at computing and network resources". While traditional, signature-based IDS often lag behind todays attacks, heuristic methods are a promising alternative. Heuristic techniques are often clustered into two categories, namely Misuse Detection and Anomaly Detection (Dokas et al. 2002). Misuse detection recognizes threats by comparing them against a set of known intrusions. Anomaly Detection discovers deviations from normal behaviour. A major advantage of anomaly detection is its ability to detect even unknown and new attacks. Misuse detection can, like traditional systems, only detect attacks which are similar to attacks already known (e.g., been previously learned by the system). The common objective of each Anomaly Detection System is to report intrusive activity. However, not all anomalous activities are also intrusive. A report of an anomalous, but not intrusive activity is called false positive. The disadvantage of heuristic procedures, especially for anomaly detection, are high false positive rates. False positives occur in particular if new types of legitimate network traffic arise such as, e.g., the installation of new distributed programs, the use of new network devices or irregular backup and remote maintenance.

Activity	Description
Not intrusive and not anomalous	True Negative (TN): there is no intrusive activity and the system does not report alerts.
Intrusive and anomalous	True Positive (TP): the activity is intrusive and is reported by the system.
Intrusive but not anomalous	False Negative (FN): The system fails to detect an intrusive activity, because it is to similar to the expected activity.
Not intrusive but anomalous	False Positive (FP): The activity is not intrusive, but different from the usual activity and reported by the system.

Table 1: Definition of possible outputs

For some IDS, up to 99% of alerts can be classified as false positives and are unrelated to network security issues (Pietraszek 2004). While the false negative rate can be improved by combining multiple IDS, it is not possible to reduce a large number of false positives by such means. It is a time-consuming task to distinguish between relevant and irrelevant alerts, which means a high workload for security analysts. A further problem of Anomaly Detection is the so called concept drift (Gates and Taylor 2006), the phenomenon of unexpected change in network traffic over time. Heuristic approaches usually have a learning phase and a productive phase. Anomaly Detection Systems learn the normal behavior of the network in the learning phase, that means they derive a statistical model, e.g., by collecting statistics of network traffic over a period of time, which can be compared later to the statistics of the productive network traffic. Here, we refer to this learned model as "sample". A high rate of false positives can have various causes, but many can be traced back to samples of low quality. The process of learning the typical network behaviour can be a challenging task: If the is training carried out at a bad time, the system might not capture the complete regular behaviour; if there is an attack in the sample, the system might not be able to detect this attack later; if the productive network is not accessible for the developer, he might not be able to create accurate samples. However, even when the current behaviour was captured perfectly, it is very likely that the sample will get outdated soon due to the continuous change of network software, devices and usage. Gates et al. (2006) critically examined current Anomaly Detection paradigms and identified these problems (summarized as problem domain, operational usability and training-data) as main issues concerning todays Anomaly Detection Systems. A possible solution for some of these problems are IDS which automatically adjust with the help of a dynamic update process to the changing network, so-called Self-Learning Systems. Thus, the detection model is updated so that it reflects the most recent network traffic. The continuous manual updating and testing by an operator would be a time-consuming task and cannot be outsourced to a central instance (like for virus scanners) as IDS updates need to be tailored to the environment they operate in and, in general, require detailed customization. Thus, there is a need for methods to be able to optimize and update systems automatically and locally. However, automatically updating such a system may open up new vulnerabilities if attacks are erroneously adjusted for, contaminating the Anomaly Detection System and preventing the detection of such attacks (Kloft and Laskov 2007). In this paper, we propose to solve these issues by combining a self-learning approach with majority voting: Instead of checking against a single model to examine the network traffic, our approach compares the traffic to several models which are continuously replaced by improved and better fitting models. At the same time, the redundancy of our training data represents an advantage over noisy data and helps to stepwise replace obsolete data. The remainder of the paper is organised as follows. In the next section, we present our method and its features. We also outline some details of our update and replacement mechanisms. Last but not least, we present the evaluations of the introduced approach. The results include a comparison of performance using different replacement strategies.

2. Related Work

Since Dorothy Denning published her initial idea about Anomaly Detection (Denning 1987), existing detection mechanisms have been continuously expanded and improved. Resulting methods include Outlier Detection (Dokas et al. 2002), Pattern Analysis (Kim et al. 2004) and Principal Component Classifier (Munz and Carle 2007). However, only few of these approaches have been adopted in productive systems. Of particular relevance to our work are methods that use multiple testing and subsequent combination of the results and methods which have gained interest especially in crowd-based image classification (Bachrach et al. 2012). Kim and Bentley (2002) tested the effect of various parameters (Sample life span, threshold) with self-updating clustering algorithms. Cretu-Ciocarlie et al. (2009) used a Self-Learning System together with n-gram analysis and a simple voting algorithm. Our approach is similar, but differs in the detection algorithm and features. Furthermore, we focused on the evaluation of replacement strategies for automatic update mechanisms. Therefore, we show more advanced strategies than full replacement.

3. Method

In the following, we will briefly outline the rationale behind our approach. Our method is based on classifying network-traffic by assigning a value from the range [0,1] indicating its abnormality to it. Depending on the value and a threshold, the traffic is then classified as normal or abnormal. Thus, if benign and malignant network traffic receive the same values during training, the result is an area in which we cannot distinguish whether the traffic is normal or intrusive. In practice, not every value is equally often represented, for simplicity we assume for now that the values are normally distributed for sufficiently large data. Yet, the normal distribution is presented merely as an illustration, the actual distribution depends of course on the feature, the user behavior and network characteristics such as the Number of hosts and Operating Systems (e.g., Mah (1997) found that the Packet Sizes for HTTP traffic a heavy-tailed distribution).

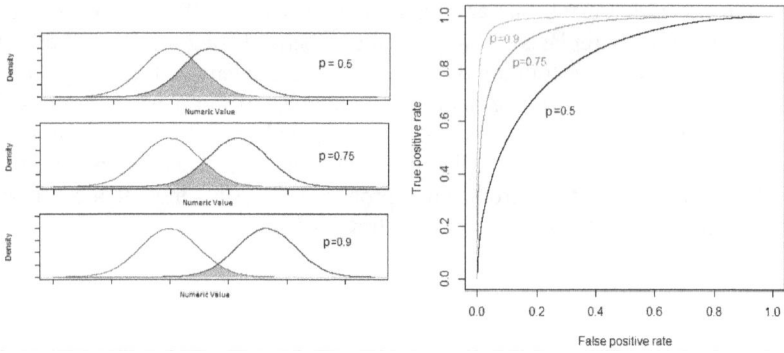

Figure 1: Relation between overlapping values and ROC-curve

The left part of Figure 1 shows such grey areas with the overlapping values with the corresponding Receiver Operating Characteristic (ROC). The red bell-curve (left) shows values representing normal traffic, the blue bell-curve shows values representing intrusive traffic. The p-value stands for the proportion of unambiguous values (the proportion of non-overlapping areas), that means p is the probability for a correct classification. The right side of Figure 1 shows the ratio of the ROC curve (i.e. true and false positive rate) in relation to the size of the grey area (i.e. grey area = 1-p) for all possible thresholds in [0,1]. For a minimal threshold, all traffic is classified as normal resulting in a point (0,0) whereas for maximal threshold all traffic is classified as abnormal resulting in point (1,1). The larger the area under the ROC curve (and thus the smaller the grey area), the better is the recognition rate. The ROC curve is a measure for the performance of a classification algorithm (in this case we classify traffic as normal or anomalous) and shows the possible combinations of true positive rate $TP/(TP+FN)$ and false positive rate $TN/(TN+FP)$. Depending on the user preferences it is possible to adjust an Anomaly Detection System a) more sensitive and report even slight deviations from the normal behaviour or b) more specific to report only deviations that are definitely intrusive. While a) leads to more false positives, b) leads to more undetected intrusive activities.

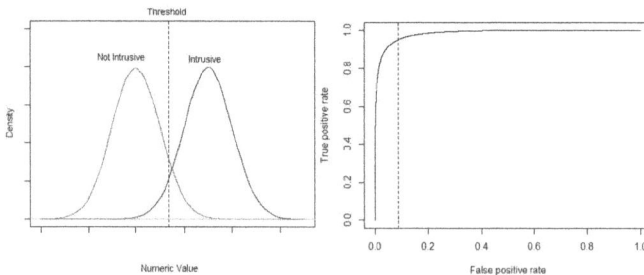

Figure 2: Threshold

Figure 2 shows the effect of the threshold. Every value on the left side of the threshold is classified as not intrusive while every value on the right side is classified as intrusive – the ambiguous values in the overlapping area included. The ROC-Cuve shows the corresponding True and False Positive Rates for this Threshold position. A ROC curve close to the diagonal line indicates a random detection rate. values close to the diagonal represent a same true and false positive rate, which corresponds to the expected detection rate of a random process. The ideal ROC curve first rises vertically to true positive rate close to 1, while false positive error rate initially remains close to 0 before the false positive rate increases. We aim to reduce the grey area by using several samples simultaneously. Thus, noise is smoothed and the influence of outliers is reduced. The following part of this paper introduces a simple algorithm derived from Packet Header Anomaly Detection (PHAD) (Mahoney and Chan 2001) and some features introduced in our earlier papers which focused on a correlation analysis and outlier detection (Hock and Kappes 2013). Our method and features may be also a valid approach detect a wide range of anomalies in practise, but our rationale for this approach is to evaluate the practical use of majority voting and Self-Learning.

3.1. The Anomaly Detection Method

In our system, traffic is classified taking into account the following features:

1. **IP.src.Entropy and Dst.Port.Entropy** show the probability for the observed distribution of IP Source Addresses and Destination Ports. For example, a Port scan with nmap, that calls 50.000 different ports a single time, generates very small entropy values.

$$value_i = \frac{\text{Number of Packets to port i}}{\text{Number of Packets}}$$

$$Entropy = \sum_{i=1}^{n} p\left(value_i\right) \log p\left(value_i\right)$$

2. **Mean.Packet.Size** is the mean-value of all packet sizes over a certain time. It can distinguish certain IP Protocols and detect some attacks with unusual small or large packet size.

$$Mean.Packet.Size = \frac{1}{n} \sum_{i=1}^{n} Packet.Size_i$$

3. **Utilization** is the number of packets over time. It can be another evidence for Denial of Service, because many DoS depend on resource exhaustion and therefore generate a lot of network traffic.

$$Utilzation = \frac{\text{Number of Packets}}{Time}$$

Using these features, PHAD determines the probability of an anomaly, called "anomaly score", based on the number and last time of previous occurrences of values. The traditional PHAD algorithm looks at the values of Packet Header fields to assign an anomaly score to each Packet. We look at the values of custom features and assign an anomaly score to each Time Window instead. PHAD calculates a probability for the observation of each value and then sums all values to an Anomaly Score. We further use a logarithm to adjust the score to a range between 0 and 1. After the anomaly score was calculated for each sample is applied majority voting. Majority voting can improve the probability of a correct result when there is an initial probability higher than 50% (i.e. random). The new probability majority voting assumes all examples are equally good. Let "p" denote the probability for a correct decision for a sample and assume that p is equal for all samples. The decision accuracy of majority voting method with n completely independent samples is given

n_i = Number of times the value was seen in training

r_i = Unique values in training

t_i = Time since last occurence

$$feature_i = \frac{t_i * n_i}{r_i}$$

$$score = 0.1\log_{10}\left(\sum feature_i\right)$$

by the binomial formula:

$$P_{Total} = \sum_{i=0}^{((n-1)/2)} \frac{n!}{i!(n-i)!} p^{n-i}(1-p)^i$$

P_{Total} is the probability for the correct classification using majority voting Figure 3 shows the total probability for a correct decision in relation to the quality and the number of samples.

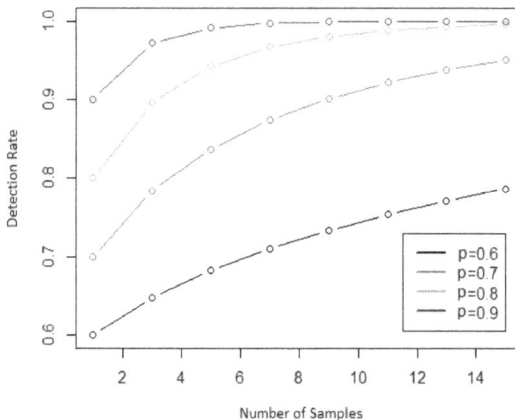

Figure 3: Theoretical improvement of quality through increase of samples

In summary, our productive phase can be broken down into three simple steps. At first, we derive our features for the current network traffic. Then we calculate the anomaly score using each of the learned samples. Each anomaly score higher then a threshold votes for "anomalous" and each score smaller then the threshold votes for "normal". The majority of these votes reveals whether the final decision for this time window is "anomalous" or "normal" in form of a value from range [0,1].

$$FinalDecision = \frac{AnomalousVote}{AnomalousVote + NormalVote}$$

As seen in Figure 3, the theoretical improvement of the quality, calculated with the binomial formula, diminishes with the number of samples used. For practical purposes, we therefore, we use this amount of samples and if there are more than 15 models, the one with most false positives is deleted to keep resources and time consumption of our method acceptable.

3.2. Update

Anomaly Detection Systems need to adept to the environment to deal with the continuously changing network traffic, the so-called concept drift. The manual definition and evaluation of adopted samples would be time consuming tasks. There is the need for an automatic update mechanism. However, a full replacement of the learned sample might lead to several problems such as an decrease of the detection performance due to outlier, noise or the unnoticed learning of attacks. Therefore, our approach evaluates different replacement strategies to update the Anomaly Detection System step by step. The Self-Learning Process first adds a new sample generated from the current traffic and then selects a deletes one of the sample to keep the original number of samples. The selection parameter is defined by the replacement strategy. Some common replacement strategies are:

Strategy	Description	Parameter
Replace worst	Deletes the sample that performed worst over an evaluation period.	Performance
Replace random	Replaces a random sample, if the new sample fulfils a minimum performance.	Performance
Replace most similar	Calculates a similarity measure and replaces one of the two most similar.	Similarity
Replace oldest	Replace the sample added first.	chronological order

Table 2: Overview of Replacement Strategies

Depending on the replacement strategy, we need to calculate the performance of one or several samples or the similarity between two samples. We consult the correlation as similarity measure:

$$corr(x, y) = \sum_{i=1}^{n}(x_i - \bar{x})(y_i - \bar{y}) / \sqrt{\sum_{i=1}^{n}(x_i - \bar{x})^2 \sum_{i=1}^{n}(y_i - \bar{y})^2}$$

The performance of a sample is approximated with the proportion of values included in the sample. Therefore, there is the need to perform an evaluation phase and compare the values from the evaluation phase with the values included in the sample:

$$Performance = \frac{\text{Number of values captured by sample}}{\text{Number of total values}}$$

4.   Results

In order to test the replacement strategies, we set up an experiment in which network traffic was monitored over a total period of 5 hours. The features, as listed in section 2.1, were calculated for traffic representing a 10 second time window. Samples were created using the features from 15 time windows. The normal network traffic has been created using a Windows PC in a test network with an Internet connection. In addition to the generated traffic from Windows (e.g. ARP, DHCP, ..) we executed typical user activities such as web radio, video streaming, browsing and e-mail. Every 100 seconds an IPv6 Router Advertisement Flood was carried out as proxy for denial of service attacks. A new sample for replacement strategies was offered once

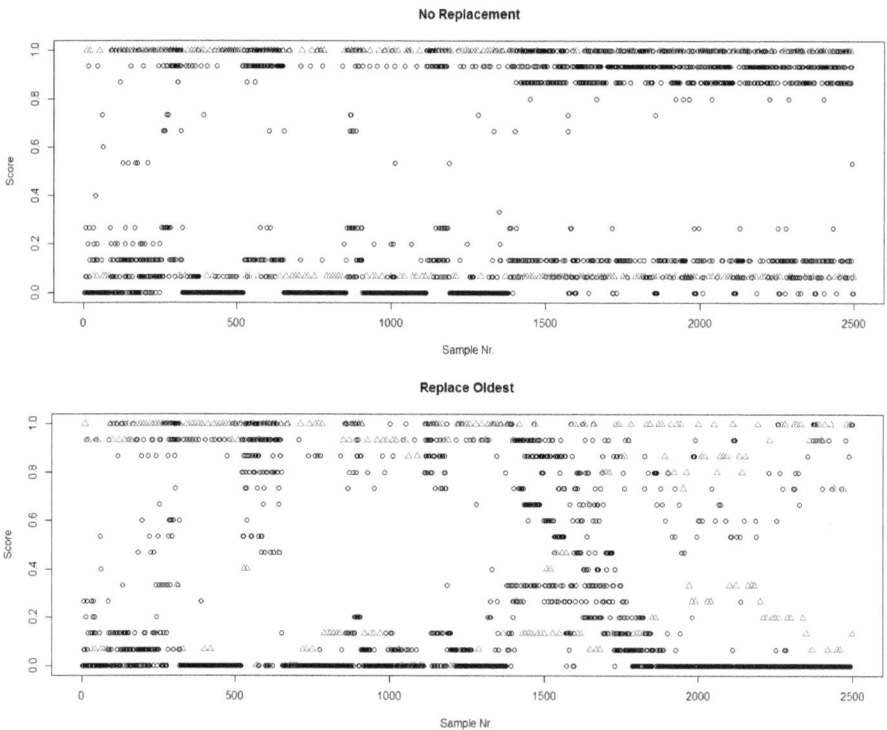

Figure 4: Anomaly Scores over Time

15 new time windows with Anomaly score < 0.5. were available.

Figure 4 shows two exemplary chosen replacement strategies over the course of time. The x-axis shows the course of time in the form of the score numbers (the traffic is rated in time slots of 10 seconds), the y-axis indicates the probability for a anomaly (given by the majority voting). The upper part of the Figure, is the plot without the exchange of samples, and the lower part shows the same experiment when the oldest sample is replaced. While the black circles show the score for normal traffic (should always be assessed with 0), the red triangles show attacks (should always be assessed with 1). The recognition rate in the upper diagram abruptly decreases after about half the time (the black cloud of points is suddenly more dense in the upper part of the plot). This behaviour usually occurs when the network behaviour changes and the samples get deprecated. The lower diagram with the replace oldest strategy shows a period of adjustment where the deprecated samples get replaced by more fitting samples. After this adaptation phase, the detection rate is again better. The detailed performance of all strategies is shown as a ROC Curve (see Figure 5). As already described in section 2, the result of classification methods (i.e. anomaly detection as well), is always a compromise of detection rate and error rate. This compromise can be generally adjusted by a threshold value. A ROC curve shows all possible combinations of recognition rate and error rate and thereby provides a better view as a single value. We use the area under curve (AUC) as a numerical quality measure (see Table 2). An AUC of 1 represents perfect detection while an AUC of 0.5 represents completely random results. The experiment without replacement achieved, as expected, the worst results. "replace oldest" archived the best results. The replace worst strategy might perform better with another measure for the sample performance.

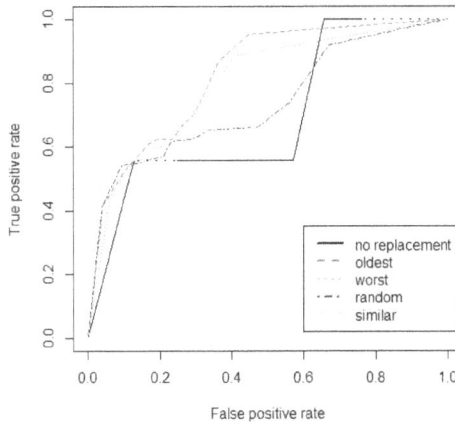

Figure 5: Experimental Results for Different Replacement Strategies

This could be archived by an additional evaluation of each new sample over a period of time or feedback by humans. The influence of additional parameters such as sample size, replacement frequency or recognition method has not been tested here. However, it is evident that the replacement strategy can have, independent from other parameter, significant impact on the quality of the anomaly detection.

Replacement Strategy	AUC
No Replacement	0.692
Oldest	0.825
Worst	0.797
Random	0.735
Most Similar	0.731

Table 3: Area under Curve

5. Conclusion and Future Work

In this paper, we evaluated Anomaly Detection in combination with majority voting by using several, dynamically updated traffic samples. Our results strongly indicate that multiple samples reduce noise and outliers. Furthermore, majority voting decreases false positives through adapting the system by self-learning. Our long-term goal is to develop and field-test a modern Anomaly Detection System based on the methods outlined in this paper. We focused on the evaluation of replacement strategies to for automatic update mechanisms and showed that the replacement strategy has impact on the quality and can prevent concept drift. The replace oldest strategy archived the best results in our experiments. This work was supported in part by the German Federal Ministry of Education and Research in scope of grant number 03FH005PA2. Responsible for the content are the authors.

6. References

Bachrach, Y., Graepel, T., Kasneci, G., Kosinski, M. and Gael, J. (2012), "Crowd IQ - Aggregating Opinions to Boost Performance", In Proc. of the 11th International Conference on Autonomous Agents and Multiagent Systems, Vol. 1, pp535-542.

Cretu-Ciocarlie, G.F., Stavrou, A., Locasto, M.E. and Stolfo, S.J. (2009), "Adaptive Anomaly Detection via Self-Calibration and Dynamic Updating", In Proc. Recent Advances in Intrusion Detection, Springer, pp41-60.

Denning, D.E. (1987), "An intrusion-detection model", IEEE Transactions on Software Engineering, pp222-232.

Dokas, P., Ertoz, L., Kumar, V., Lazarevic, A., Srivastava, J. and Tan, P. (2002), "Data mining for network intrusion detection", In Proc. NSF Workshop on Next Generation Data Mining, pp21-30.

Gates, C. and Taylor, C. (2006), "Challenging the anomaly detection paradigm: a provocative discussion", In Proc. of the 2006 workshop on New security paradigms, ACM, pp21-29.

Hock, D. and Kappes, M. (2013), "Using R for anomaly detection in network traffic", In Proc. ITA 13, Fifth International Conference on Internet Technologies and Applications.

Kim, J. and Bentley, P.J. (2002), "Towards an Artificial Immune System for Network Intrusion Detection - An Investigation of dynamic Clonal Selection", In Proc. of the 2002 Evolutionary Computation CEC'02, IEEE, Vol. 2, pp1015-1020.

Kim, M., Kong, H., Hong, S., Chung, S. and Hong, J.W. (2004), "A flow-based method for abnormal network traffic detection", In Proc. NOMS 2004, A Network Operations and Management Symposium, IEEE/I-FIP, Vol. 1, pp599-612.

Kloft, M. and Laskov, P. (2007), "A poisoning attack against online anomaly detection", In Proc. NIPS Workshop on Machine Learning in Adversarial Environments for Computer Security.

Kruegel, C., Valeur, F. and Vigna, G. (2005), "Intrusion detection and correlation: challenges and solutions", Springer, Vol. 14.

Mah, B.A. (1997), "An empirical model of HTTP network traffic", In Proc. INFOCOM'97, IEEE, Vol. 2, pp592-600.

Mahoney, M. and Chan, P.K. (2001), "PHAD: Packet header anomaly detection for identifying hostile network traffic", Florida Institute of Technology technical report, pp1-17.

Munz, G. and Carle, G. (2007), "Real-time analysis of flow data for network attack detection", In Proc. IM'07, 10th IFIP/IEEE International Symposium on Integrated Network Management, IEEE, pp100-108.

Pietraszek, T. (2004), "Using adaptive alert classification to reduce false positives in intrusion detection", In Proc. Recent Advances in Intrusion Detection, Springer, pp102-124.

Richardson, R. (2011), "CSI computer crime and security survey"

An Overview of Interworking Architectures in Heterogeneous Wireless Networks: Objectives, Features and Challenges

O.Khattab and O.Alani

School of Computing, Science & Engineering, University of Salford, UK
e-mail: o.khattab@edu.salford.ac.uk; o.y.k.alani@salford.ac.uk

Abstract

Loose coupling and tight coupling are two main interworking architectures have been proposed by European Telecommunication Standards Institute (ETSI) for integrating between the different types of technologies (3GPP, non-3GPP) such as Global System for Mobile Communication (GSM), Wireless Fidelity (Wi-Fi), Worldwide Interoperability for Microwave Access (WiMAX), Universal Mobile Telecommunications System (UMTS) and Long Term Evolution (LTE). On the other hand, Media Independent Handover IEEE 802.21 (MIH) and IP Multimedia Subsystem (IMS) frameworks have been proposed by IEEE group and 3GPP, respectively to provide seamless Vertical Handover (VHO) between the aforementioned technologies by utilizing these interworking architectures to facilitate and complement their works. In this paper, we overview loose and tight coupling interworking architectures and highlight their objectives, features, and challenges. Then, we conclude that loose couple is more suitable with MIH and contributes for enhancing its vital role in heterogeneous wireless environment.

Keywords

Heterogeneous Wireless Networks, IP Multimedia Subsystem (IMS), Loose Coupling, Media Independent Handover (MIH), Tight Coupling, Vertical Handover (VHO).

1. Introduction

With the advancement of wireless communication and computer technologies, mobile communication has been providing more versatile, portable and affordable networks services than ever. Therefore, the number of users of mobile communication networks has increased rapidly as an example; it has been reported that "today, there are billions of mobile phone subscribers, close to five billion people with access to television and tens of millions of new internet users every year" (International Telecommunication Union [ITU], 2013) and there is a growing demand for services over broadband wireless networks due to diversity of services which can't be provided with a single wireless network anywhere anytime (Angoma et al. 2011), (Chiu et al. 2011), (Ma et al. 2011) and (Dimitriou et al. 2011). This fact means that heterogeneous environment of wireless systems such as Global System for Mobile Communication (GSM), Wireless Fidelity (Wi-Fi), Worldwide Interoperability for Microwave Access (WiMAX) and Universal Mobile

Telecommunications System (UMTS) will coexist providing Mobile User (MU) with roaming capability across different networks. One of the challenging issues in Next Generation Wireless Systems (NGWS) is achieving seamless Vertical Handover (VHO) while roaming between these technologies; therefore, telecommunication operators will be required to develop a strategy for interoperability of these different types of existing networks to get the best connection anywhere anytime. To fulfill these requirements of seamless VHO two main interworking architectures have been proposed by European Telecommunication Standards Institute (ETSI), namely; loose and tight coupling for integrating between the different types of technologies. In this paper, we are going to present loose coupling and tight coupling as well as highlight their objectives, features, and challenges. Finally, we conclude that loose couple interworking architecture is more suitable with Media Independent Handover (MIH) and contributes for enhancing its vital role in heterogeneous wireless environment.

The rest of the paper is organized as follows: section 2 describes the VHO procedure. In section 3, we present MIH and IMS frameworks. In section 4, we describe the loose coupling and tight coupling interworking architectures with their objectives, features, and challenges. In section 5, a comparison between the two interworking architectures is presented. In section 6, the relation of loose and tight coupling with MIH is highlighted and finally, we conclude the paper in section 7.

2. Vertical Handover (VHO) Procedure

The mechanism which allows the MUs to continue their ongoing sessions when moving within the same Radio Access Technology (RAT) coverage areas or traversing different RATs is named Horizontal Handover (HHO) and VHO, respectively. In the literature most of the research papers divide VHO procedure into three phases: Collecting Information, Decision and Execution (Abdoulaziz *et al.* 2012), (Busanelli *et al.* 2011), (Gondara and Kadam, 2011), (Louta *et al.* 2011) and (Zekri *et al.* 2010), as described below.

A. Handover collecting information

In this phase, all required information for VHO decision is gathered, some related to the user preferences (e.g. cost, security), network (e.g. latency, coverage) and terminal (e.g. battery, velocity).

B. Handover decision

In this phase, the best RAT based on aforementioned information is selected and the handover execution phase is informed about that.

C. Handover execution

In this phase, the active session for the MU will be maintained and continued on the new RAT; after that, resources of old the RAT are eventually released.

3. Media Independent Handover (MIH) and IP Multimedia Subsystem (IMS) Frameworks

In a previous work (Khattab and Alani, 2013), we have classified the VHO approaches proposed in the literature into four categories based on MIH and IMS frameworks (MIH based VHO category, IMS based VHO category, MIP under IMS based VHO category and, MIH and IMS combination based VHO category) in order to present their objectives in providing seamless VHO. It has been concluded in (Khattab and Alani, 2013) that MIH is more flexible and has better performance providing seamless VHO compared with IMS framework; hence, the majority of approaches in the literature were based on MIH framework. The IEEE group has proposed MIH to provide a seamless VHO between different RATs (Neves *et al.* 2009) and (Lampropoulos *et al.* 2008). The MIH defines two entities: first, Point of Service (PoS) which is responsible for establishing communication between the network and the MU under MIH and second, Point of Attachment (PoA) which is the RAT access point. Also, MIH provides three main services: Media Independent Event Service (MIES), Media Independent Command Service (MICS) and Media Independent Information Service (MIIS) (Marquez *et al.* 2011) such that MIH relies on the presence of mobility management protocols, e.g., MIPv4 and MIPv6. In a previous work (Khattab and Alani, 2013), we have classified the VHO approaches proposed in the literature into two categories based on the mobility management protocols (MIPv4 and MIPv6) for which we have presented their performances and characteristics. It has been concluded in (Khattab and Alani, 2013) that providing service continuity through MIPv4 category under MIH will allow the operators to diversify their access networks take into account advantages of this category, while MIPv6 category under MIH requires future work improvements in terms of VHO decision criteria, additional entities, complexity, diversity of RATs and evaluation using empirical work real environment.

A.   Media Independent Event Service (MIES)

It is responsible to report the events after detecting, e.g. link up on the connection (established), link down (broken), link going down (breakdown imminent), etc. (IEEE Group, 2013).

B.   Media Independent Information Service (MIIS)

Figure 1 shows that MIIS is responsible for collecting all information required to identify the need for handover and provide them to MUs, e.g. available networks, locations, capabilities, cost, etc. (IEEE Group, 2013).

C.   Media Independent Command Service (MICS)

It is responsible to issue the commands based on the information which is gathered by MIIS and MIES, e.g. MIH handover initiate, MIH handover prepare, MIH handover commit and MIH handover complete (IEEE Group, 2013).

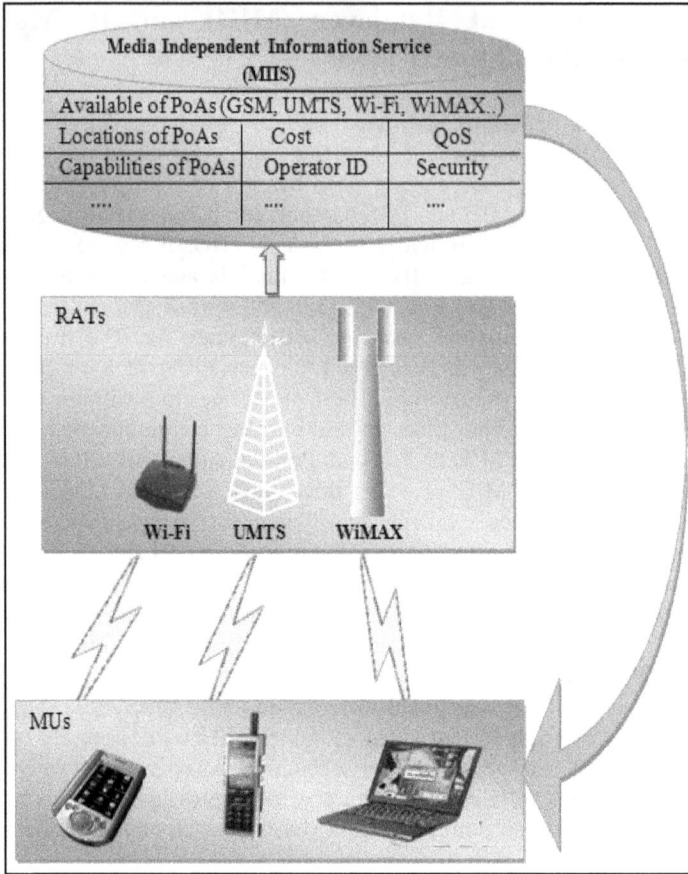

Media Independent Information Service (MIIS)		
Available of PoAs (GSM, UMTS, Wi-Fi, WiMAX..)		
Locations of PoAs	Cost	QoS
Capabilities of PoAs	Operator ID	Security
....	....	....

Figure 1: Media Independent Information Service (MIIS) Passing Information about Radio Access Technologies (RATs) to Mobile Users (MUs)

4. Interworking Architectures

The NGWS will consist of heterogeneous wireless access networks, such as UMTS, Wi-Fi, WiMAX and LTE, these different RATs have significant different capabilities in terms of supported data rate, coverage area, cost, etc. For example, The UMTS provides high coverage area, high cost and low data rate from 144 Kbps to 2 Mbps at 10 Km/h to maximum 500 Km/h depending on propagation channel, while the Wi-Fi provides low coverage area, low cost and high data rate from 1 Mbps to 54 Mbps at 30 m to maximum 450 m (Haji *et al.* 2009). Therefore, complementarity of these technologies through interworking architectures is essential to provide ubiquitous Wireless access abilities with high coverage area, high data rate and low cost to MUs. Consequently, the challenge would be the ability to move MUs seamlessly between these different types of wireless technologies. The two main interworking architectures found in the literature are loose coupling and tight coupling (Nguyen-Vuong *et al.* 2007), (Lampropoulos *et al.* 2007) and (Kassab *et al.* 2010); these are discussed next.

A. Loose coupling

In loose coupling architecture, each of the existing access wireless networks, such as UMTS, Wi-Fi and WiMAX is independently deployed. Both of WiMAX and Wi-Fi data do not pass through 3rd Generation Partnership Project (3GPP) core network this in turn means, there is no need to modify any architectural change, no additional cost and the interworking point occurs after 3GPP core network in particular, follow Gateway GPRS Support Node (GGSN) with internet. Also, the networks interconnection in this architecture based on MIP while for roaming service the Authentication, Authorization and Accounting (AAA) server connects between different RATs which allows the Wi-Fi and WiMAX data go directly to the internet without requiring for direct link between their components and 3GPP core network (Ronald, 2009).

B. Tight coupling

In tight coupling architecture, the Wi-Fi and WiMAX data pass through 3GPP core network before going to the internet and significant modifications of existing access wireless networks are necessary for providing seamless service to the MU to move from one network to another (Fangmin *et al*. 2007), this in turn impacts the 3GPP core network performance in terms of complexity, congestion and packet loss due to the overload. The networks interconnection in this architecture is based on the existing 3GPP core network functionalities (e.g. core network resources, subscriber databases and billing systems) that ensure MUs to continue their ongoing sessions when moving within different RATs. There are two types of tight coupling (Benoubira *et al*. 2011):

- Tight coupling integration at the GGSN level.
- Tight coupling integration at the RNC level.

- Tight coupling integration at the GGSN level

In this architecture, all of the RATs are connected together by Virtual GPRS Support Node (VGSN) which is responsible to exchange subscriber information and route packets between the wireless access networks, the handover duration (latency) is equivalent with loose coupling where MIP is used (no need of MIP functionalities) and it requires less complexity modification in 3GPP core network (Ronald, 2009).

- Tight coupling integration at the RNC level

In this architecture, Access Point (AP) and Base Station (BS) in Wi-Fi and WiMAX, respectively are connected with Radio Network Controller (RNC) by Interworking Unit (IWU). The IWU main functionality is to translate protocol and signalling exchange between RNC and another RATs interface, such as AP and BS (Benoubira *et al*. 2011).

5. Loose Versus Tight Coupling Comparison

In section 4, we have presented two main interworking architectures: loose coupling and tight coupling and their purposes, features and challenges have been discussed. To provide comparison of the two interworking architectures, we summarize their specifications on: efficiency of handover duration, probability of packet loss, mobility management, congestion, complexity, overload, additional modification, and additional cost, this is shown in Table 1.

According to our comparison between interworking architectures in Table 1, loose coupling seems to supersede tight coupling for the majority of the compared characteristics in terms of probability of packet loss, congestion, complexity, overload, additional modification and additional cost. It provides the same efficiency for handover duration when MIP is used and lower probability of packet loss than tight coupling which is incurred due to overload in 3GPP core network.

Characteristics	Tight Coupling	Loose Coupling
Efficiency of Handover Duration	Low	Similar with MIP
Probability of Packet Loss	High	Low
Mobility Management	3GPP Core Network Functionalities	MIP
Congestion	High	Low
Complexity	High	Low
Overload	High	Low
Additional Modification	High	No
Additional Cost	High	No

Table 1: Comparing Loose VS. Tight Coupling

6. MIH with Loose and Tight Coupling

The IEEE group presented MIH to provide seamless VHO between different RATs such as UMTS, Wi-Fi and WiMAX. To facilitate its work the interworking architectures contribute for enhancing MIH vital role in heterogeneous wireless environment.

After fair comparison in section 5 (Table 1), a better performance is provided by loose coupling compared with tight coupling which makes loose coupling the interworking architecture of choice to complement MIH vital role in heterogeneous wireless environment to achieve a seamless VHO in conjunction with applying MIPv4.

7. Conclusion

In this paper, we have described two main interworking architectures: loose coupling and tight coupling and their objectives, features and challenges have been discussed.

Fair comparison based on their performance in terms of latency, probability of packet loss, mobility management, congestion, complexity, overload, additional modification requirement and additional cost requirement has been made. We have described MIH framework which provides seamless VHO between different RATs by utilizing aforementioned interworking architectures to facilitate and complement their works. Also, we have concluded that loose couple interworking architecture is more suitable to work with MIH and enhance its vital role in heterogeneous wireless environment. Therefore, we can say that in the near future, providing service continuity through MIPv4 category under MIH will allow the operators to diversify their access networks take into account advantages of loose coupling interworking architecture.

8. Reference

Abdoulaziz, I.H., Renfa, L. and Fanzi, Z. (2012), "Handover Necessity Estimation for 4G Heterogeneous Networks", *International Journal of Information Sciences and Techniques*, vol. 2, no. 1, pp. 1-13.

Angoma, B., Erradi, M., Benkaouz, Y., Berqia, A. and Akalay, M.C. (2011), "HaVe-2W3G: A Vertical Handoff Solution between WLAN, WiMAX and 3G Networks", *7th International Wireless Communications and Mobile Computing Conference 2011 (IWCMC 2011)*, pp. 101-106.

Benoubira, S., Frikha, M. and Tabbane, S. (2011), "Hierarchical Mobile IPv6 Based Architecture for Heterogeneous Wireless Networks Interworking", *3rd International Conference on Communication Software and Networks 2011 (ICCSN 2011)*, pp. 422-426.

Busanelli, S., Martalo, M., Ferrari, G. and Spigoni, G. (2011), "Vertical Handover between Wi-Fi and UMTS Networks:Experimental Performance Analysis", *International Journal of Energy, Information and Communications*, vol. 2, no. 1, pp. 75-96.

Chiu, K.L., Chen, Y.S. and Hwang, R.H. (2011), "Seamless session mobility scheme in heterogeneous wireless networks", *International Journal of Communication Systems*, vol. 24, no. 6, pp. 789-809.

Dimitriou, N., Sarakis, L., Loukatos, D., Kormentzas, G. and Skianis, C. (2011), "Vertical Handover (VHO) Framework for Future Collaborative Wireless Networks", *International Journal of Network Management*, no. 6, vol. 21, pp. 548–564.

Fangmin, X., Luyong, Z. and Zheng, Z. (2007), "Interworking of Wimax and 3GPP Networks Based on IMS [IP Multimedia Systems (IMS) Infrastructure and Services]", *IEEE Communications Magazine*, vol. 45, no. 3, pp. 144-150.

Gondara, M. and Kadam, S. (2011), "Requirements of Vertical Handoff Mechanism in Wireless Networks", *International Journal of Wireless and Mobile Networks*, vol. 3, no. 2, pp. 18-27.

Haji, A., Ben Letaifa, A. and Tabbane, S. (2009), "Integration of WLAN, UMTS and WiMAX in 4G", *16th International Conference Electronics, Circuits, and Systems 2009 (ICECS 2009)*, pp. 307-310.

IEEE Group (2006), "IEEE 802.21 Tutorial", http://www.ieee802.org/21/, (Accessed 15 Nov 2013).

International Telecommunication Union (ITU) (2013), "Our vision: Committed to connecting the world", http://www.itu.int/en/about/Pages/vision.aspx, (Accessed 15 Nov 2013).

Kassab, M., Bonnin, J.M. and Belghith, A. (2010), "Technology Integration Framework for Fast and Low Cost Handovers-Case Study:WiFi-WiMAX Network", *Journal of Computer Systems, Networks, and Communications, Hindawi Publishing Corporation*, vol. 2010, no. 9, pp. 1-21.

Khattab, O. and Alani, O. (2013), "A Survey on Media Independent Handover (MIH) and IP Multimedia Subsystem (IMS) in Heterogeneous Wireless Networks", *International Journal of Wireless Information Networks (IJWIN)*, vol. 20, no. 2, pp. 215-228.

Khattab, O. and Alani, O. (2013), "Survey on Media Independent Handover (MIH) Approaches in Heterogeneous Wireless Networks", *IEEE 19th European Wireless 2013 (EW 2013)*, pp. 1-5.

Lampropoulos, G., Salkintzis, A.K. and Passas, N. (2008), "MediaIndependent Handover for Seamless Service Provision in Heterogeneous Networks", *IEEE Communication Magazine*, vol. 46, no. 1, pp. 64-71.

Lampropoulos, G., Passas, N., Kaloxylos, A. and Merakos, L. (2007), "A Flexible UMTS/WLAN Architecture for Improved Network Performance", *Wireless Personal Communications Journal*, vol. 43, no. 3, pp. 889- 906.

Louta, M., Zournatzis, P., Kraounakis, S., Sarigiannidis, P. and Demetropoulos, I. (2011), "Towards Realization of the ABC Vision: A Comparative Survey of Access Network Selection", *IEEE Symposium on Computers and Communications(ISCC)*, pp. 472-477.

Ma, X., Liu, J. and Jiang, H. (2011), "On the design of algorithms for mobile multimedia systems: A survey", *International Journal of Communication Systems*, vol. 24, no. 10, pp. 1330-1339.

Marquez-Barja, J., Calafate, C.T., Cano, J.C. and Manzoni, P. (2011), "Evaluation of a Technology-Aware Vertical Handover Algorithm Based on the IEEE 802.21 Standard", *IEEE Wireless Communications and Networking Conference 2011 (WCNC 2011)*, pp. 617-622.

Neves, P., Soares, J. and Sargento, S. (2009), "Media Independent Handovers:LAN, MAN and WAN Scenarios", *IEEE GLOBECOM Workshops*, pp. 1-6.

Nguyen-Vuong, Q.T., Agoulmine, N. and Ghamri-Doudane, Y. (2007), "Terminal-Controlled Mobility Management in Heterogeneous Wireless Networks", *IEEE Communication Magazine*, vol. 45, no. 4, pp. 122- 129.

Ronald, B. (2009), "Integration of Heterogeneous Wireless Access Networks", in Ekram, H. (Ed.) *Heterogeneous Wireless Access Networks Architectures and Protocols*, US: Springer, 978-0-387-09777-0.

Zekri, M., Jouaber, B. and Zeghlache, D. (2010), "Context Aware Vertical Handover Decision Making in Heterogeneous Wireless Networks", *35th Conference on Local Computer Networks 2010 (LCN 2010)*, pp. 764-768.

Connected In-Car Multimedia: Qualities Affecting Composability of Dynamic Functionality

A.Knirsch[1,2], J.Wietzke[2], R.Moore[2] and P.S.Dowland[1]

[1]Centre for Security, Communications and Network Research,
Plymouth University, Plymouth, United Kingdom
[2]ICM Labs, Faculty of Computer Science,
University of Applied Sciences Darmstadt, Darmstadt, Germany
e-mail: andreas.knirsch@h-da.de

Abstract

In-Car Multimedia systems have become a fundamental part of a car's human-machine interface. Recent developments within the domain of mobile consumer electronics create demands for flexible functionality by use of after-market applications, also within the automotive sector. Further, current systems already provide connectivity to enable dynamic data using cellular access networks. Future systems will provide comparable features not only for data, but also for functionality. The capabilities for modification or enhancement of functionality using network connectivity requires a thorough consideration of certain software qualities, also with respect to operation within a safety critical environment and provisioning of an adequate user experience. This paper characterises relevant software qualities with a strong focus on composability. The objective is to provide a base for building a modular system that appears as a homogenous whole, while providing sufficient dependability. An architecture is proposed to illustrate the applicability of those qualities to a particular software system.

Keywords

Embedded systems, automotive software engineering, infotainment, composability

1. Introduction

In recent years the significance of automotive information and entertainment (aka. infotainment) systems has grown rapidly. They represent the central information interface between the car and its occupants and already affect a prospective customer's purchase decision. They combine an increasing number of software-based functionalities of different importance and purpose, developed independently by multiple suppliers and integrated onto a shared hardware (HW) platform (a.k.a. the 'head-unit'). The aim is to provide guidance and assistance, while enabling the driver to configure and control automotive functions and offer a rich variety of entertainment functionalities. This evolution has led to large-scale complex software systems of >20 million lines of code (MLOC), decomposed into software components to tackle the complexity and integrated into the head-unit to achieve cost efficiency in production. The head-unit features various interfaces to other systems and the occupants of the car, and their mobile or storage devices. Figure 1 depicts some common components and interfaces of next generation systems.

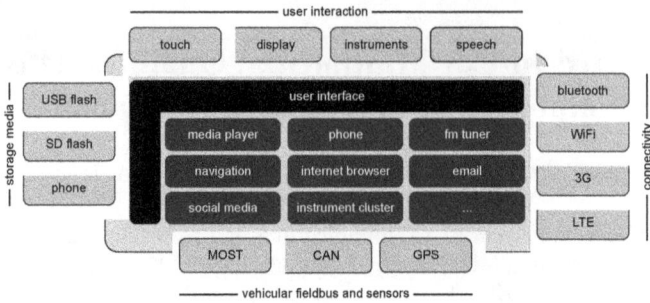

Figure 1: Exemplary components and interfaces.

Whereas the scope of past systems were limited to In-Vehicle Infotainment (IVI), current developments led to systems where the distinction of safety critical software functionalities, like e.g. the instrument cluster, becomes blurred due to integration. The instrument cluster provides functionality (e.g. indicators for gear, exterior light, speed control) that is classified safety critical using level ASIL B (Automotive Safety Integrity Level) following ISO 26262 "Road vehicles – Functional safety". Currently there are already systems available that display IVI content within a fully digital instrument cluster. Those systems are realised using several distinct platforms (aka. electronic control units (ECU)) interconnected by in-vehicle bus systems (e.g. CAN, MOST) and direct links to achieve an efficient video transport (e.g. LVDS).

It is the intention of the car manufacturers to reduce the number of ECUs, while utilizing available multi-core HW architectures (Monot et al., 2012). A decreasing number of dedicated HW units increase the integration density at the software level for a single HW platform while using a multi-source code base. In result the head-unit evolves into a mixed critical system (MCS), combining distinct levels of assurance against failure (Burns and Davis, 2013). Nevertheless, safety critical and non-safety critical functions may be still separated at the software level to prevent unwanted mutual interference. The objective is to maintain the necessary reliability of vehicular software, with a failure rate of about one part per million in a year (Mössinger, 2010).

Future IVI is anticipated to go beyond just information and entertainment due to the fusion with other existing and upcoming functionality to build an integral UI for the occupants. In the following the broader term In-Car Multimedia (ICM) is used to differentiate from IVI. Despite this heterogeneity at the software (SW) level, the user interface has to provide all functionality in a comprehensive and uniform way, blended into the car-manufacturer's usage concept. To achieve an adequate and purpose-oriented user experience (UX), both the allocation and the presentation of the content has to respect the car's operating state, the user's preferences, and interaction with the system, while considering a multi-display environment. Additionally, the software system has to meet specific temporal requirements while being deployed to a resource constrained embedded HW platform. Moreover, the system contains safety critical components and is operating within a safety relevant environment and therefore has to provide sufficient dependability, or more simply: it must work as intended.

The impact of these challenges is amplified by the demands and needs for dynamic content and functionality, available through wireless access networks (i.e. 3G, LTE). This enables ICM systems to dynamically update both data (e.g. geographical maps, traffic information) and functionality (e.g. 'apps') as provided for consumer electronics (CE) using 'app-stores/-markets'. Mössinger (2010) formulates this as follows:

> *"The next software revolution in vehicles is imminent as multimedia and consumer electronics enter the automotive world. Vehicles will be connected to the Internet and to all kinds of nomadic and home-based devices as new sources for automotive software, such as open source, emerge."*

Such SW deployment provides new opportunities for after-market solutions and maintenance, to reflect the relatively long product life cycle of automotive systems in comparison to CE. This also implies a new dimension of customisation by providing the 'user' freedom to choose what to integrate on the system. The consequence is an increased independency from and between suppliers of SW functionality. This raises additional issues regarding composability and the integration onto a common HW platform while maintaining a deterministic predefined temporal behaviour (i.e. dynamic aspects), to reflect the different degrees of importance of the integrated SW components.

In the following, we name and analyse relevant qualities and their relationships that have impact on the composability of dependable modular systems - using ICM systems connected to infrastructure-based wireless access networks as an illustrative example. Further, we match those qualities to a SW architecture for demonstrating the applicability onto practical systems.

2. Related Work

Burns and Davis (2013) provide a comprehensive review on MCS. They classify the prevention of interference between tasks from different components as primary concern with the implementation of MCS. Further, they name AUTOSAR as software standard of the European automotive industry for addressing mixed criticality issues. As foundation to standardisation they address research questions on how to reconcile the conflicting requirements of partitioning for assurance and sharing for efficient resource usage as fundamental:

> *"[...] how, in a disciplined way, to reconcile the conflicting requirements of partitioning for (safety) assurance and sharing for efficient resource usage."*

AUTOSAR provides mature means for partitioning and hence prevention of interference between different components (Mössinger, 2010). Hence it supports the shift from the "one function per ECU" paradigm to more centralized architecture designs (Monot et al., 2012). But it is rather static and does provide the necessary capabilities to integrate software components (i.e. dynamic content) originated from the CE domain. However, an AUTOSAR operating system (OS) may complement a system architecture to contain safety critical components, which is hosting multiple parallel containers with less critical software to support the demands for dynamic data and functionality.

Chung and do Prado Leite (2009) provide a comprehensive overview on the treatment of non-functional requirements (NFR). They claim the concept of quality is fundamental to software engineering. Both functional and non-functional characteristics must be taken into consideration during development, because functionality is not useful or usable without provisioning the necessary non-functional characteristics or quality attributes. They provide definitions to clarify terms related to NFR, describe differences to non-SW systems, and reason about the lop-sided emphasis in functionality:

> *"However, partly due to the short history behind software engineering, partly due to the demand on quickly having running systems fulfilling the basic necessity, and also partly due to the 'soft' nature of non-functional things, most of the attention [...] has been centred on notations and techniques for defining and providing the functions [...]."*

Attiogbé et al. (2006) propose the verification of composability using a formal model. They define such a model based on components' characteristics. In detail those are an *identifier*, a *state*, and an *interface* made of services that realise the interaction with the environment (i.e. other components). They define composability by considering the links between the components' services and their behavioural compatibility. The focus is basically limited on the system's functionality. Although the *interface* may contain details on characteristics, they omit an explicit modelling of NFRs.

Component-based software engineering (CBSE) has been a research area for many years. Hence, there are already a number component models with different aims and targeted for different domains available. A component model essentially consists of rules defining the construction of the components and their assembly. Crnković et al. (2011) provides a comprehensive overview on many of those and proposes a classification framework to support differentiation based on different dimensions to factor in the different aspects of the development process using an expressive formal model. They specify a component by a set of 'component properties', which covers both functional and non-functional properties (referred to as 'extra-functional properties' (EFP)): a component consists of a functional interface providing or using services, and a set of non-functional properties. Bindings define the connections between interfaces, whereas bindings are distinguished into connections between components and platform (i.e. those which enable component integration by use of an adequate abstraction layer) and into connections between components (i.e. those which enable component interaction by use of interoperable functional interfaces). Further, they provide information on specification, management, and composition of NFRs. Those ideas and their terminology are adopted for the concepts provided below.

3. Software Qualities related to Composable Systems

Modular systems are rendered by use of more or less distinct and heterogeneous components. To form an integrated whole those components have to be composable. This feature is expressed by the quality 'composability', which has to be reflected by the system's requirements to define targeted characteristics. The requirements also have to consider other non-functional qualities, referred to as non-functional requirements (NFR). While functional requirements reflect the purpose of the SW system (Chung and do Prado Leite, 2009), NFRs express the SW system's characteristics and attributes to make it useful and usable under stated conditions.

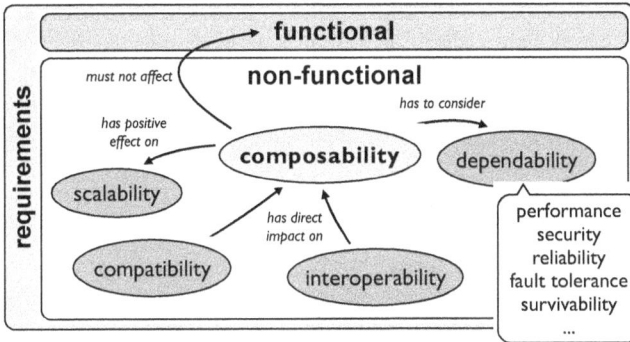

Figure 2: Qualities related to composability.

3.1. Composability

Composability is a complex quality. To make this term more tangible and also support the classification of whether a system meets a certain degree of composability, it is decomposed into the most significant and related qualities and characteristics, which are detailed in the following sections. Unfortunately, most classification schemes for NFRs are inconsistent with each other (Chung and do Prado Leite, 2009) and do not sufficiently recognize potential interactions between requirements. Hence, in the following sections the focus is kept on composability.

3.2. Compatibility and Interoperability

Composability mainly depends on compatibility and interoperability. Following the definition of Neumann (2004), compatibility implies the possible coexistence of different components (or entities) without adverse side effects. Interoperability addresses the ability of those different components to work constructively with one another. Both compatibility and interoperability are constructive aspects of SW engineering and therefore have to be considered already during the system design phase. This also implies that a system that lacks compatibility and/or interoperability might not be able to be refactored for improvement of those qualities without significant efforts. This statement is also supported by Chung and do Prado Leite (2009), who propose that NFRs play a critical role for architectural design.

3.3. Scalability

Further, composability and its derived qualities compatibility and interoperability have an effect on the scalability of a modular system. This is mainly related to the extendibility regarding the number of composed components. Also the reusability of the system's components increases with improved composability and therefore may have positive effects on the efficiency of the development process due to the possible reuse of already existing or legacy components.

3.4. Dependability

With regards to the operation within a safety relevant environment and containing safety critical functionality, the ICM system's dependability takes on a special role, which has to be considered throughout system development, maintenance and deployment of dynamic functionality. This includes, but is not limited to, the system's security, reliability, fault tolerance, survivability and performance.

4. Applied Development of ICM Systems

Based upon the information gathered through involvement in several multi-national development projects of ICM systems at different Original Equipment Manufacturers (OEMs), it can be observed that the industry does not apply a comprehensive approach to achieving composable systems. The system qualities and characteristics described above are not addressed adequately (if they are addressed at all) during the constructive design and development phase. In reality, the composing of components is mainly seen from a functional viewpoint, covering the components' interfaces with respect to the functional interdependencies. This is necessary but not sufficient to achieve composable systems. The following section describes some of the most critical issues that have been observed.

4.1. Temporal Behaviour

During the operation of the system the computational requirements and hence the computational load varies for different components, depending on the current system state, user interaction, or external events (i.e. triggered by automotive systems and sensors or through network communication). This may result in high-load (or peak-load) situations, where the system behaviour is not defined due to shared use of both computational and non-computational resources (e.g. input/output devices). Further, the system behaviour is difficult to test, due to various potential permutations of load distributions regarding the actual state of the components and depending on the actual integrated components. The latter gains significance for dynamic functionality (i.e. on user request), because neither the constellation of integrated components nor their potential mutual interferences are foreseeable. This may result in sporadic temporal interferences between components, violating the components' compatibility. Components that dynamically adjust the priorities of their executing threads and hence bias the scheduling without knowledge of other components' current state or their importance related to their semantics with a view on the overall system amplify such effects. Even more adverse is the circumstance that usually temporal behaviour isn't defined on the granularity of components. Latency requirements and performance characteristics serve as examples here. Hence, a violation of the required temporal behaviour often does not appear before integration of all components. With dynamic functionality for connected head-units this can cause unpredictable behaviour during the product-lifecycle, affecting the compatibility.

4.2. Memory Footprint

Similar to the computational resources, the platform's memory capabilities are also limited whereas the actual demands vary during system operation. While the footprint of a component can be estimated based on static analysis of the source code (if available), it is unlikely that the platform will provide as much memory as the overall system may theoretically demand. For dynamic functionality it is impossible to anticipate how much memory the platform has to provide to the components. The available memory may not be sufficient to cover all functionalities. A solution is provided by use of over-commit (aka. over-booking) (Urgaonkar et al., 2002) which also affects deterministic temporal behaviour and hence the component's compatibility.

4.3. User Interface

The automotive user interface (UI) provides multiple input and output facilities to enable a multi-modal interaction with various software components in parallel use. Many of those provide a graphical front end using the car's multi-display environment and concurrently utilise available graphical processing units (GPU) for HW acceleration. Due to a lack of the availability of multi-GPU platforms, this implies a bottleneck with potential adverse temporal effects for parallel computed components that rely on graphical output. Furthermore, as each of the components provide only a portion of the graphical user interface (GUI), the independent artefacts need to be blended to provide the car's occupants a consistent and uniform look and usage concept. The compositing of UI artefacts is related to both the components' compatibility and interoperability. A valid solution may be to implement the whole UI within a distinct component that relies on distinct "functional" components (this is basically the current approach). However, such an approach inhibits the modification and extension of those "functional" components without adaptation of the UI component. Hence this centralised UI approach is not applicable for dynamic functionality.

4.4. Tools and Techniques

Unfortunately, based on the experience gathered in industry projects, the applied business project management tools or techniques do not provide significant assistance. They may help to mitigate effects by adding transparency and traceability to the development process but also obfuscate the root cause: Insufficient addressing of composability throughout the constructive phases of the system development. This also applies to use of coding standards. Although they may help to improve maintainability and reliability by defining how the code must be structured and which language features should and should not be used, and hence represent an important building block for complex systems, composability lies beyond such non-software-architectural implementation rules. Nevertheless, coding standards can be used for automated checking of the components' sources statically for compliance with clear results to support the reliability of the system under development (Holzman, 2013), positively affecting the system's dependability.

The increasing system complexity and the heterogeneous functionality makes the consideration of composability throughout the system development overdue. This gets even more emphasised with the perspective on integration of dynamic functionality while considering an adequate degree of dependability.

5. Proposed Architectural Features

Based upon the problems detailed above, several suggestions can be made to aim for the goal of a more deterministic component integration and prevention of adverse component interactions. The intention is to assemble building blocks that bridge the gap between the conceptual approaches to an applicable solution (or at least significant improvements) for ICM systems that integrate dynamic functionality. However, a single building block may improve the system but also introduce some drawbacks. Hence it is recommended to utilise all suggestions in combination to both: benefit from the improvements while mitigating individual negative effects. The following proposed architectural features were evaluated using a prototype implementation, based upon OpenICM (Knirsch et al., 2012a).

5.1. Component Containment (CON)

Following the classification of Crnković et al. (2011) an exogenous management of extra-functional properties (i.e. NFRs) using containers to encapsulate the components is suggested. While the components concentrate on functional aspects, the containers take care of the NFRs by preventing unwanted interference. This obviates any modification to the components for system integration and effectively implements a separation of concerns. The functional binding between the components is independent of the management of the NFRs. This corresponds to the concept of execution domains (ED), whereas such containers for managing temporal NFRs are implemented using CPU affinity techniques in multi-core environments, virtualisation techniques, or both in combination (Vergata et al., 2011). For a stricter encapsulation Schnarz et al. (2014) describe an asymmetric multiprocessing (AMP) approach in combination with a multi-OS environment. Whereas EDs provide containment within a given OS, approaches based upon a multi-OS environment support containment using an OS domain (OSD), and vOSD for virtualisation respectively. Containment domain (CD) is used as generic term for ED, OSD and vOSD. Figure 3 illustrates containment using distinct CDs, whereas the execution platform depends on the actual implementation of the CD (i.e. ED, OSD, or vOSD).

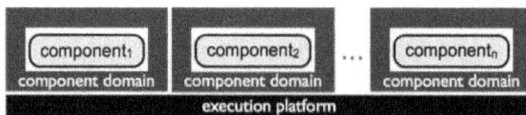

Figure 3: Using CDs for component containment.

An assembly of components sharing a single CD is refereed to as 'composite component'. Although the NFRs of a composite component are derived from the individual components, the characteristics of the composition are not. The composition is a set of components that interact together and hence also interfere with each other affecting compatibility. The possibly resulting adverse behaviour depends e.g. on the current system state, user interaction, component interaction and system load. This leads to a non-deterministic behaviour that may violate super-ordinated NFRs, and potentially affect functional requirements. However, clustering components based on certain characteristics (i.e. similarities) like criticalness, component provider, or semantics may provide adequate means to limit the propagation of adverse interaction. Such containment for dynamic functionality introduced after-market can be realised by use of a CD.

Figure 4 illustrates an exemplary ICM design using different types of CDs. Those are arranged hierarchically to demonstrate the flexibility in assembling mixed approaches for component containment. This means a particular CD may contain one or more other CDs. The depicted system consists of three distinct OSDs for very strict isolation, relying on an AMP based approach: AMP_1 contains instrument cluster components (i.e. classified ASIL B), AMP_2 contains the infotainment subsystem, whereas AMP_3 realises a OSD for an Android OS that provides capabilities to add, update and run dynamic functionality (i.e. 'APPs'). The HW platform provides four CPU cores, with two of them assigned to AMP_2. The latter host two EDs, while one ED contains a vOSD for creating a sandboxed Linux environment and providing four virtual cores. The vOSD then again contains two further EDs, utilizing the vcores.

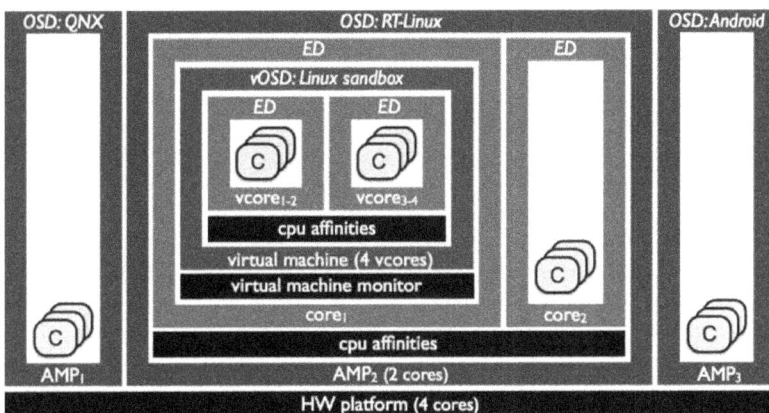

Figure 4: Exemplary composition of different containment techniques.

Similar concepts for data and non-computational resource accesses are already in use and approved for CE devices (e.g. Android Application Sandbox, Apple App Sandbox), while the focus is not set on multiple in-parallel user-operated applications (or components). Also other operating system specific solutions like 'adaptive partitioning' for QNX focussing on the platforms computational resources and the even more elaborate 'cgroups' on Linux feature the implementation of a containing model. For a portable implementation the use of a generic system interface or the abstraction within a domain specific software framework might be advantageous.

However, they may aid the partitioning within a particular component, but inadequately separate components of different safety criticalness. For the latter only multi-OS based containment might provide the required rigid partitioning.

5.2. Component Communication (COM)

Containment isolates the components, but they need to be able to interact with each other; they are interdependent. Basically, the connections in between are realised through functional interfaces, which enables component composition (also referred to as binding). Those interfaces provide the services of the respective components, i.e. implementing actions that both the provider and the consumer of the interface understand. Hence the interfaces realise interoperability.

ICM Systems are highly interactive, communicating with users and other in-vehicle systems. Hence, they rely on an event-based system based on event-triggers. However, some system components have to fulfil strict temporal requirements and therefore implement time-triggered behaviour of real-time systems. Nevertheless the communication between the components is event-based, which affects both the interfaces of the components and the communication channels. The latter have to be implemented efficiently to reflect the required qualities like performance and responsiveness of the system and the limited available HW resources. This leads to the application of shared memory (SHM) communication, which provides flexibility and adequate throughput. Events are processed using a central dispatching service to relay messages from sender to addressee using synchronised queues (Knirsch et al., 2012a). More complex communication is realised using synchronised data structures (aka. 'data containers') within SHM. This implements a loose coupling of components, while fostering an efficient communication flow and functional interoperability.

5.3. Management of Shared Resources (SHR)

Compatibility means coexistence without adverse side effects. Components are integrated into the head-unit and therefore share common resources. Although the next generation multi-core HW provides more computational resources to the system, components have to compete for other shared resources (SHR). Even worse, the access to SHR was implicitly managed through the system's task scheduler and applied thread priorities and scheduling strategies on single-core HW. This is not the case for in-parallel computed components on multi-core systems. The result is a non-deterministic behaviour due to unmanaged access to SHR and the related latencies. Important (i.e. high priority) components have to wait for unimportant. This affects the compatibility of the components, independent of an applied concept for component containment (e.g. the above described). A management layer as described with the Shared Resource Arbiter (SHARB) in (Knirsch et al., 2012b) is able to make the temporal behaviour related to the access to SHR more deterministic. Hence, resource access management has positive effect on the compatibility.

5.4. Composite User Interface (CUI)

The user interface (UI) has to address the required flexibility for future systems as outlined in 4.3. It constitutes a SHR with special characteristics: multiple components may use the UI in parallel. For the graphical part, several components may render a subset of the visualised frontend, to be blended and mixed on multiple displays (e.g. centre console, instrument cluster, rear mirrors, head-up display). Usually only one single HW graphic accelerator is available to support an appealing presentation of information and entertainment content. The containment of components creates requirements for a specific communication for UI (i.e. streaming of video and audio). To prevent adverse interference while maintaining an efficient communication, a SHM based compositing architecture provides an adequate solution. Notwithstanding a partitioning of components using vOSDs (CDs based on virtualisation techniques), subsets of the UI rendered by different components can be composited while utilising multiple HW graphic accelerators (Knirsch et al., 2013). This facilitates the compatibility due to the opportunity to build a homogeneous UI while partitioning the components into CDs.

5.5. Software Framework (SWF)

The features proposed here leverage composability by affecting derived qualities. It is not recommended to apply a single feature only due to negative or not sufficient effects. A SW framework is able to combine those to simplify their application. Additionally, such a framework is able to cover additional constructive aspects that may have positive impact on composability. In accordance to (Neumann, 2004) this includes modularity and encapsulation (i.e. containment), clean hierarchical and vertical abstraction, separation of policy and mechanism, object orientation and strong typing. Table 1 maps those aspects with the proposed architectural features. Hence, a framework considering and effectively addressing the constructive aspects by use of those features leads to improved composability.

constructive aspects	5.1 CON	5.2 COM	5.3 SHR	5.4 CUI	5.5 SWF
modularity and encapsulation	■	■			
clean hierarchical and vertical abstraction	■	■			
separation of policy and mechanism			■	■	
object orientation					■
strong typing					■

Table 1: Constructive aspects mapped to architectural features.

6. Conclusions and the Future

In the past dynamic content for ICM systems was limited to data. Next generation systems will provide capabilities to install and update functionality during the whole product life cycle (i.e. after-market). At the same time, safety critical applications are integrated onto the same platform, constituting systems of mixed criticality. This puts emphasis on non-functional qualities, in particular on dependability and composability, affected by parallel usage of shared resources (e.g. GPU, I/O, etc.) on multi-core HW. This work is intended to provide guidance for the design of ICM systems and related SW frameworks. Therefore qualities related to composability, their interplay and effects were characterised.

Further, a set of architectural features needed to improve composability, while also considering ICM system's safety requirements and demands for appealing UIs have been proposed. In summary, the combination of certain constructive aspects by use of those features leverages the system's SW components' composability. This provides support for the integration of dynamic functionality and hence prepares ICM systems for future demands while ensuring a deterministic behaviour.

7. References

Attiogbé, C., André, P. and Ardourel, G. (2006), "Checking Component Composability", Software Composition, LNCS, Vol. 4089, Springer, pp. 18-33.

Burns, A. and Davis, R. (2013), "Mixed Criticality Systems - A Review", 3rd Ed., Department of Computer Science, University of York, 2013.

Chung, L. and do Prado Leite, J.C.S. (2009), "On Non-Functional Requirements in Software Engineering", Conceptual Modeling, LNCS, Vol. 5600, Springer, pp. 363-379.

Crnković, I., Sentilles, S., Vulgarakis, A. and Chaudron, M.R.V. (2011), "A Classification Framework for Software Component Models", IEEE Transactions on Software Engineering, Vol. 37, No. 5, pp. 593–615.

Holzmann, G.J. (2013), "Landing a Spacecraft on Mars", IEEE Software, Vol. 30, No. 2, pp. 83–86.

Knirsch, A., Vergata, S. and Wietzke, J. (2012a), "Strukturierung von Multimediasystemen für Fahrzeuge", Echtzeit 2012, Informatik Aktuell, Springer, pp. 69-78.

Knirsch, A., Schnarz, P. and Wietzke, J. (2012b), "Prioritized Access Arbitration to Shared Resources on Integrated Software Systems in Multicore Environments," 3rd IEEE International Conference on Networked Embedded Systems for Every Application, pp. 1–8.

Knirsch, A., Theis, A., Wietzke, J. and Moore, R. (2013), "Compositing User Interfaces in Partitioned In-Vehicle Infotainment", Mensch & Computer 2013, Oldenbourg, pp. 63–70.

Monot, A., Navet, N., Bavoux, B. and Simonot-Lion, F. (2012) "Multi-source software on multicore automotive ECUs - Combining runnable sequencing with task scheduling," IEEE Transactions on Industrial Electronics, Vol. 59, No. 10, pp. 3934–3942.

Mössinger, J. (2010), "Software in Automotive Systems", IEEE Software, Vol. 27, No. 2, pp. 92–94.

Neumann, P.G. (2004), "Principled Assuredly Trustworthy Composable Architectures", Computer Science Laboratory, SRI International, Menlo Park, CA, USA.

Schnarz, P., Wietzke, J. and Stengel, I. (2014), "Towards Attacks on Restricted Memory Areas through Co-Processors in Embedded Multi-OS Environments via Malicious Firmware Injection", 1st Workshop on Cryptography and Security in Computing Systems, Vienna.

Urgaonkar, B., Shenoy, P. and Roscoe, T. (2002), "Resource Overbooking and Application Profiling in Shared Hosting Platforms," SIGOPS Oper. Syst. Rev., Vol. 36, No. SI, pp. 239–254.

Vergata, S., Knirsch, A. and Wietzke, J. (2011), "Integration zukünftiger In-Car-Multimedia-systeme unter Verwendung von Virtualisierung und Multi-Core-Plattformen", Echtzeit 2011, Informatik Aktuell, Springer, pp. 21–28.

Node Status Detection and Information Diffusion in Router Network using Scale-Free Network

A.W.Mahesar, A.Messikh, A.Shah and M.R.Wahiddin

Department of Computer Science, Institute of Information and Communication Technology, International Islamic University Malaysia
e-mail: Abdul.waheed@live.iium.edu.my;
{messikh|asadullah|mridza}@iium.edu.my

Abstract

In the field of computer networks various routing and internetworking algorithms and protocols have been introduced according to many performance metrics like network topology, scalability, speed, and congestion control requirements. In this paper we have used the concept of scale-free network theory to design a more robust data dissemination approach which can be used in one dynamical Autonomous System (AS) to know the appearance and disappearance of nodes, and speedily propagate the information to all nodes in the routers network. By taking advantage of the features of scale-free network behavior as found in inhomogeneous structure, short path lengths, highly clustered and epidemiological spreading an enhanced algorithm has been introduced which effectively finds the node status in the network and speedily broadcasts the information of status to all nodes in the network.

Keywords

Scale-free networks, degree distribution, preferential attachment, graph theory

1. Introduction

The concept of scale-free nature of many artificial (manmade) or natural complex networks in the world has been extensively studied during the last decade (Strogatz, 2001) (Barabasi, 2001) (Wang, 2002). In the category of technological networks the Internet (Faloutsos et al. 1998), World Wide Web (Reka Albert, Hawoong Jeong, 1999) and electrical power grid (Amaral et al. 2000), are scale-free networks. Similarly, the transportation networks of airways (Barrat et al. 2004), movie-actor collaboration network (Newman et al. 2001), scientific collaboration network (Dame, 2002) and web of human sexual contacts (Liljeros et al. 2001) have been proved to be scale-free networks. The complex structure of these networks has introduced great thrust and interest among the researchers to investigate the internal and hidden organizing principles or rules behind the emergence of these complex networked systems, and their resilience towards breakdown.

Complex networks formation has been seen and observed in many fields of life due to availability of vast amount of data gathered and analyzed with the help of high processing and storage capabilities of modern processing systems. Unfortunately, in spite of the availability of a huge amount of data, there are still many microscopic phenomena needed to fully understand the complexity level and dynamic behavior of these networks. Therefore, there is a severe need to understand the dynamics inside these networks, once understood then it will be easy to fully analyze the behavior with topology of these complex networks.

The most convenient way to represent any network is the graph theory. In graph theory, vertices represent the nodes and edges represent the links in the network. For example, the complex network of internet is a network of domain or routers. The Erdos and Renyi (ER) (A.Renyi and P.Erdos,1959) introduced the concept of random graph theory in the classical mathematical graph theory. According to them, complex networks topology can be best described by random graph. For example, if we have a large number of nodes in the network, and if we connect pair of nodes with the equal probability p then ultimate outcome will be physical example of ER random graph. The (ER) model remained very popular from late fifties to late nineties and, the modeling of almost all complex networks was based on random graph theory. According to this model the nodes degree distribution follow the uniform distribution. In this way, the network will be homogeneously connected with long length paths and low clustering coefficient. These features show that the connectivity distribution is homogeneous in networks as shown in Figure 1. In (ER) model the node degree distribution shows very different behavior as compared to real world complex networks. The Barabasi and Albert analyzed the network of World Wide Web (Albert-Laszlo Barabasi and Albert Reka, 1999) and found that the node degree of WWW does not follow random graph connections rather, it is scale-free graph and its degree distributions follow power law form as given in equation (1).

$$p(k) \sim k^{-\gamma} \tag{1}$$

Where $p(k)$ is the probability of node degree distribution and γ is scaling exponent which is a numerical parameter called connectivity distribution exponent. In fact, γ is a scale-free parameter in the sense that it does not depend on a characteristic scale of the network. Further, exponent gamma γ has been measured as well as confirmed in a number of research studies to be approximately 2.1 (Goh et al. 2005). It means, the node degree k and the number of links a node can have, follows the power-law distribution relation. Thus power-law implies that few nodes in the network can have large number of links whereas majority of nodes have very small number of connections. Also, (Faloutsos et al.1998) has shown that, from the autonomous systems perspective internet is also scale-free network.

Therefore, for explaining the power law distribution in complex networks Barabasi and Albert (Albert-Laszlo Barabasi and Albert Reka, 1999) proposed the model that is known as Barabasi-Albert (BA) model in short. According to them there are two main features of scale free behavior of any growing complex network. These features are continuous growth and preferential node attachment. Later they noticed this behavior in many real world networks. Due to these two features, the node with many connections tends to have more chances to acquire links in future like also known as rich get richer phenomenon. Therefore, this is the reason for creation of giant nodes in the network with high node degree distribution. Both these factors influence the creation of inhomogeneous or heterogeneous structure of network topology with hubs and make networks more robust under random node failures.

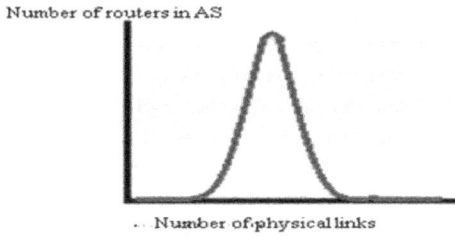

Figure 1: Bell shape curve distribution of routers linkages

Also, the inhomogeneous topological structure allows rapid information diffusion in networks due to short path lengths. Figure 1 shows the nodes degree distribution in ER random graphs, where it follows the Poisson distribution with bell shape curve. Figure 2 shows power law distribution with continuously decreasing curve as fat tailed curve behavior in (a) and decreasing slope on log-log scale of scale-free model in (b).

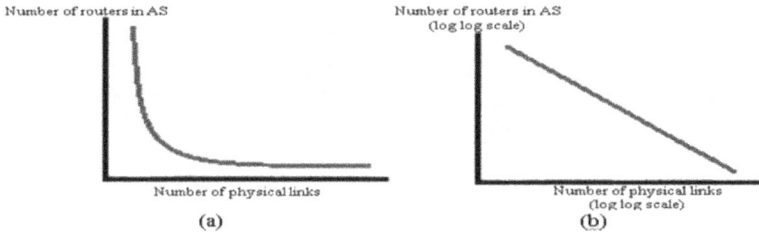

Figure 2: Power law distributions of routers linkages

According to the BA network model, the preferential node attachment plays crucial role in degree distribution of nodes in the network, with assumption that highly connected nodes have more chances to get more and more links. Figure 3 shows the preferential node attachment rule. It can be clearly seen that all the nodes have different importance and this scale-free behavior is the cause of inhomogeneous structure in the growing complex networks.

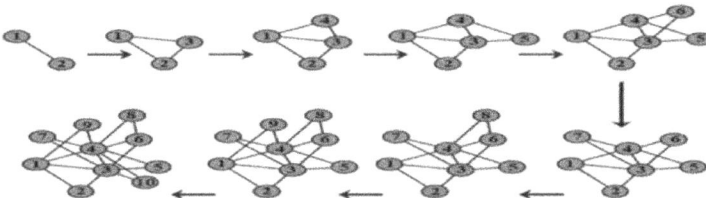

Figure 3: The formation of a scale-free network as an effect of the preferential node attachment (Oliver Hein, 2006)

Therefore, the formation of routers network in autonomous system based on preferential attachment can lead the network towards the scale-free topology. This formation allows the nodes in the network to form inhomogeneous structure and create short path lengths between nodes. In this way by taking advantage of these features and by using them properly, optimum results can be achieved in routers network. The figure 3 shows the network formation as a result of preferential attachment. The rest of the paper is organized as follows. In Section 2 we present scale-free model of routers network. In Section 3 we present the mathematical modeling to know the appearance and disappearance of nodes, ratio based technique and SFN dynamic node status detection algorithm. In Section 4 we discuss simulation results and finally, Section 5 concludes the paper with future work.

2.   Scale-free model for routers network

As scale free networks are based on two main features namely growth and preferential attachment, and this behavior has been shown in Internet from the autonomous systems perspective as well as routers perspective as given in (Romualdo Pastor-Satorras 2007). If we analyze this pattern of increasing nodes in the network of routers we can have network of routers as given in figure 4.

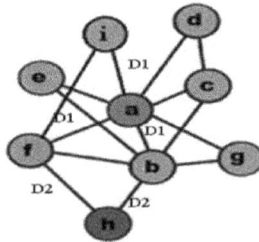

Figure 4: Schematic representation of scale-free network of routers connected in the Internet with D1 (Green) directly attached with a and D2 (h) (Blue) indirectly attached nodes with *a* as main node.

The scale-free network of the routers in the Internet can be represented by graph G (V, E). Where V is the set of vertices or nodes represented by circles, and E is the set of links between nodes represented by lines. Further, D1 are directly connected routers with main router a (Red) and D2 is indirect neighbor or second degree router from a. Also, we can represent the total number of nodes N (t) and the total number of links L (t) as a function of time t. As we are concerned with the dynamic networks therefore the behavior of above network is assumed to be dynamic, as addition or deletion (appearance / disappearance) of nodes makes it highly dynamic, evolving or growing network. Moreover, we can observe the behavior of a network in case of appearance/disappearance of routers in the network by both the dynamical rules governing the nodes and flow occurring along the links in terms of information diffusion. For example, in such network we assume the preferential attachment rule for acquiring the links and information updates of (appearance/disappearance) between nodes as a flow of routing updates.

According to BA model of preferential attachment, there are two main steps as given below: (Barabasi, 2001)

- Growth: Starting with a small number (m_0) of nodes, at every time step, we add a new node with $m \leq (m_0)$ edges that link the new node to m different nodes already present in the system as shown in (Barabasi, 2001).

- Preferential attachment: When choosing the nodes to which the new node connects, we assume that the probability that a new node will be connected to node i depends on the degree Ki of node i, such that

$$\prod i = k_i \div \sum_j k_j \qquad (2)$$

where k_i is the degree of node i and k_j is the sum of the degrees of all nodes in the network.

After t time steps, there are

$$N(t) = \lim_{t \to \infty}(t + m_0)$$
nodes (3)

and

$$L(t) = \lim_{t \to \infty}(mt)$$
edges (4)

Now, we represent the above network in Figure 4 with the help of the adjacency matrix X= {xij}. This will be the NxN matrix defined such that

$$X_{ij} = \begin{cases} 1 & \text{if } (i, j), \text{ is directly connected} \\ 0.5 & \text{if } (i, j), \text{ is connected through second degree node connection} \\ 0 & \text{if } (i, j), \text{ is not connected} \end{cases}$$

where, i and j are any nodes in the network.

	a	b	c	d	e	f	g	h	i
a	0	1	1	1	1	1	1	0.5	1
b	1	0	1	0.5	1	1	1	1	0.5
c	1	1	0	1	0.5	0.5	0.5	0.5	0.5
d	1	0.5	1	0	0.5	0.5	0.5	0.25	0.5
e	1	1	0.5	0.5	0	0.5	0.5	0.5	0.5
f	1	1	0.5	0.5	0.5	0	0.5	1	1
g	1	1	0.5	0.5	0.5	0.5	0	0.5	0.5
h	0.5	1	0.5	0.25	0.5	1	0.5	0	0.5
i	1	0.5	0.5	0.5	0.5	1	0.5	0.5	0

Figure 5: Mathematical representation of network in Figure 4 as undirected graph, where 0.5 represents the second degree node from main node a.

3. Mathematical modeling of the concept "node detection or disappearance and appearance of nodes in the network".

To know the appearance and disappearance of nodes in the network, the main node will have to send the periodic update or keep alive messages to all nodes in the network. Let us assume that the sending period to keep alive messages is 10ms (milli seconds (it can be varied depending on the sensitivity or rapid response of nodes in the network). It means after each 10ms update message will be sent to all nodes in the network. In case of second degree or indirect nodes the message will be sent through nearest neighbor node from main node in the network.

Further, if we have two nearest neighbors then less congested or more reliable route can be selected as in many traditional routing protocols. In above network of figure 4, there are two routes to node h (Blue) from node a, first from node a (Red) via node b (green), and second from node f (green). So, in traditional routing the preferred route will be fastest for example, which has more bandwidth or less congestion or it can be any other network metric depending on the type of networks like social network, covert (terrorist) network, airport- air flight network etc. But, here we find the shortest route based on the probability of degree distribution of neighboring nodes, for example from the probability of (a to b) or (a to f) in above scenario of network given in figure 4. If probability from a $\rightarrow$ b with respect to links of b is high as compared to a $\rightarrow$ f, then the route from a$\rightarrow$ b $\rightarrow$h will be selected as shortest route for h. mathematically,

$$\Pi_{a \rightarrow b} = \frac{Kb}{\Sigma_j Kj} \tag{5}$$

Where k_b is the degree of node b and k_j is the sum of the degrees of all nodes in the network.

Or

$$\Pi_{a \rightarrow f} = \frac{Kf}{\Sigma_j Kj} \tag{6}$$

Where, k_f is the degree of node f and k_j is the sum of the degrees of all nodes in the network.

3.1. The ratio based technique for node detection:

To know the presence and absence of nodes, we find the value of the ratio **r** between sending and receiving messages among nodes from the main node to all. The result of ratio will decide the appearance and disappearance of nodes. Also we set threshold value of ratio **r** to further know the stability of nodes in the network. Based on the values of ratio, we can have three cases.

First case:

If the main node sends three messages after each 10ms and if it gets three replies from the receiving nodes in 30ms interval then it will be assumed that the nodes are alive from the ratio of sending and receiving messages. The ratio of messages like three messages and three replies, so ratio is 1, and this ratio will trigger the appearance of node in the network.

Second case:

If main node sends three messages and receives two replies then the ratio will be 3:2 and it will be assumed that the node now may be present in the network. Similarly, if main and receiving node has 3:1 ratios, it will be assumed that the node is not in good condition or it is trying to reduce the chances to get connected or the node is not stable in the network.

Third case:

If main node doesn't receive any reply and the ratio is 3:0, then main node will be able to know that the particular node has disconnected or disappeared and main node will broad cast the message accordingly to all nodes that particular node is no more part of the network now. This can be represented as

Let R represent the ratio, if R= (N received messages / N sent messages) > 0.5 it implies that the node is connected.

If the ratio R= (N receive / N sent) > 0.0 and R < 0.5, then we can assume that node is in unstable condition.

But, if ratio R= (N receive / N sent) is 0.0 it means that node has disappeared from the network.

This effect can be shown mathematically in the adjacency matrix with (0 as disappeared and 1 as present) entries in the rows and columns of the matrix for connectivity. And the value 0.5 represents the presence of indirect nodes in the network. When main node observes from the result of ratio that the particular node is approaching a low threshold, it will be assumed that node is going to reduce the participation in the network in advance.

Further, if we observe from the epidemic modeling perspective, as scale-free nature allow the presence of hubs and giant structure due to power-law distribution, therefore the information in main node can propagate to all nodes like infection propagates. Therefore, by taking advantage of this behavior and disseminating information in an epidemic way in the network can be more effective and threshold value of ratio decides the triggering effect for the main node to decide when to propagate. Also, we can assume that the main router *a* in the figure 4 or the router with second largest connections of links *b* in figure 4 has advanced configuration like high bandwidth, high processing speed and large buffer size for handling incoming and outgoing information. Moreover, we can say that there are two scenarios, first when the main node try to receive the message from the nodes as pull based. It is something like when node tries to extract new information from its neighbors in above case to know the status (Ganesan et al. 2002). In second scenario when a node sends new information to a selected or all neighbors as push based. Finally, as we have to deal with dynamic or evolving networks, therefore the proposed algorithm for above case must rapidly propagate updates, because some tasks or information have to be activated as soon as possible and newly assigned tasks make the older one useless or obsolete.

3.2. SFN node status detection dynamic routing algorithm.

Algorithm 1: The algorithm for detecting the disappearance and appearance of nodes in scale-free based topology of routers network.

VARIABLE Mn =Main node, Dn =Direct neighbor, In = Indirect neighbor

Step1. Every node in the network will send or exchange their degree distribution to

their neighbor's at each time interval of addition of links.

Step2. Node with higher degree Max: f (Ki) will be selected as the main node (Mn)

of network from degree distribution probability.

Step3. Mn (Main) node will send its IP and node degree to all nodes (direct Dn/

Indirect In) in the network.

Step4. If node is directly connected neighbor THEN

Update will be send directly.

ELSE

In case of indirect neighbor, probability of neighbor's degree distribution

will decide the path.

IF the degree of node b is higher THEN

b will be selected as next route.

ELSE

'f' will be the next route.

Step5. Mn will send periodic message k three times to all connections after each 10

seconds.

Step6. After receiving reply messages from all nodes ratio will be calculated.

IF ratio R=1 THEN

node is connected

ELSE

IF ratio is zero THEN

node will be considered as disappeared

ELSE

IF ratio is in between threshold 0.5< and >0.3 THEN

the node is not in stable condition.

Step7. The unstable node information will be used to select best path in advance in

network.

Step8. The disappearance will be disseminated as broad cast message to all nodes in

the network epidemically.

4. Results and findings

We have implemented and tested this algorithm in Java2SE as research tool. The following graphs show the relation between time in milliseconds and number of nodes in the network as it grows based on preferential node attachment concept. The graph in Figure 7(a) shows the time taken by main node after addition and dissemination of this information to all nodes as network grows. The result shows as network grows based on preferential link attachment and due to inhomogeneous topology caused by few hubs in the network, the time is decreasing to diffuse the information in network as it is growing. In graph 7(a) vertical axis represents time in milliseconds and horizontal axis shows the number of new nodes attached as it grows.

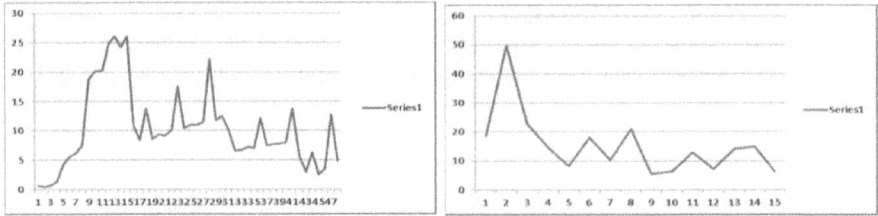

(a)   (b)

Figure 7: (a) Node appearance and information diffusion time. (b) Node disappearance and information diffusion time

The graph in Figure 7(b) shows node disappearance from network and its information diffusion time is decreasing as network grows based on preferential link attachment. In graph 7(b) vertical axis represents time in milliseconds and horizontal axis shows number of nodes deleted from the network.

5.   Conclusion and future work

Based on scale-free features like preferential node attachment and growth, the routers network has been analyzed. By taking advantage of heterogeneous topology formation from preferential node attachment, an efficient way of data transmission to many nodes at once has been achieved. Further, this paper has added the link detection algorithm in this type of topology, which will greatly help to know the status of their detached as well as newly added nodes in the network. Also, the stability of nodes can be determined from the results of ratio and better route can be decided in advance for future configuration in the network. The nodes sudden appearance and disappearance also can be analyzed in many real as well as artificial complex networks and better strategies can be formulated to properly know the behavior and effects in these networks. Also, epidemic spreading and other features in scale free networks can be used in various networks like sensor, ad hoc and wireless networks to better devise powerful and robust algorithms and this may constitute a future work.

6.   Acknowledgement:

This research is funded by the Malaysian Grant No. FRGS 11-042-0191

7.   References

A.Renyi and P.Erdos, 1959. On Random Graphs. *Publ.Math.Debrecen* 6, p.290-297.

Amaral, L. A. N., A. Scala, M. Barthélémy, and H. E. Stanley, 2000. Classes of behavior of small-world networks. *Proc. Natl. Acad. Sci.* U.S.A. 97, 11 149.

Barabasi, A.L and Albert, R, 1999. Emergence of Scaling in Random Networks. *Science* 286 (5439): 509-12

Barabasi, A.L. and Albert.-R., 2001. Statistical Mechanics of Complex Networks. *Review of Modern Physics*, 77, pp.41–71.

Barrat, A., Barth, M. & Vespignani, A., 2004. Weighted evolving networks: coupling topology and weights dynamics.,(1), pp.1-4.

Dame, N., 2002. Evolution of the social network of scientific collaborations. *Physica A 311*, 3(4), pp.590–614.

Ganesan, D. et al., 2002. An Empirical Study of Epidemic Algorithms in Large Scale Multihop Wireless Networks. *Intel Research, Berkeley Technical Report, IRB-TR-02-003*.

Goh, K., Kahng, B. & Kim, D., 2005. Evolution of the Internet Topology and Traffic Dynamics of Data Packets. , pp.235–250.

Liljeros, F., Edling, C.R. & Stanley, H.E., 2001. Distributions of number of sexual partnerships have power law decaying tails and finite variance. *Nature*, 1(6), pp.1–6.

Michalis Faloutsos, Petros Faloutsos, C.F., 1998. On Power-Law Relationships of the Internet Topology. *ACM SIGCOMM Computer Communication Review*, 29(4), pp.251–262.

Newman, M.E.J., Strogatz, S.H. & Watts, D.J., 2001. Random graphs with arbitrary degree distributions and their applications.

Oliver Hein, M.S. and W.K., 2006. Scale-Free Networks The Impact of Fat Tailed Degree Distribution on Diffusion and Communication Process. , 48, pp.267–275.

Reka Albert, Hawoong Jeong, A.-L.B., 1999. Diameter of the World-Wide Web Growth dynamics of the World-Wide Web Global methylation in eutherian hybrids. *Nature*, 401(September), pp.398–399.

Romualdo Pastor-Satorras, A.V., 2007. *Evolution and Structure of the Internet*, Cambridge University Press.

Strogatz, S.H., Watts, D.J, 1998. Collective dynamics of small-world networks.*Nature* 393 (6684) 409-10.

Wang, X.F., 2002. Complex Networks: Topology, Dynamics and Synchronization. *International Journal of Bifurcation and Chaos*, vol. 12, no. 5, pp. 885–916.

Achieving Improved Network Subscriber Geo-Location

T.O.Mansfield, B.V.Ghita and M.A.Ambroze

School of Computing and Mathematics, Plymouth University, Plymouth, UK
e-mail: {thomas.mansfield|bogdan.ghita|m.ambroze}@plymouth.ac.uk

Abstract

Future disaster and emergency management requirements are currently under discussion in the US and Europe that will require mobile phone network operators to locate their subscribers to a high level of accuracy within a short time period. Current deployed mobile phone geo-location systems are required to locate the caller to within 125 m. Future systems will require an order of magnitude better accuracy.

This paper proposes a method to achieve improved location accuracy with the addition of carrier phase analysis and accurate time of flight techniques to current systems. The resulting combination of technologies has been analysed using a simplified model to benchmark and compare the subscriber location estimate against existing solutions.

The system described in this paper shows the potential to meet the emerging disaster and emergency management requirements in complex radio frequency environments.

Keywords

Geo-location, SyncE, IEEE1588 PTP, RF navigation, carrier phase analysis.

1. Introduction

Current disaster and emergency management applications require mobile phone network providers to locate the physical position of their subscribers if they contact the emergency services; in the case of US, the enhanced emergency alert (E911) legislation requires the network providers to locate the caller to within 125 m 67 % of the time (Reed et al. 1998). Next Generation 911 (NG911) is likely to require more accurate and more reliable position estimation of the user calling the emergency services, likely to be < 10 m up to 95% of the time (DTRITA 2013). This legislation will lead to a requirement for network operators to be able to quickly locate subscribers in many challenging environments.

One of the main challenging environments of operation is likely to be locating users in dense urban environments and urban canyons (ground level urban areas with very limited direct visibility of the sky/satellites). These areas typically have very dense subscriber populations and complex radio frequency (RF) environments.

Typical RF problems encountered in dense urban environments include high multipath effects, poor line of sight (Including poor GPS coverage), localised areas of low signal strength and considerable inter-channel interference.

This paper will investigate the viability of combining mature and developing technologies in order to provide a more accurate subscriber location estimate over a wider range of environments than can be obtained from any single technology.

The remainder of this paper is broken into the following sections. Section 2 reviews the current deployed capability for mobile phone geo-location. Section 3 provides a summary of the commonly applied approaches to coupling mature technologies to provide geo-location services. Section 4 provides an overview of a novel system that could be deployed in addition with current geo-location systems to provide an increased level of system accuracy. Method of overcoming the main challenges of this system are described in section 5. Section 6 details the simulation work carried out to verify the described approach. The results obtained from this simulation are provided in and section 7. Sections 8 and 9 provide information on future work and conclusions gained from the paper.

2.   Current Deployed Capability

Current E911 compliant geo-location based systems are largely based on time difference of arrival (TDoA) systems. The most accurate and widely deployed system currently used is the AT&T uplink TDoA (U-TDoA) system. (AT&T 2013).

This system relies on sensitive time synchronised location measurement units (LMUs) located at each base station. The LMUs monitor each subscriber's uplink data channel when placing a call. The individual LMUs are time synchronised by GPS and communicate over the inter-base station network to calculate a subscribers position. This system commonly provides geo-location accuracy of around 50 m when the subscriber has a line of sight view of at least 3 network base stations. (True Position 2011).

3.   Current Research Areas

The current state of the art in mobile phone subscriber geo-location can be separated into three main areas: RF based, peripheral device based and hybrid of both systems. Many peripheral and hybrid systems require the use of ancillary sensors within the subscriber's handset. Due to a lack of standardisation in the peripheral devises available on any mobile phone and the high coverage required to meet the emerging requirements, this review will cover RF based systems which use typical mobile phone RF devices only.

The network based approach relies on using the characteristics of both the mobile phone network and other RF systems, such as Wi-Fi, to provide a geo-location estimate.

Perhaps the most commonly applied technique to provide a geo-location estimate for subscribers within a mobile phone network is to use timing based techniques such as time of arrival (ToA) (van der Bij and Lipinski 2012) or time difference of arrival (TDoA) (Locata 2013). All time based systems however suffer from several drawbacks. Firstly in areas with poor line of sight from the transmitter to the receiver, the signal cannot take a direct path. This causes significant error at the receiver. Additionally, the reflection of signal produces a multipath environment and associated reading, leading to further measurements errors.

Another approach to network based geo-location is to use an angle of arrival (AoA) approach. This approach commonly requires the calculation of the angle that a signal is received from (Niculescu and Nath 2003). If the angle of the subscriber is known from three or more base stations, the users location can be calculated by creating an intersect. Again this approach has several inherent problems, firstly a non-line of sight signal path will cause intersect errors. Secondly, the method of accurately locating the angle of arrival is not trivial and involves the use of sectored, rotation or electronically steerable antennas, all of which have considerable angular measurement errors.

Frequency and carrier phase analysis may also be used to estimate a subscriber's location (Roxin et al. 2007). Frequency based analysis typically relies on the motion of the subscribers to allow the Doppler shifts in their signals to be tracked. The drawback to this method is the fact that the location of slow moving or stationary subscribers will drift over time. Meanwhile, carrier phase analysis relies on the monitoring of the carrier signal phase of a source RF signal. The drawbacks of this technique are that the signals monitored need an accurate clock to provide reliable phase analysis and that the carrier signal can be affected lowering positional accuracy.

Another RF based approach that can be taken is to monitor certain network properties, from generic signal strength to data recognition, including such as cell IDs or signal fingerprinting (Kjaergaard 2010). This family of approaches has one main drawback: The subscriber system must have either a pre-determined database of network topology data or have acquired it via a lengthy simultaneous localisation and mapping (SLAM) procedure. Both of these approaches are difficult to implement in practical scenarios where either RF topology changes rapidly without the network operators knowledge or there is no time to build up a complex SLAM calibration scheme.

GPS receivers are currently integrated on many mobile phones. The task of relaying the GPS information over the network to the network operator is trivial. There are however limitations to using GPS in urban environments. To operate successfully, the receiver needs a clear line of sight view of at least 4 GPS satellites. In most locations, this requires a wide field view of the sky, which is not available in many urban canyon environments. It is worth noting at this point that, although there are many urban areas where there are less than 4 satellites in direct line of sight, many densely populated areas are likely to still allow visibility of 1 or more satellites due to the good constellation spread of existing GPS satellite networks.

Success has been made in combining a single GPS receiver with ToA and carrier phase analysis to determine a geo-location estimation [9]. This approach combines mobile phone network ToA and carrier phase analysis to provide a position estimate in the absence of a full set of GPS satellites. Due to limitations in the measurement accuracy of the phone network component of this system, location estimates only provided an uncertainty of 345 m 95% of the time.

The concept of combining GPS and terrestrial RF systems can be improved selecting a terrestrial signal with better transmission properties than those found in mobile phone networks.

4.   Improving U-TDoA Resolution with Short Wave Radio Phase Analysis

The proposed method relies on several layers of techniques with varying accuracy levels that complement each other in a typical urban environment, starting with U-TDoA for coarse acquisition and adding in other techniques to provide added robustness and accuracy.

The system assumes that a U-TDoA system is in operation and can achieve a positional accuracy of < 50 m in good conditions with a clear line of sight to the subscribers. It is also assumed that the area has a good level of coverage from a short wave digital Digital Radio Mondiale (DRM) signal. The DRM radio service is a shortwave radio service that uses a modulated carrier wave frequency of 5-6 MHz (ETSI 2009), providing a wavelength of approximately 50 m. Due to the commercial nature of the DRM service, transmitter location is optimised in urban environments to allow good population coverage.

It is possible in non-multipath environments, with GPS clock accuracy, to carry out phase analysis on the recovered transmission carrier wave with a phase noise of <10 % (Carvajal et al. 2011). This provides a location accuracy of ≈ 5 m if a clear signal is received.

It has been mentioned that the carrier phase technique requires a GPS level clock accuracy of ≈ 100 ns (Dana 1990). This only requires visibility of 1 GPS satellite. This external time source may also be provided in indoor environments by a GPS time repeater system.

It can be seen that DRM carrier phase analysis, supported by the GPS clock pulse, can be overlaid onto the existing U-TDoA system and can improve the locational accuracy by an order of magnitude.

The problem still remains that the system would provide poor results in an area of high multipath propagation of the DRM signal.

5.   Combatting Multipath

To combat the effects of multipath in the signal, an extra layer of geo-location techniques is required in the system. A typical multipath environment is considered in Figure 1.

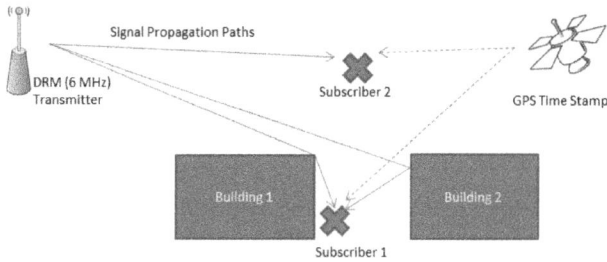

Figure 1: Typical Urban Environment with Multiple Signal Paths

It can be seen in Figure 1 that subscriber 1 does not have a direct line of sight with the DRM transmitter and is receiving both a reflection and a refraction of the transited signal. Receiving both signals, with a slight time delay increases carrier phase noise and makes the position estimation within the DRM signal less accurate.

If the phase analysis is carried out sufficiently frequently (at least 8 samples per sine wave), the subscriber system can calculate the quality of the carrier phase analysis. In the scenario shown in Figure 1, subscriber 2 has a good line of sight with the DRM transmitter, so consequently could easily determine that it has a good Gaussian distributed positional accuracy. Conversely subscriber 1 knows that it has a poorly distributed carrier phase signal and is likely to have a poor positional accuracy distribution.

In this case, subscriber 1 can gain a relative position from subscriber 2. This is possible by using the IEEE 1588 precession time protocol (PTP) in conjunction with ITU Synchronous Ethernet (SyncE) standard. The combination of the PTP time plane and SyncE frequency plane to estimate ToA can provide timing accuracies of ≈ 4.5 ns. (Ouellette et. al. 2011) proving a relative positional accuracy of < 2 m between the two users. From this relative navigation solution, it is possible for subscriber 2 to maintain a geo-location with an estimation error of < 10 m, even in an area of high multipath and poor line of sight with any external reference.

6. Simulation Details

The aim of the simulation is to calculate the positional estimation accuracy of subscribers in a system where carrier phase analysis and ToA geo-location are used simultaneously to determine a user's geo-location in areas of both low and high multipath.

The following major limitations and assumptions have been applied to the simulation model; the subscribers are not moving; During reflections and refractions there is no frequency shift to the affected signal; The received signal strength is suitably high and free from interference, including atmospheric effects, throughout the simulation; Subscriber 1 and 2 are free to share their positional estimate in real time with each other. While these limitations may have minimal impact in certain environments, these limitations are likely to affect the simulation accuracy when compared with most real world environments. The accuracy results derived from the model should be considered a 'best case' example.

The case environment to be simulated is that shown in Figure 1. The simulation will assign typical signal generation errors (ETSI 2009) and free space delays to estimate the positional accuracy and confidence level in a multipath environment. The simulation will be broken into two stages. Stage 1, as shown in Figure 2, will simulate the system relying on DRM phase analysis alone. The second stage of the simulation, as shown in Figure 3, will add the layer of system that relies on relative geo-location between subscriber 1 and 2. This will allow the final positional estimate of subscriber 2 to be calculated after combing the uncertainty of subscriber 1 and the uncertainty of the relative position of subscriber 2 from subscriber 1.

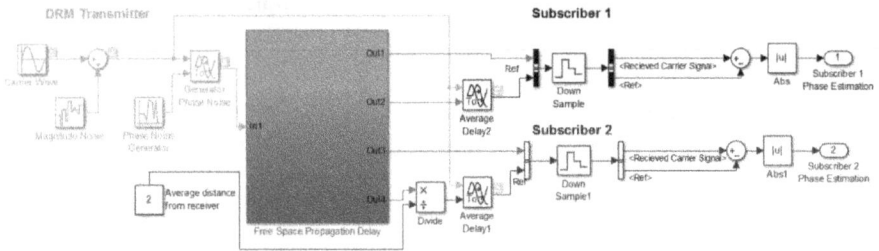

Figure 2: Simulink Simulation of DRM Phase Analysis System

Figure 4 simulates the maximum likely geo-location accuracy of the DRM based system in an area of good RF line of sight to subscriber 1 and while in an area of high multipath, as seen by subscriber 2. The DRM transmitter, comprising of a carrier wave with amplitude and phase noise added is shown in green. The red blocks calculate typical errors of free space transmission in direct path, reflection and refraction environments. The black and blue blocks simulate the receiving and time stamping errors of subscriber 1 and 2 respectively.

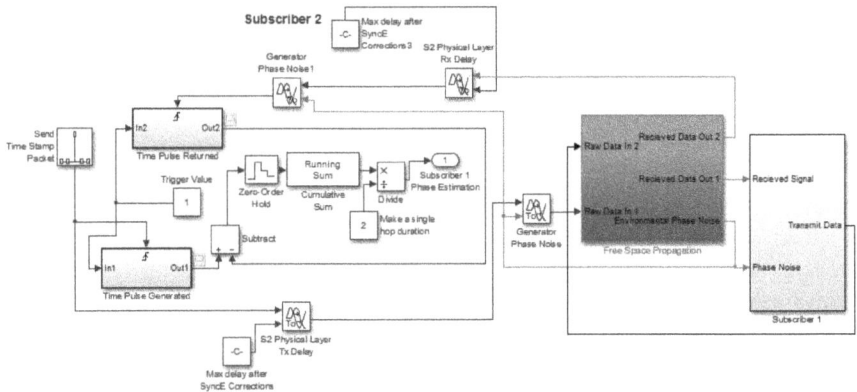

Figure 3: Simulink Simulation of SyncE and PTP Link

Figure 3 shown the simulation model used to estimate the ToA jitter during relative geolocation via a combination of SyncE and PTP. The red blocks simulate typical errors expected from the free space transmission after the corrections applied by SyncE have been applied. The black blocks attribute the reception, processing and transmission errors expected from the subscriber 1 hardware. Subscriber 2, represented by the blue blocks, simulates the appropriate hardware transmission and reception errors of the system. In addition to this, subscriber 2 also monitors the jitter and delay in the system by comparing the difference in the network layer transmission and reception of a pre-determined packet header.

7.   Simulation Results

7.1. DRM Phase Analysis

The simulation shown in Figure 2 and Figure 3 was run by Simulink®. The resulting carrier phase analysis noise can be seen in Figure 4.

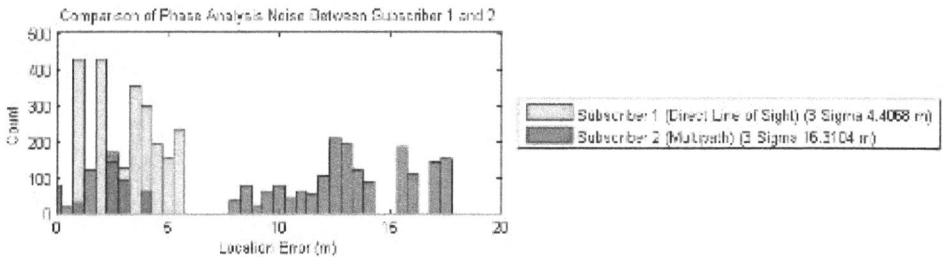

Figure 4: Comparison of Subscriber 1 and Subscriber 2 with DRM Carrier Phase Geo-Location Only

It can be seen in Figure 4 that subscriber 2, the subscriber that is coping with multipath signals, has a significantly wider spread of signal noise. Analysis of the data revealed that the 3σ estimate of position was 4.41 m for subscriber 1 and 16.31 m for subscriber 2.

7.2. PTP and SyncE

The simulation shown in Figure 3 was run. The resulting ToA jitter, causing positional uncertainty in the relative position of subscriber 2 from subscriber 1, can be seen in Figure 5.

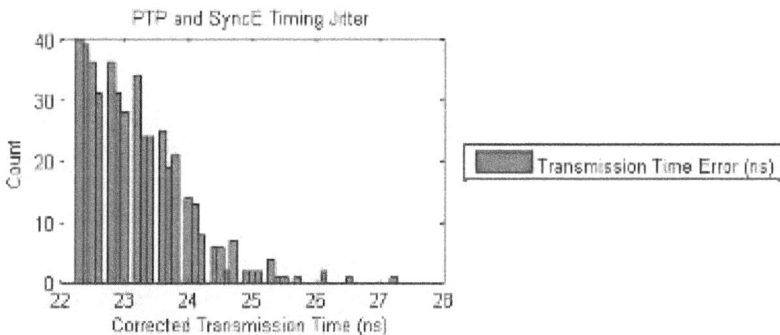

Figure 4: PTP and SyncE Message Timing Jitter

The PTP and SyncE message jitter has been plotted in Figure 4. The 3σ error of the system between subscriber 1 and 2 is 25.489 ns. This equates to a 3σ relative location error of 7.45 m.

As the absolute positional accuracy of subscriber 2 is a combination of the uncertainty of subscriber 1 and the relative position of subscriber 2, the resulting probability density functions (PDFs) have been multiplied together to produce the distribution shown in Figure 6.

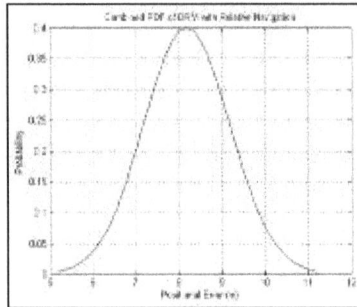

Figure 5: Subscriber 2 Absolute Positional Accuracy

This provides subscriber 2 with a 3σ geo-location accuracy of 10.52 m.

7.3. Summary

Subscriber 1 DRM Geolocation Estimate (3σ) (m)	4.4
Subscriber 2 DRM Geolocation Estimate (3σ) (m)	16.3
Subscriber 2 Combined relative and DRM Geolocation Estimate (3σ) (m)	10.5

Table 1 - Simulation Results Summary

It can be seen in Table that the DRM phase analysis, in the absence of multipath, can provide an order of magnitude improvement over the existing U-TDoA systems used in current E911 systems and could provide the coverage required by NG911 legislation in the simulated environment. In the multipath environment at subscriber 2, the system alone does improve on the existing U-TDoA systems, but is unlikely to provide accurate enough readings for future NG911systems alone.

With the addition of the PTP and SyncE relative geo-location technology, the positional accuracy of subscriber 2 after combining all system uncertainties provides an absolute uncertainty that is significantly better than that found in existing subscriber geo-location systems and may well provide the coverage required by NG911 legislation

8.   Future Work

There is potential for the simulation model to be improved by working to remove some of the significant limitations previously highlighted.

9. Conclusion

It has been demonstrated that combining several layers of complimentary geo-location techniques that are either in existence on mature products or emerging from research NG911 geo-location accuracy in dense urban environments could be achieved.

Although each of the technologies used in isolation have significant drawbacks in their ability to provide a geo-location estimate, combining several layers of techniques may allow users to estimate their location in a range of complex environments.

10. References

AT&T, "Legacy Location Based Services FAQ", (2014) https://developer.att.com/developer/forward.jsp?passedItemId=3100156. Updated 13th December 2013. Accessed December 2013.

True Position Inc (2013) "True Position Guide to Location Technologies", http://www.trueposition.com/resource-center/white-papers/trueposition-guide-to-location-technologies/DownloadSecured Accessed December 2013.

Reed, J. H., Krizman, K. J., Woerner, B. D., and Rappaport, T. S. (1998)"An Overview of the Challenges and Progress in Meeting the E-911 Requirement for Location Service". Virginia Tech, 1998. Published in the IEEE Communications Magazine, April 1998.

Carvajal, R., Aguero, J. C., Godoy, B. I., and Goodwin, G. C., (2011) "On the Accuracy of Phase Noise Bandwidth Estimation in OFDM Systems". 2011. The University of Newcastle, Australia. Published in the 2011 IEEE 12th International Workshop on Signal Processing Advances in Wireless Communications, 2011.

Dana, P. H., (1990) "The Role of GPS in Precise Time and Frequency Dissemination". Published in GPSWorld, July-August 1990.

Ouellette, M., Ji, K., Li, H., and Liu, S. (2011) "Using IEEE 1588 and Boundary Clock Synchronisation in Telecom Networks". Huawei Technologies Inc and China Mobile Research Institute. Published in the IEEE Communications Magazine, Feb 2011.

The US Department of Transportation Research and Innovative Technology Adminsitration (DTRITA) (2013), "Research Success Stories Next Generation 9-1-1". Updated Dec 4th 2013. http://www.its.dot.gov/ng911/index.htm. Updated Dec 4th 2013. Accessed Jan 2014.

ETSI (2009) "Digital Radio Mondiale (DRM); System Specification" V3.1.1 (2009-08) 2009. European Telecommunications Standards Institute and European Broadcasting Union.

Soliman, S., Agashe, P., Fernandez, I., Vayanos, A., Gaal, P., and Oljaca, M. (2000) "gpsOne™: A Hybrid position location system", IEEE Sixth International Symposium on Spread Spectrum Techniques and Applications, Sep 2000.

Locata (2013) "Locata Tech Explained", Locata Corporation PTY Limited, Locata Commercial Website, http://locata.com/technology/locata-tech-explained/ . Accessed August 2013.

van der Bij, E., and Lipinski, M, (2012) "Network fir European Accurate Time and Frequency Transfer". Hardware and Timing Section, CERN, 2012.

Niculescu, D. and Nath, B., (2003) "Ad Hoc Positioning System (APS) UsingAoA", Proceedings of INFOCOM 2003.

Kjaergaard , M. B. (2010) "Indoor Positioning with Radio Location Fingerprinting" PhD Thesis, University of Aarhus, Denmark, 2010.

Roxin, Gaber, J., Wack, M., Nait-Sidi-Moh, A. (2007) "Survey of Wireless Geolocation Techniques" Proceedings of IEEE Globecom Workshop 2007.

A Privacy-Aware Model for Communications Management in the IP Multimedia Subsystem

J.Ophoff[1] and R.A.Botha[2]

[1]Centre for Information Technology and National Development in Africa (CITANDA), Dept. of Information Systems, University of Cape Town, South Africa
[2]School of ICT, Nelson Mandela Metropolitan University, South Africa
e-mail: jacques.ophoff@uct.ac.za; ReinhardtA.Botha@nmmu.ac.za

Abstract

Never before have people been so connected to one another. Today we have the ability to communicate with almost anyone, anytime, anywhere. Our increased connectivity and reachability also leads to new issues and challenges that we need to deal with. When we phone someone we expect an instant connection, and when this does not occur it can be frustrating. On the other hand it is equally disruptive to receive a call when one is busy with an important task or in a situation where communication is inappropriate. Social protocol dictates that we try to minimize such situations for the benefit of others nearby and for ourselves.

This management of communications is a constant and difficult task. Using presence – which signals a person's availability and willingness to communicate – is a solution to this problem. Such information can benefit communication partners by increasing the likelihood of a successful connection and decreasing disruptions. This paper addresses the problem of staying connected while keeping control over mobile communications.

The paper presents a model for privacy-aware communications management, extended to the IP Multimedia Subsystem (IMS). The model stresses the privacy of potentially sensitive presence information. A unique perspective based on social relationship theories is adopted. The use of relationship groups not only makes logical sense but also assists in the management of presence information and extends existing standards. Thus the model presents a solid foundation for the development of future services. In these ways the proposed model contributes positively towards balancing efficient mobile communications with the need for privacy-awareness.

Keywords

IP Multimedia Subsystem, Communications management, Privacy

1. Introduction

Without control mobile communications risk becoming disruptive and disorganizing (Rennecker and Godwin, 2005). These consequences can be far-reaching. Ling (2004) states that many people find mobile phones disturbing, and there are numerous situations where the use of mobile phones are seen as inappropriate.

According to Ling (2004, pp. 125–142) there are three general domains in which mobile communications can cause disruption: public settings with extensive norms governing behaviour (such as restaurants), interpersonal interactions and on an individual, internal level. It is clear that the disruption caused by an incoming communication affects the recipient, people in the immediate vicinity, and also changes the social status and behaviour patterns.

The problem of disruptions is extremely relevant when we frame it against the current state of information overload. Having to deal with a multitude of facts and tasks as efficiently as possible has meant that our attention has become scarce – put another way we are trading in the economics of attention (Davenport and Beck, 2000). Operating in this environment requires us to manage our attention, and correspondingly our communications, as efficiently as possible if we want to lead a productive life.

In the face of these challenges people often reconsider their perception of acceptable use and adopt a more tolerant attitude (Palen et al., 2000; Love and Perry, 2004). Research suggests that a range of dynamic factors influence our communications: the communications medium, relationship between caller and receiver, status differences, affinity towards a contact, expectations of reciprocity and culture all play a role (Rennecker and Godwin, 2005). Perhaps this explains why an effective solution to this problem is yet to be found.

While the convergence of communication channels with the Internet is delivering richer communication experiences no standards exist to communicate context between the caller and receiver. 'Call manager' mobile applications allow a degree of rule-based control over communications and enable users to pull social networking data about a caller, but are not based on standards and are reliant on interfaces to third-party websites. Thus the Caller ID feature is still the only reliable context indication and is only available to the receiver. However, it is often unavailable because it can be switched off by the caller. Centralised analysis and management of a wide variety of context data is needed to overcome these problems (Baladrón et al., 2012).

In mobile communications a fundamental conflict exists between the desire for availability and the wish to maintain a high level of control over communication and personal privacy. Parties need a way to balance availability, interruptions leading to disruption as well as privacy requirements. This balance needs to be addressed on a technological and social level. The objective of this paper is the development of a prescriptive model for controlling disruptions in mobile communications using established presence standards in the IMS.

The paper proceeds with an overview of privacy concerns related to mobile communications, focusing on the sharing of context information. Thereafter, in Section 3, social relationships are examined as a contributing factor to our perception of privacy. Following this Section 4 presents and discusses a model for communications management in the IMS taking the previous points into consideration. A key aspect of the model is the use of presence as a service. Finally, Section 5 concludes the paper.

2. Privacy Concerns

As context information is of a highly personal nature it is natural to assume that users will be concerned about who has access to such information. It may be said that social networking and media is changing this attitude and that users are more willing to share personal information. However, further research is needed to confirm this – users may just be limited in their knowledge of the risks or lack good alternative applications which respect privacy. Three salient points are given by Schmidt et al. (2000) which summarize many of the privacy concerns people perceive:

1. People want to be in control of what about them is visible to others.
2. People want to know what others know about them.
3. People like to share information selectively.

In general, research indicates that privacy is less important than is currently thought and that users are willing to share personal information in exchange for useful services (Khalil and Connelly, 2006; Raento and Oulasvirta, 2008; Ophoff and Botha, 2008). However, this does not mean that the privacy of information is not valued (Danezis et al., 2005). Rather, the social relationship as well as the type of information influences privacy.

Research has shown that privacy concerns depend significantly on the relationship between caller and receiver (Consolvo et al., 2005; Khalil and Connelly, 2006; Raento and Oulasvirta, 2008). Users are more likely to share availability information with social relations such as significant other, family and friends (Khalil and Connelly, 2006). Similar findings have been shown for the sharing of location information (Consolvo et al., 2005).

It has also been shown that different kinds of context are perceived with varying levels of privacy. Information such as location and activity are perceived as more sensitive than company and conversation (Khalil and Connelly, 2006). However, it has been found that users often share such information in as much detail as possible, or not at all (Consolvo et al., 2005). This is in contrast to other projects which have found allowing granular information to be important (De Guzman et al., 2007; Raento and Oulasvirta, 2008). Controlling the granularity of information displayed to different groups and having the ability to fake some or all context information is an important aspect in giving users full control over their information (Raento and Oulasvirta, 2008).

3. Social Relationship Groups

The users in a contact list often express a social relationship with the user in charge of it. Relationships affect our knowledge of another user as well as our availability for communication with a user. Relationships also influence our perception of privacy and will determine how much information we are willing to share.

It is generally accepted that relationships are not innate, but are formed and develop gradually over time as exchanges between people take place (Roloff, 1981, pp. 61–

62). These social relationships are greatly influenced by the time or the need we have to develop a relationship (Trenholm and Jensen, 1996, p. 352). Consequently, many unique relationships develop between people.

Hartley (1993, p. 177) observes that in everyday life we often recognize complex, individual relationships arranged into groups. He proposes, for example, three such groups: family, friends, and co-workers. Such groups are easily expressible classifications of the type of relationship we have with a specific person. For example, instead of saying that one has a confiding, respectful relationship with someone, we would abstract it and simply call each other friends.

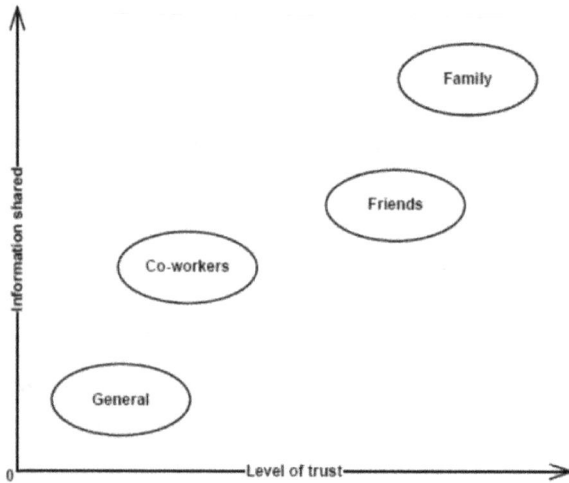

Figure 1: Social Relationship Groups

It is acknowledged that many types of relationships exist in the real world and it is left up to users to define the relationships which apply to them. However, it is common to identify general groups of relationships which apply to almost all users. As example four groups are suggested in Figure 1: general, co-workers, friends and family. The figure presents an illustrative example of how a user may classify relationships.

Social relationships move through various stages characterized by changing levels of communication and self-disclosure. DeVito (1992, p. 428) explains that these stages range from initial contact and involvement to intimacy, possibly followed by deterioration and, finally, dissolution. While trust increases when a relationship is growing, it is an almost universal truth that a deterioration of a relationship leads to a marked decrease in trust (DeVito, 1992, p. 426). The amount of information being shared is dependent on the state of the relationship as well as the sensitivity of the information (DeVito, 1992, p. 368).

Thus social relationships play an important role in our perception of privacy. It is likely that we would share more context information with someone we are familiar with or who reciprocates the act. Thus, in the long term, it may be possible to automatically adapt the level of information sharing, based on the amount of reciprocated information and the sensitivity thereof.

4. A Model for Communications Management in the IMS

The IMS is a service enabling platform, offering features which services can build upon (Cuevas et al., 2012). On top of the core network various application servers reside which host and execute services. The main protocol linking all these components and responsible for establishing and managing sessions (referred to as calls in traditional telephony) is the Session Initiation Protocol (SIP) (Rosenberg et al., 2002). In addition the Session Description Protocol (SDP) plays an important role in describing multimedia sessions (Handley and Jaconson, 1998).

The ability to create advanced services is one of the most important features of the IMS. One of the most significant services that the network will provide is presence.

4.1. Presence as a Service

At a fundamental level presence conveys a user's availability and willingness to communicate. In the context of this research presence refers to whether a user can be contacted right now. Knowing about presence is useful because it saves communication time.

IMS presence can provide a much more detailed description of the current user state than currently available in applications, where presence information is limited to user availability. This description can include communication address information, such as email or mobile phone, the terminal capabilities, for example video support, and location information, all distributed in real time to authorized users. Information is transmitted in real time meaning enriched communications and a better end user experience.

In the network presence information is not only available to end-users, but also to other services which can benefit from the information. Figure 2 illustrates how, in addition to the data and sensors on the mobile phone, services used by the receiver can publish context information. These services can share context with each other and also publish presence information to the presence service. Another feature which increases the available context in the IMS is the session protocol, which is examined next.

4.2. Session Description Protocol

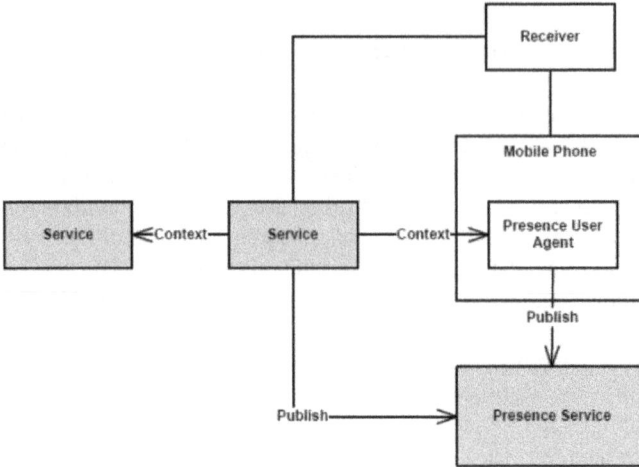

Figure 2: Service Context

In the network SDP provides a complete description of the session to be established. This description can be further classified into session- and media-level information. SDP makes session information, such as the subject of the session and the time at which the session is to take place, available. In addition, information about the media requirements for the session, such as port numbers and codecs, can also be retrieved.

The PUA or user can use this additional information for further decision making regarding the session. When combined with presence and a SIP message, which contains information such as the user address, routing and security requirements, this creates a comprehensive set of data which can be used as the basis for a decision model in a communications management service. In addition, a lot of information can be obtained from the network automatically.

4.3. Presence for Communications Management in the IMS

The model prescribes that callers be assigned into one or more groups, based on social relationship. Groups are implemented through authorization policies and rules. The existing standards which define authorization policies do not allow for user defined groups as part of the conditions of an authorization rule. Thus the model uniquely extends these rules by adding the group condition. This provides a mechanism by which a receiver can define a privacy list by groups of contacts and apply presence authorization accordingly.

A user would create and maintain a group document which is stored alongside presence information and authorization rules. When examining a rule set the presence server would identify whether a group (list element) exists as an identity condition. If a group does exist the presence server imports all the corresponding callers as specified in the document, before applying the necessary actions and transformations to the presence information. This is illustrated in Figure 3.

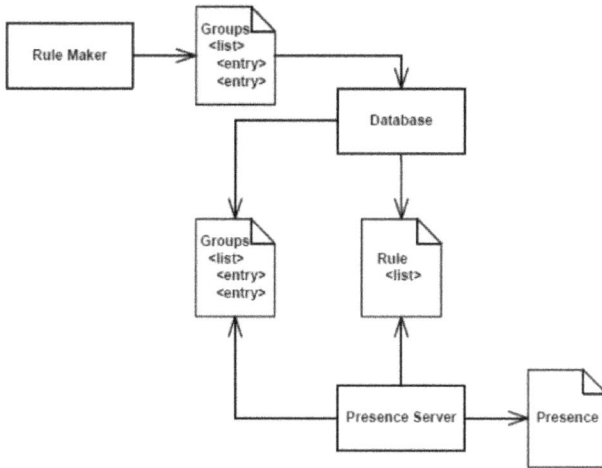

Figure 3: Groups Extension to the Presence Authorization Framework

Several entities in the IMS provide additional privacy to the user. This extends the functionality available through presence standards. The information contained by the SDP can be used as conditions for authorization rules. For example, the type of session can be used to filter requests for presence information when connected to anything other than a voice call. The filter criteria in the Home Subscriber Server can also be used as part of a presence authorization policy. The filter criteria is similar to the conditions part of authorization rules. However, in addition to specifying when a permission applies, the filter criteria can specify specific services to be invoked.

Figure 4 illustrates the proposed model. Standard IMS components are not elaborated, but numeric labels indicate the points of extension for communications management. Below each extension point is discussed:

1. IMS services used by a user can provide additional context information to a PUA or other services. A service can also publish information directly to a presence service.
2. Session information exposed by SDP further extends the information available to entities in the IMS. Together with service context this extends the information available to make communications management decisions.
3. The user profile information located on the Home Subscriber Server can be used for decision making by services in the IMS. The Serving Call/Session Control Function is the main entity that makes use of this information. The user profile can be updated via a SIP Application Server.
4. User profile information can also be used as an availability indicator to callers. However, in this case the omission of authorization rules must be taken into consideration as a potential loss of privacy can occur.
5. Services can assist users in managing communications. A SIP Proxy Server can be used to manage incoming communications and provide forwarding to a new endpoint. Thus the receiver can remain connected for communication using a single identity on the network.

6. The model call profile construct can be extended by using a SIP Terminating User Agent. This allows communications to be screened and routed in a preferred manner, including blocking calls. The caller may also be informed of any action and given additional options to proceed.
7. The IMS extends privacy features by allowing user profile information to be used as part of presence authorization rules.
8. Services can provide additional filtering of presence or session information before sending it to a caller. An example is a SIP Back-to-Back User Agent.

The model requires context, captured as presence information. This allows a receiver to present an availability state to potential callers. The model prescribes three approaches in using presence to manage communications. These approaches allow the receiver to indicate availability for communication, the caller to present call cues and the automatic handling of calls for the receiver. These mechanisms allow the caller to make an informed decision about whether to proceed with an intended call. Such knowledge can not only minimize receiver disruptions, but also save the caller from fruitless attempts to contact an unreachable target.

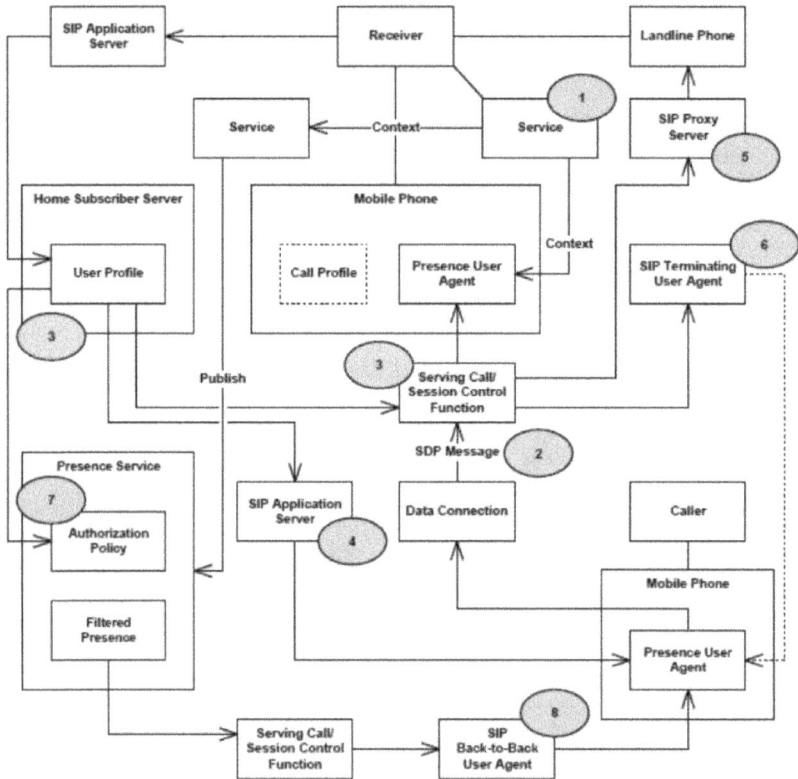

Figure 4: A Model for Communications Management in the IMS

The model also addresses how the receiver can maintain privacy of presence information. Requests for information can come from multiple sources, not all of them trusted. Thus the use of groups based on social relationships is prescribed. This allows for authorization rules which closely relate to trust relationships in the real world. Authorization rules allow requests to be evaluated according to several conditions and can filter the final presence document before it is returned to a caller.

From the above it can be concluded that the model fits well into the IMS network and can be extended to meet the needs of communications management. Thus the model looks promising for providing value in next generation networks.

5. Conclusion

This paper presented an abstract IMS model based on presence standards, while incorporating privacy and social relationship theories. To facilitate a concise model a discussion of privacy based on context and relationships was given. This allowed the model's core functionality to be defined in a clear and consistent way. While the IMS creates the opportunity for implementing innovative features specifically relating to communications management, it is important to remember that such services are only available to users in the IMS.

Unfortunately relationships are not always the only consideration when deciding if personal information should be shared. Certain situations may force users to share information irrespective of their personal feelings. An example may be a company forcing employees to remain logged on to a communications system and displaying their availability status. These situations are acknowledged by the model and require further research.

6. References

Baladrón, C., Aguiar, J. M., Carro, B., Calavia, L., Cadenas, A. and Sánchez-Esguevillas, A. (2012). Framework for Intelligent Service Adaptation to User's Context in Next Generation Networks, *IEEE Communications Magazine* 50(3), pp. 18–25.

Consolvo, S., Smith, I. E., Matthews, T., LaMarca, A., Tabert, J. and Powledge, P. (2005). Location Disclosure to Social Relations: Why, When, & What People Want to Share, CHI '05: *Proceedings of the SIGCHI Conference on Human Factors in Computing Systems*, ACM Press, pp. 81–90.

Cuevas, A., Nicoll, W. and Schroder, K. (2012). The challenges of IMS deployment at Telefonica Germany, *IEEE Communications Magazine* 50(8), pp. 120–127.

Danezis, G., Lewis, S. and Anderson, R. (2005). How Much is Location Privacy Worth?, *Proceedings of the Fourth Workshop on the Economics of Information Security*.

Davenport, T. H. and Beck, J. C. (2000). Getting the Attention You Need, *Harvard Business Review* 78(5), pp. 118–126.

De Guzman, E. S., Sharmin, M. and Bailey, B. P. (2007). Should I Call Now? Understanding What Context is Considered When Deciding Whether to Initiate Remote Communication via Mobile Devices, *GI '07: Proceedings of Graphics Interface 2007*, ACM Press, pp. 143–150.

DeVito, J. A. (1992). *The Interpersonal Communication Book*, 6th edn, HarperCollins Publishers.

Handley, M. and Jaconson, V. (1998). *SDP: Session Description Protocol*, RFC 2327, Internet Engineering Task Force.

Hartley, P. (1993). *Interpersonal Communication*, Routledge.

Khalil, A. and Connelly, K. (2006). Context-aware Telephony: Privacy Preferences and Sharing Patterns, *CSCW '06: Proceedings of the 2006 20th Anniversary Conference on Computer Supported Cooperative Work*, ACM Press, pp. 469–478.

Ling, R. (2004). *The Mobile Connection: The Cell Phone's Impact on Society*, Morgan Kaufmann.

Love, S. and Perry, M. (2004). Dealing with Mobile Conversations in Public Places: some implications for the design of socially intrusive technologies, *CHI '04: CHI '04 Extended Abstracts on Human Factors in Computing Systems*, pp. 1195–1198.

Ophoff, J. and Botha, R. (2008). Mobile Communications: User Perception and Practice, *South African Computer Journal* 40, pp. 63–73.

Palen, L., Salzman, M. and Youngs, E. (2000). Going Wireless: Behavior & Practice of New Mobile Phone Users, *CSCW '00: Proceedings of the 2000 ACM Conference on Computer Supported Cooperative Work*, pp. 201–210.

Raento, M. and Oulasvirta, A. (2008). Designing for privacy and self-presentation in social awareness, *Personal and Ubiquitous Computing* 12(7), pp. 527–542.

Rennecker, J. and Godwin, L. (2005). Delays and interruptions: A self-perpetuating paradox of communication technology use, *Information and Organization* 15(3), pp. 247–266.

Roloff, M. E. (1981). *Interpersonal Communication: The Social Exchange Approach*, Sage Publications.

Rosenberg, J., Schulzrinne, H., Camarillo, G., Johnston, A., Peterson, J., Sparks, R., Handley, M. and Schooler, E. (2002). *SIP: Session Initiation Protocol*, RFC 3261, Internet Engineering Task Force.

Schmidt, A., Takaluoma, A. and Mäntyjärvi, J. (2000). Context-Aware Telephony Over WAP, *Personal and Ubiquitous Computing* 4(4), pp. 225–229.

Trenholm, S. and Jensen, A. (1996). *Interpersonal Communication*, 3rd edn, Wadsworth Publishing Company.

Issues of Adoption: Can Health Services Designed for Developed Countries be Adopted in Developing Countries?

R.Ssembatya[1, 2] and S.Zawedde[3]

[1]Faculty of Science and Technology, Uganda Christian University, Uganda
[2]Institute of Computer Science, Mbarara University of Science and Technology,
[3]Faculty of Business and Management, Uganda Martyrs University, Uganda
e-mail: richssembatya@gmail.com; szawedde@umu.ac.ug

Abstract

Electronic health record (EHR) systems are a popular mechanism for accessing health records in the developed world and have contributed towards improved and cost-effective health care management. However, the development of appropriate and scalable EHR systems in developing countries has been difficult to achieve because of certain limitations inherent in the technological infrastructure. For instance, bandwidth limitations and power outages make it difficult to guarantee dependability in terms of accessibility to the data. This paper presents a comparative study of 19 EHR systems in terms of the security and usability of these systems within the context of the developing world. The evaluation is based on a number of dimensions such as development environment, system platform, type and access control standards found in the National Institute for Standard and Technology (NIST) and Certification Commission for Health Information Technology (CCHIT). Our research indicates that all the systems evaluated require online access control decisions. Access to data on a central server is controlled by a mechanism that verifies/authenticates users or parties wanting to view/modify/edit patient records. However, solely relying on an online access control system is limiting, particularly in developing countries where access to the server can be disrupted by a number of disastrous events. Additionally, literature also reveals that all the evaluated tools were developed with the user contexts in the developed World and therefore do not represent the needs of the patients and medical practitioners in the developing countries.

Keywords

Security, Measurement, Performance, Usability.

1. Introduction

An Electronic Health Record (EHR) is a record of health-related information on an individual that is created, gathered, managed, and consulted by authorized healthcare professionals in a digital format (HIPAA, 2009). EHRs can exist on standalone computers, networked server computers, removable disks or mobile devices and can be accessible online from interconnected network systems providing the opportunity for healthcare organizations to improve health care delivery. Electronic health records enable the efficient communication of medical information and thus reduce operating costs and administrative workload (Gunter & Terry, 2005).

Over time, researchers have made significant efforts to design and implement EHR systems of which some are employer sponsored (Dossia, sponsored by Wal-Mart, BP and AT&T), provider sponsored (MyHealtheVet, sponsored by the United States Department of Veterans Affairs), and others are independent products (Microsoft HealthVault and Google Health, which were developed for profit making and open source projects respectively). However, the development of appropriate and scalable EHR systems in developing countries has been difficult to achieve (Omary, Lupiana, Mtenzi, & Wu, 2009; Tierney et al., 2010). The literature reveals many EHR systems that have not survived the test of time. Such systems include MEDCAB (Kamadjeu, Tapang, & Moluh, 2005) and FUCHIA (Tassie et al., 2002). All the available literature indicates that these systems are no longer actively in use or development.

Similarly, with the explosion of open-source EHR systems, more patients and physicians in developed countries are shifting towards accessing health information online. The $34 billion of incentives provided by the American Recovery and Reinvestment Act (ARRA) (2009) has greatly increased the development of open-source EHR systems in developed countries. The ARRA further stresses that healthcare providers should deploy EHR systems that are certified for "meaningful use" (www.healthit.gov) criteria, which includes the implementation of access control (Smith et al., 2010). The intent of meaningful use criteria is to ensure that EHR systems can interoperate with other systems in order to enable electronic exchange of health information in accordance with all laws and standards.

While previous studies have widely documented the success and failure factors of information and communication technology (ICT) solutions in developing countries, there appears to be a gap in specifically answering the question; can online health services designed for developed countries be adopted for EHR systems in developing countries? Studies conducted by Mars and Seebregts (2008), Yogeswaran and Wright (2010), and Forster et al. (2008) deal with broader issues of adoption such as technology investments, early stakeholder's participation and training. Other studies focus on policy and regulatory issues for EHR systems and give less attention to technological barriers (Coleman, 2010; Jacucci, Shaw, & Braa, 2006). In addition, most studies have been conducted for developed countries (Greenhalgh et al., 2010; Sanders et al., 2012; McGinn et al., 2011). From the perspective of the health digital divide, the available literature does not yet seem to adequately answer whether health services designed for developed countries can be adopted in developing countries. Therefore, our study seeks to answer this question, and guide researchers, development teams and regulatory organizations by assessing the potential and applicability of the current EHR systems in developing countries. The paper classifies and summarizes EHR systems and provides a framework for researchers to extract assertions and provide guided decisions. A set of assessment criteria was established to ascertain the degree to which the evaluated systems address technology constraints in developing countries, NIST (www.nist.gov) meaningful use and CCHIT certification (www.cchit.org). Using these evaluation criteria, we evaluated 19 EHR systems extracted from online search databases.

The rest of this paper is organized as follows; Section 2 presents background work on digital divide and related healthcare requirements as specified by NIST and CCHIT certification. Section 3 presents definitions and the methodology behind our evaluation. Section 4 details the evaluation results followed by conclusions based on the results of the evaluation.

2. Background

In this section, we review literature on the digital divide as it applies to E-Health systems and the NIST and CCHIT requirements for developing secure EHR systems to protect patients' records from compromise.

2.1. E-Health and Digital Divide

In the context of this study, developing countries are countries with various challenges such as frequent power outages, intermittent connectivity and lack of centralised services in addition to other Information and Communication Technology (ICT) constraints. When compared to developed countries, the gap is described as the digital divide (Brodie et al., 2000; Hsu et al., 2005). In relation to E-health, the digital divide is a form of health disparity in healthcare's access to and use of both the information technologies and health information online (Brodie et al., 2000). Barriers to the emergence of an equitable information society have led to the existence of the digital divide (Liff & Shepherd, 2004). According to "Glocal" eHealth Policy context (www.rockefellerfoundation.org), developing countries trail far behind developed countries in E-health services and the widening gap has been attributed to several challenges: failure to develop E-health roadmaps by the Governments resulted from insufficient political will, lack of e-health experts or leaders to champion E-health projects, corruption, limited resources to finance the development of the project, poverty, frequent power outages among others (Hogberg, 2005; Omary et al., 2009; Kalogriopoulos et al., 2009).

2.2. International Standards and Regulations

According to Oppliger (1996), international standards can be defined as documented agreements containing precise criteria that must be followed consistently as rules, guidelines or definitions of characteristics to ensure that any products, materials, processes or services are fit for their purpose. The acceptance and adoption of these standards is recognized by very many states and governments in Europe, Asia, Canada and some African countries (Tuyikeze, 2005; Tuyikeze & Pottas, 2005). Due to lack of standards and regulations specific to individual countries, Tuyikeze and Pottas (2005) from South Africa recommended that it is necessary to adopt other standards such as HIPPA, NIST or CCHIT certification to overcome some of the criticisms of ISO standards, such as being too general and therefore not providing stringent solutions to specific healthcare requirements. Therefore, we assembled eight evaluation criteria to represent legal requirements of the EHRs from NIST and CCHIT certification.

2.3. NIST Meaningful Use

The National Institute of Standards and Technology (NIST), known between 1901 and 1988 as the National Bureau of Standards (NBS) is an agency in US that works with industries to develop and apply technology, measurements and standards. NIST provides certification programs to ensure that E-health systems offer the necessary functionality to help healthcare providers meet meaningful use criteria. NIST provides four criteria: the first criteria requires that users be given a unique name and/or identification number for tracking; the second criteria requires that controls should be established to permit only authorized users accessing patient's records; the third criteria requires that a user authorized for emergency situation be granted a set of privileges applicable only for emergency situation and lastly, the ability to activate emergency access roles.

2.4. Certification Commission for Health Information Technology (CCHIT)

The combination of NIST and CCHIT meaningful criteria are the driving force behind the implementation of access control in E-health systems. The goal of access control within E-health systems is to provide systems access control by ensuring that only authorized users have access to patient's information (Tuyikeze, 2005; Smith et al., 2010). In order to accomplish this goal, CCHIT provides four criteria: the first criteria requires that EHR systems must implement permissions such that users are only given least privilege; the second criteria requires administrative facilities to assign privileges to users and groups; the third criteria requires that EHR systems must implement either one of user-based access control (UBAC), context-based access control (CBAC) or role-based access control (RBAC); and lastly, EHR systems should allow a user to have their permissions removed without having to delete the user from the system. We use these criteria to analyse the systems we found in our literature search.

3. Selection criteria

Below are the criteria we used for selection and inclusion of articles in our research.

i. We did a literature search based on the following keywords; Electronic health record systems\tools\software, patient health record systems, electronic medical record systems, and personally controlled health record systems). Various databases were used to select our primary studies.

ii. We surveyed tools developed from 1999 to 2010 because it is during this time that EHR systems had gained much wider attention.

iii. The review excludes magazines, student's dissertations, newspapers and books among others. We were mostly interested in analysing tools that are currently in use. We also excluded tools and publications not written in English and studies without a sufficiently concrete description of implementation procedures. This means that the results may not be generalised to other E-health tools.

3.1. Selection Procedure

Initially, 6 online search databases were selected and a total of 157 EHR articles and systems were generated. Based on the titles, abstracts and procedures for the implementation of online health record systems, a total of 89 articles and tools were excluded. 68 articles met the selection criteria and were presented for further review. 44 articles were then excluded because despite having relevant titles, abstracts and full text, they did not present relevant tools for this study. The procedure for the selection of our articles is illustrated in figure 1.

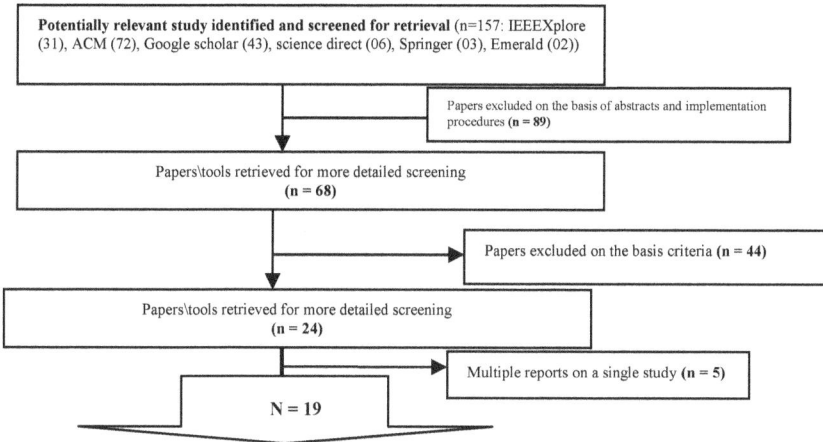

Figure 1: Review flow diagram

3.2. Evaluation Criteria

In this section, we introduce the evaluation criteria which offers an analysis of EHR systems based on three general dimensions i.e. technology, NIST meaningful use and CCHIT certification. Technological features are sub divided into development environments (DE), system platform and type. System platform (Platform) classifies tools based on web/client-server platform or desktop platform. Desktop platforms enable health care providers to record and store health information on a desktop based application. Client-server platforms use powerful servers with a high bandwidth connection to the network to hold centralized health information. System type (Type) classify tools based on whether they are meant to be purchased (p), have a complete free software downloadable version (dv) and/or meant for demonstration (d).

NIST meaningful use provides four criteria for our evaluation: **NIST-U1:** Users given unique name and/or number; **NIST-U2:** Access controls with defined user privileges; **NIST-U3:** Emergency-time only privileges for user roles; **NIST-U4:** The ability to activate emergency access roles

CCHIT certification defines four criteria for our evaluation: **CCHIT-M1:** Users are given least privilege permission set; **CCHIT-M2:** Administrative facilities to assign privileges to users; **CCHIT-M3:** Context-based access control (CBAC), user-based access control (UBAC), or role-based access control (RBAC); **CCHIT-M4:** User role revocation without deleting a user

Table 1 illustrates a classification of various EHR systems obtained from our review based on the dimensions described above.

4. Discussion

In this section, we provide a description of 19 EHR systems analyzed in table 1 and summarize information about the applicability of these tools in developing countries. We also provide information on whether the systems passed or failed each of the 11 evaluation criteria presented in section 3.2.

From the technological perspective, the biggest number of tools analysed are open source tools – those that have a complete free software downloadable version (HealthVault (www.healthvault.com), Indivo (indivohealth.org), Open EMR (www.oemr.org), iTrust (http://agile.csc.ncsu.edu/iTrust/wiki/doku.php?id=start), WorldMedcard (www.worldmedcard.com), Tolven (www.tolven.org), Myhealthfolders (myhealthfolders.com), MediCompass (https://www.medicompass.com/mcweb/default.aspx) and Dossia (dossia.org)), followed by proprietary tools – those that are owned by companies and the source code is not accessible (HealthConnect, FIS' HealthManager (www.fisglobal.com), VitalChart (www.vitalchart.com), SmartPHR (www.thesmartphr.com), Sharedhealth (www.sharedhealth.com) and Mymedicalrecords.com (www.mymedicalrecords.com)). The study further indicates that only one tool was designed for demonstration only (Mitamura et al., 2005). This therefore implies that the majority of tools in the matrix are open source tools. Dalle and Jullien (2002) argue that the openness of the source code is a key feature, which together with compatibility allows open source software to be advantageous over proprietary software. Increasingly, a vast number of proprietary tools do not mention their development environments and hence the use of "??" in the matrix.

Despite the flexibility proposed in the NIST and CCHIT certification in regard to access control, all the tools analysed used RBAC. Ferraiolo et al. (2001) highlighted that RBAC's flexibility provides the ability to simplify policy customization and make security policy management a none-technical job. The evaluation indicates that all the tools analysed are actively seeking to meet both NIST and CCHIT certification. All tools evaluated provide a set of pre-defined roles and permissions that an administrator can assign to users or groups of users. The pre-defined roles in the system represent a common role within the healthcare settings e.g. physician role, technician role etc. A user may be assigned one or more roles. Healthcare administrators have the ability to add any arbitrarily named role and assign it any number of privileges.

The evaluation further indicates that all tools met the first two NIST meaningful use criteria (NIST-U1 and NIST-U2), and only HealthVault, Indivo, VitalChart, and Dossia support emergency-time only privilege for user roles (NIST-U3). The lack of emergency access roles (NIST-U4) causes all the evaluated tools to fail to meet NIST meaningful use criteria. From the CCHIT certification, all the tools evaluated provide users with a given set of least privileges (CCHIT-M1), enables the administrator to define roles for the users that guide information access in the system (CCHIT-M2) and also allows user revocation without first having to delete users from the systems (CCHIT-M4).

Daglish and Archer (2009) argue that patients need to be in control of their data such that those responsible for patients' care can perform their duties efficiently. Other reasons why patients need access to their health records include: records at the hospital server could be unreachable due to frequent power outages and/or unreliable Internet connections. Similarly, if the patient cannot give a new doctor access to his/her existing records, redundant tests may end up being used, resulting to different portions of patient's data being scattered among multiple EHRs. This makes it difficult for the doctors to have a complete picture of the patient's treatment history.

System/Dimension	Technology			NIST-Use	Meaningful	CCHIT Criteria	
	DE	Platform	Type	NIST-U1, U2	NIST-U3, U4	CCHIT-M1, M2	CCHIT-M1, M2
HealthConnect	PerlOracle DB	Web based	p	yes	no	Conf. dependant, yes	RBAC, yes
Google Health	Java, .Net, XML, PHP, python	Web based	dv	yes	no	Conf. dependant, yes	RBAC, yes
Tool A	??	Web based	d	yes	no	yes	RBAC, yes
MEDIS	HTML, XML, JSP script language, Java? Apache & Tomcat web servers	Web based	p	yes	no	Conf. dependant, yes	RBAC, yes
Microsoft. HealthVault	.Net, Java, XML	Web based	dv	yes	Conf. dependant, no	yes	RBAC, yes
Indivo	Java, PHP, Tomcat, Apache Web Server 2.0, MySQL, PHP-Java Bridge 4.1.2	Web based	dv	yes	Conf. dependant, no	yes	RBAC, yes
FIS HealthManager	PIP, GT.M	Web based	p	yes	no	Conf. dependant, yes	RBAC, yes
VitalChart	??	Web based	p	yes	Conf. dependant, no	Conf. dependant, yes	RBAC, yes
OpenEMR	PHP, JavaScript, MySQL	Web based	dv	yes	no	Conf. dependant, yes	RBAC, yes
SmartPHR	XML??	Web based	p	yes	no	yes	RBAC, yes
Sharehealth	??	Web based	p	yes	no	yes	RBAC, yes
Dossia	XML, .Net (C#), Java, PHP	Web based	dv	yes	Conf. dependant, no	yes	RBAC, yes
iTrust	Java/MySQL, Apache Tomcat webserver	Web based	dv	yes	no	yes	RBAC, yes
WorldMedcard	PHP, .Net, Windows Server 2008, SQL server, ASP.Net, ISS,	Web based	dv	yes	no	yes	RBAC, yes
MyMedicalrecords.com	??	Web based	p	yes	no	yes	RBAC, yes
Tolven	J2EE framework, JBOSS application server, OpenLDAP	Web based	dv	yes	no	Conf. dependant, need LDAP	RBAC, yes
Myhealthfolders	.Net (aspx)	Web based	dv	yes	no	yes	RBAC, yes
Dr. I-Net	.Net (aspx)	Web based	dv	yes	no	yes	RBAC, yes
MediCompass	.Net (aspx)	Web based	dv	yes	no	yes	RBAC, yes

Table 1: Summarized Classification Matrix Showing EHR Systems versus Dimensions

However, all tools in the matrix are designed for healthcare providers – patients have little or no access to their health records. Electronic health record systems such as Microsoft HealthVault, Indivo[tm] and Dossia empower users with some access but the access must be online. In addition, all tools evaluated require online access control decisions. Solely relying on an online access control system is limiting, particularly in developing countries where access to the server is disrupted by a number of disastrous events. When the server becomes unavailable, for example due to power outages that is common in developing countries, access control decision cannot be made, making EHRs unreachable. Studies conducted by Sunyaev, Chornyi, Mauro and Kremar (2010), Daglish and Archer (2009) highlights that any security mechanism needs to be usable; otherwise users will not use the system at all.

Furthermore, the infrastructure in developing countries is characterized by little or no Internet bandwidth, unreliable and intermittent main electricity and limited user expertise, among others (Omary et al., 2009). This implies that developing countries require context relevant tools – tools developed with the unique constraints of the developing world in mind. However, all the tools explored are developed with user contexts in the developed world and thus do not represent the needs of the users in developing world. This can be witnessed by the existing manual paper based health records in most healthcare organizations in developing countries (Omary et al., 2009; Tierney et al., 2010; Kalogriopoulos, Baran, & Nimunkar, 2009).

5. Conclusion

Despite the potential of EHR systems to address the challenges facing health systems in developing countries, the majority of EHR systems designed for developed countries cannot be adapted for implementation in developing countries. The failure of adoption is attributed to many factors including: 1) **Online Access Control:** The majority of EHR systems require online access control decision. When the server/database is unavailable, for example due to frequent power outages that is common in developing countries, access control decisions cannot be made, making health records unreachable; 2) **Users' Context:** The majority of EHR systems designed for developed countries were developed with the user contexts in the developed World and therefore do not represent the needs of the patients and medical practitioners in the developing countries.

We therefore feel that in order for EHR systems to satisfy the intended users specifically in developing countries, existing systems needs to be extended on mobile phones such that records can be made available when hospital servers are offline. Akinyele et al. (2011) affirmed that mobile phones (also called small handheld computers) can be used to provide health records without the need for a single server.

6. References

Akinyele, A., Lehmann, C. U., Green, M. D., Pagano, M. W., Peterson, Z. N. J., & Rubin, A. D. 2010. Self-protecting electronic medical records using attribute-based encryption on mobile device. Technical report, Cryptology ePrint Archive, Report 2010/565, 2010. http://eprint. iacr. org/2010/565.

American recovery and reinvestment act 2009, u.s.c. 111-5, 2009.

Brodie, M., Flournoy. R. E., Altman, D. E., Blendon, R. J., Benson, J. M., and Rosenbaum, M. D. 2000. Health information, the Internet, and the Digital Divide. *Health Affairs*, 19, 255–265.

Coleman, A. 2010. *Developing an e-health framework through electronic healthcare readiness assessment.* Doctoral Thesis. Nelson Mandela Metropolitan University http://www.nmmu.ac.za/documents/theses/Alfred%20Coleman.pdf. Accessed 10/08/2012.

Daglish, D. and Archer, N. 2009. Electronic Personal Health Record Systems: A Brief Review of Privacy, Security, and Architectural Issues"*Proceedings of the IEEE 2009 World Congress on Privacy, Security and Trust and the Management of e-Business*, pages 110-120.

Dalle, J. M. and Jullien, N. 2002. *Open-Source vs. Proprietary Software.* Working paper, 2002. www.flosshub.org/system/files/dalle2.pdf. Accessed 17/04/2012.

Dr. I-Net. http://www.drinet.com/. Accessed 13/08.2013.

Ferraiolo, D., Sandhu, R., Gavrila, S., Kuhn, D. and Chandramouli, R. 2001. Proposed NIST standard for role-based access control. *ACM Transactions on Information and System Security (TISSEC),* 4(3):224–274.

Forster, M., Bailey, C., Brinkhoff, M.W. G., Graber, C., Boulle, A., Spohr, M..., and Egger, M. 2008. Electronic medical record systems, data quality and loss to follow-up: Survey of antiretroviral therapy programs in resource-limited settings. *Bulletin of the World Health Organization, 86,* 939-947. http://dx.doi.org/10.1590/S0042-96862008001200011. Accessed 15/08/2012.

Greenhalgh, T., Stramer, K., Bratan, T., Russell, J., and Potts, H. 2010. Adoption and nonadoption of a shared electronic summary record in England: A mixed-method case study. *British Medical Journal, 340.* doi: 10.1136/bmj.c3111.

Gunter, T and Terry, N. 2005. The Emergence of National Electronic Health Record Architectures in the United States and Australia: Models, Costs, and Questions. *Journal of Medical Internet Research,* 7(1):3.

HIPAA.com. The definition of electronic health records. http://www.hipaa.com/2009/05/the-definition-of-electronic-health-record/. Accessed 06/08/2012.

Hogberg, U. 2005. The World Health Report 2005: Make every mother and child count – including Africans. *Scand J Public Health.* 33: 409–411.

Hsu, J. H., Huang, J., Kinsman, J. et al. 2005. Use of e-Health services between 1999 and 2002. A growing digital divide. *J Am Med Inform Assoc.* 12:164 –71. DOI 10.1197/jamia.M1672. Accessed 12/04/2012.

Jacucci, E., Shaw, V. and Braa, J. 2006. Standardization of health information systems in South Africa: The challenge of local sustainability. *Information Technology for Development, 12,* 225–239. Doi: 10.1002/itdj.20044. Accessed 1/08/2012.

Kalogriopoulos, N. A., Baran, J., Nimunkar, A. J. and Webster, J. G. 2009. Electronic medical record systems for developing countries: review. *Conference Proceedings of the IEEE Engineering in Medicine and Biology Society,* September 2009; 1730–3.

Kamadjeu, R. M., Tapang, E. M. and Moluh, R. N. 2005. Designing and implementing an electronic health record system in primary care practice in sub-Saharan Africa: a case study from Cameroon. *Inform Prim Care (*Jan 2005*),* 13(3):179-186.

Liff, S. and Shepherd, A. 2004. *An Evolving Gender Digital Divide?* Internet Issue Brief no 2. Oxford: Oxford Internet Institute. http://educ.ubc.ca/faculty/bryson/565/genderdigdiv.pdf. Accessed 02/08/2012.

Mandl, K. D. and Kohane, I. S. 1999. HealthConnect: Clinical Grade Patient-Physician Communication, Informatics Program and Divisions of Emergency Medicine and Endocrinology Children's Hospital, Harvard Medical School, Boston, MA.

Mandl, K. D., Simons, W. W., Crawford, W. C. R. and Abbett, J. M. 2007. Indivo: a personally controlled health record for health information exchange and communication. *BMC Med Informatics and Decision Making* 2007; 7(1):25. doi: 10.1186/1472-6947-7-25. http://www.biomedcentral.com/1472-6947/7/25.1472-6947-7-25.

Mars, M. and Seebregts, C. 2008. Country case study for e-health: South Africa. http://archive.k4health.org/system/files/County%20Case%20Study%20for%20eHealth%20So uth%20Africa.pdf. Accessed 11/08/2012.

McGinn, C. A., Grenier, S., Duplantie, J., Shaw, N., Sicotte, C., Mathieu, L... Gagnon., M. P. 2011. Comparison of user groups' perspectives of barriers and facilitators to implementing electronic health records: A systematic review. *BMC Medicine, 9*doi:10.1186/1741-7015-9-46.

Mitamura, Y., Yamamoto, A., Hayashi, H., Namioka, T., Tsuduki, Y., Shimono, T., Hirokawa, H., Yamakami, H. and Yoshida, A. 2005. A peer-to-peer-based medical information sharing system. CCECE/CCGEI, Saskatoon.

Omary, Z., Lupiana, D., Mtenzi, F. and Wu, B. 2009. Challenges to E-Healthcare adoption in developing countries: A case study of Tanzania. *Networked Digital Technologies*, 2009.

Oppliger, R. 1996. *Authentication System for Secure Networks*, Artech House, Boston, MA.

Sanders, C., Rogers, A., Bowen, R., Bower, P. Newman, S. P. 2012. Exploring barriers to participation and adoption of telehealth and telecare within the Whole System Demonstrator trial: a qualitative study. *BMC Health Services Research*, doi: 10.1186/1472-6963-12-220.

Smith, B., Austin, A., Brown, M., King, J. T., Lankford, J., Meneely, A., and Williams, L. (2010, October). Challenges for protecting the privacy of health information: required certification can leave common vulnerabilities undetected. In *Proceedings of the second annual workshop on Security and privacy in medical and home-care systems* (pp. 1-12). ACM.

Sunyaev, A., Chomyi, D., Mauro, C., and Krcmar, H. 2010. Evaluation Framework for Personal Health Records: Microsoft HealthVault vs. Google Health. *In Proceedings of the Hawaii International Conference on System Sciences (HICSS 43), Kauai, Hawaii.*

Tassie, J. M., Balandine, S., Szumilin, E., Andrieux-Meyer, I., Biot, M., Cavailler, P., Belanger, F., and Legros, D. 2002. Fuchia: a free computer program for the monitoring of hiv/aids medical care at the population level. *Int Conf AIDS*, (14:C11029).

Tierney, W., Achieng, M., Baker, E., Bell, A., Biondich, P. ... Braitstein, P. 2010. Experience implementing electronic health records in three east African countries. *In Safran C, Marin H, Reti S, editors.* Partnerships for effective ehealth solutions. 13th ed. Amsterdam: IOS Press; 2010. pp. 371–6. World Congress on Medical and Health Informatics.

Tuyikeze, T. 2005. *A model for information security management and regulatory compliance in the South African health sector.* MSc thesis. Nelson Mandela Metropolitan University. http://www.nmmu.ac.za/documents/theses/Thesis_TITE.pdf. Accessed 01/08/2012.

Tuyikeze, T. and Pottas, D. 2005. Information Security Management and Regulatory Compliance in the South African Health Sector. *Proceedings of the ISSA 2005 New Knowledge Today conference.*

Yogeswaran, P. and Wright, G. 2010. EHR implementation in South Africa: How do we get it right? *Studies in Health Technology and Informatics,* *160*, 396-400. http://munin.uit.no/bitstream/handle/10037/1567/thesis.pdf?sequence=4. Accessed 15/08/2012.

An Investigation into User Perceptions of Privacy and Trust and their Real-World Practices

R.Stockton and S.Cunningham

Creative and Applied Research for the Digital Society (CARDS), Glyndŵr University, North Wales, UK
e-mail: {r.stockton|s.cunningham}@glyndwr.ac.uk

Abstract

Internet security is a well-researched and understood topic. However, the concept of online privacy is a less well-defined issue, particularly with the advent of mass email and social networking interactions. This paper presents results from a user survey to determine perceptions of privacy and trust in online environments. Results suggest that users have often-contradictory views of their privacy in the online world, but that the content of personal messages are perceived as the most sensitive data exchanged online. There is recognition of a number of security mechanisms available in the web domain. We go on to investigate personal messaging security in email. This is done by an investigation into the adoption of Transport Layer Security (TLS) encryption facilities in Internet mail servers, split into a pilot study and larger-scale piece of work. Results show that the majority of email servers sampled utilise TLS and that this majority is only somewhat more than 60% of all servers tested.

Keywords

Privacy; trust, security, encryption.

1. Introduction

This paper provides an initial investigation into user perceptions of privacy and trust in the online world and undertakes an initial examination of technologies that may be deployed to secure the information deemed most at-risk by user groups. In doing so, we seek to map out the current landscape of Internet privacy and to demonstrate that online privacy is an area in its infancy and one that needs significant further research to determine models of best practice for policymakers and security technologists.

2. Background

2.1. Online Privacy

Kemp and Moore (2007) discuss privacy as being a difficult to define, that it has quite clearly been eroded in the USA with legislation such as the PATRIOT act since the terrorist attacks of September 2011, and a similar situation is in place in the UK. The work represents Solove's (2002) six conceptions of privacy: 1) the right to be let alone; 2) limited access to the self; 3) secrecy; 4) control of personal information; 5) personhood; 6) intimacy; and adds a seventh term: 7) privacy as a cluster concept. These definitions have their problems, but are all clearly issues in the online society.

Warren (2002) analyses the legal context, provision of the UK Data Protection Act of 1998 and provides an evaluation of the approaches that have been taken by organizations to action the DPA requirements. The body of the work in the paper looks at the approaches taken by organizations to implement the DPA. The researcher uses three methods to examine the organizations. These are: a questionnaire survey of 14 organizations; 30 interviews of experts from across government and public sector organizations; and case studies compiled from in-depth interviews with employees from organizations including health, police and education. Warren finds that the scope of the right to privacy under this new legislation remains untested and contested by employer bodies. The paper identifies a variation in investment in compliance with the DPA from £75 to £10,000 per year and that awareness raising and training throughout an organization is important to comply with this legislation.

Yee (2006) states that privacy protection approaches are in early stages of research, treating the problem as an access protection one through technology and rights management. Yee argues it is important to measure the trust that the service user can have in the web service, as without trust, the service will not be used. Yee references the Goldberg *at al.* (1997) definition of privacy: *"privacy refers to the ability of individuals to control the collection, retention, and distribution of information about themselves."* Yee takes this statement and outlines the following definitions: 1) privacy refers to the ability of individuals to control the collection, use, retention, and distribution of information about themselves; 2) a service's protection of user privacy refers to the service's use of provisions to give the user control over the service's collection, retention, and distribution of information about the user; and 3) a measure of a service's protection of user privacy is a numerical value that indicates the degree of the user's control (or some aspect of that control) over the service's collection, retention, and distribution of information about the user.

Yee states there must be an understanding between the service provider and the service user as defined by a number of rules. Without consequences by a legal or governance framework then the trust by the users towards the service provider will not be a strong. Yee outlines some basic provisions that need to be in place and measured to control the trust and privacy of the service user's information and states that the list is not exhaustive:

- Use of a privacy policy that automatically ensures that the user's privacy policy is not violated;

- Use of a cryptographically secure log (this log can be later inspected to check for policy violations) to record each provider action involving the user's private data;

- Use of employee background checks when they are hired to try to exclude dishonest people from the provider's organization;

- Use of reputation mechanisms to record and indicate the past performance of the provider in terms of integrity (e.g. Better Business Bureau);

- Use of seals of approval that attest to the fact that the provider has undergone and passed rigorous inspections of its business processes.

Yee concludes with two outcomes, relevant to the research undertaken here. The measures serve at least two important functions: 1) they help the consumer to choose services that are more effective at protecting privacy, and 2) they let web service developers or managers know if more countermeasures are needed to achieve a predefined level of privacy protection effectiveness.

Kosa (2010) explores the current state of thinking in privacy related to computer systems. Work on formalizing trust in computer systems dates back to the mid-nineties, in contrast, however, work on formalizing privacy in computer systems is in its infancy. Kosa's work notes that privacy, unlike trust, is legislated [in Canada]. However, in regard of trust, the following statement is made:

"Trust, on the other hand, is the Wild West; almost anything goes. Early attempts at formalizing privacy in computer systems have been largely restricted to P3P initiatives and other policy developments."

Kosa explains that privacy is historically treated as an emotional and ethical concept. Whereas trust is more about the acceptance of risk to support action. In the realm of computer systems computational trust tends to be about transactional reliability and authenticity. For the concepts of trust and privacy to be enabled at the technical level for computer systems to operate with, both need to be formalized.

2.2. Secure Messaging

Farrell (2009) discusses why users are not routinely encrypting their e-mail. It outlines that e-mail sent between a Message User Agent (MUA) and Message Transfer Agent (MTA) is normally unencrypted. Encryption systems for e-mail include: OpenPGP which can be installed as a plug in to most e-mail clients; and Secure Multipurpose Internet Mail Extensions (S/MIME), which is built into most e-mail clients. These protocols have been around for a long time. S/MIME has been implemented into MS Outlook since 2000 and Open PGP has been in existence since 1997. These encryption products can provide two services: origin authenticity and encryption. The paper outlines that to enable the use of any of these systems the user has to first arrange to exchange encryption keys between parties to allow the system to operate. This hurdle for the end user is the problem as they either don't know how to do this, don't know the option exists, or finds the steps too hard. Both systems also insist that users include proof of who you are to enable the origin authenticity element of the process.

Robison (2012) outlines a secure overlay feature implemented in a Javascript Bookmarklet. The overlay is used to provide an encrypted chat session in Facebook using Facebook chat as the communications channel and the Bookmarklet acting as the input and output window. All communications are encrypted and not viewable by Facebook. The paper explains the usability of the system and how it addresses the key problem with security in ease of use. A trail of the software showed that over 50% of people were able to use the system with relative ease. The paper describes a survey conducted with a small sample size of 65 users that finds that people are unaware of any privacy issues associated with using online chat but assume that the phone and e-mail are more secure. This is a good clear piece of work showing how an overlay system can be used to hide communications across an untrusted system such as Facebook in this example. More work would be valuable in this area to include a generic system that could overlay many different web applications to secure the messages that pass through them.

Even though privacy is becoming a key requirement, frameworks that consider privacy in a comprehensive way are still missing. Most of the work in the literature focuses on a few aspects of privacy only. Moreover, much of the research has been devoted to anonymity metrics for privacy-preserving micro data releasing.

Colombo (2012) presents a model-based framework MAPaS. The MAPaS model is intended for developers of information systems to be able to create a privacy and access relationship model for the system under development. This model describes the information types in a schema with roles, skills and requirements of users of the system under development. Building access and information relationship rules in the system the developer is able to analyze and test the design for privacy weaknesses. Asking a number of questions of the model, it is possible to examine if the information and role allocation and access design is robust and meets the developers' intentions. An example given in the paper is attempting to allocate an access role to an inappropriate member of staff. If the privacy model description of the information system is correctly configured then the inappropriate staff member should be denied the inappropriate access role. If this is not the case the system logic can be amended. Using such as system over much iteration can assist a system developer to understand how the privacy logic of a system will respond before the expensive phase of actual systems development and testing.

3. Investigating User Perceptions of Privacy & Protection

3.1. Methodology

An online survey was devised to investigate the perceptions that users have of trust, security and privacy in their online activities. The survey was sent to all staff in a University as well as several JISC mailing lists including UCISA (Universities and Colleges Information Systems Association) and HEWIT (Higher Education Wales Information Technology). As such, it is acknowledged that the majority of respondents are people employed in the UK higher education sector. A total of 218 responses were received. A cross section of ages was represented in the survey with results mainly coming from the 35-50 age group category. When working with Chi-Square statistics, in our analysis, for less than 2 degrees of freedom, we apply Yates' correction.

3.2. Survey Results

Initial questions focused around the typical application uses of users surveyed. E-mail was the most used Internet application, followed closely by online web searching. Online shopping and banking were used extensively. There was a spread of other applications being used by significant percentages of respondents. To determine the area where users felt their privacy is most vulnerable, they were each asked to select the three areas that concerned them most, from a pre-defined list of options. A summary of the responses is shown in Figure .

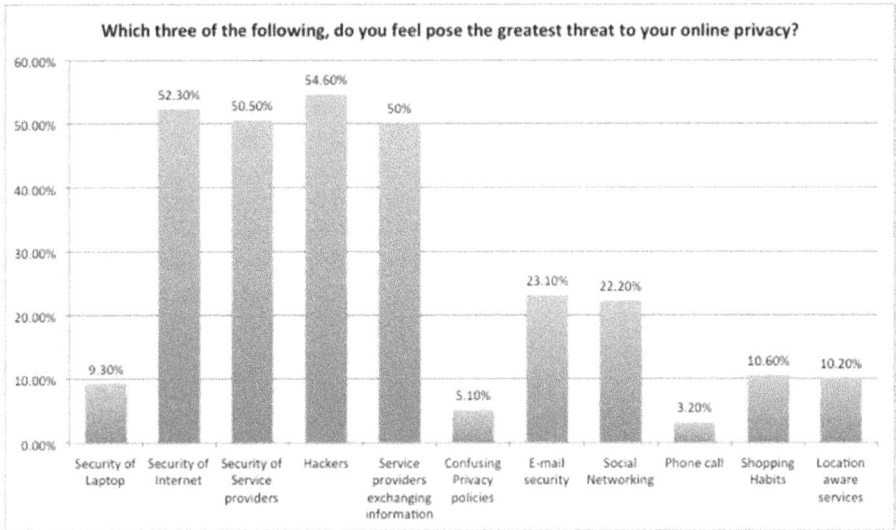

Figure 1: Threats to Online Privacy (N=216)

Hackers were the main concern at 54.6% followed closely by Security of Internet (52.3%) and Security of Service Providers which you send information to (50.5%). Curiously e-mail security (23.1%) and social networking (22.2%) were lower down the concerns. Shopping Habits (10.6%), Location aware services (10.2%) Laptop security (9.3%) and Phone calls (3.2%) had low concerns. Respondents seem to put greater importance on security and malicious threats from third parties than on the services providers not complying with privacy policies or having suitable or relevant privacy policies in place.

The UK Data Protection Act (1998) makes provision for the way in which organisations are entitled to store and use individuals' information. Part of the Act entitles individuals with access to this information, partly to ensure that it remains current and correct. However, we hypothesise that correctness of information does not equate to a sense of privacy or trust, since it remains in the possession of third party, whose uses of the information may not be as transparent to the end user. As such, we posed the question: "*As long as the information stored about you is correct then you have nothing to be concerned about". Do you agree with this statement?*". The results were that 86.2% responded negatively, indicating that the significant majority disagree, χ^2_{Yates} (1, N=218)=113.07 p<0.01. It is clear that there are concerns on storage of information, which would indicate a lack of trust between users and data controllers.

In terms of users being aware of the privacy polices and terms of use, we asked participants "*Have you read the privacy policies provided by web sites you use and *the software you install?"*. 41.3% responded Yes and 57.8% responding No (*N*=218) it is clear that a larger number than expected do read the privacy statements provided by the sites which shows they are interested in privacy online. This is not to say that they were satisfied with what they found in those statements. As a follow-up to this question, we asked the participants *"Have you refrained from using a service due to a requirement to provide them with what you consider to be personal or private information? Perhaps during a sign up stage or during a purchase."* The results here were extremely significant, with 92.2% of respondents replying that they had refrained from using a service due to a requirement to provide what they considered to be personal or private information, χ^2_{Yates} (1, *N*=218)=153.62 p<0.01.

To follow-on, it was decided to determine how frequently users divulge what they consider to be private information, in return for receiving a product of service, which they might otherwise prefer to not to share. To this end, a specific question employed was *"Have you revealed information about yourself to a service provider which you would have preferred not to, but did so to access the service?"*. The breakdown of responses is shown in Figure 2. The results do not indicate specifically whether a majority of users do, or do not, reveal private information in return for a service, however, the low percentage of users reporting in the Don't Know category, indicates that the majority of users do manage to make an informed decision about the private information they may or may not reveal, χ^2 (2, *N*=218)=69.61 p<0.01.

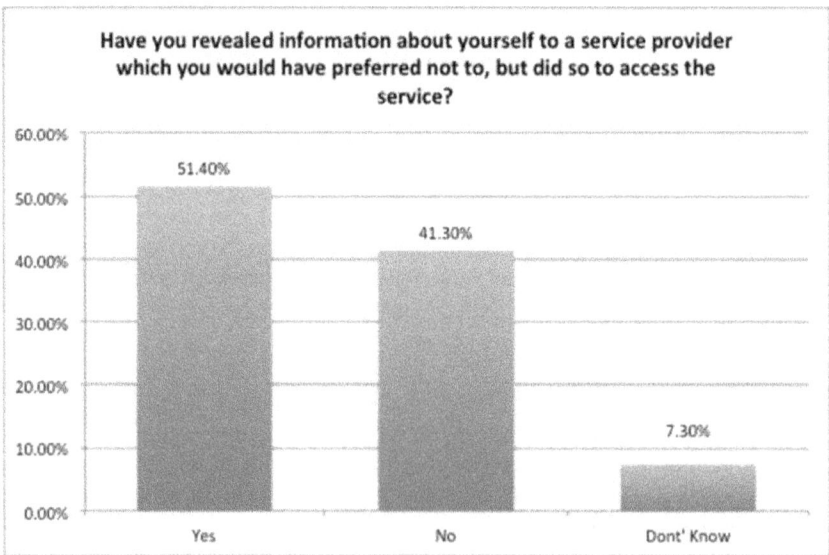

Figure 2: Revealing Private Information to Receive a Service (*N*=218)

To obtain an insight into technical features that users perceive as providing them with security features, participants were asked to select a technical security feature that would provide them with the most confidence in using an online service. The results can be seen in Figure 3, indicating a significant confidence amongst participants in in the use of Secure Socket Layer (SSL) χ^2 (3, *N*=218)=269.93 p<0.01. Results suggest that users value the recognized presence of SSL services almost universally across online services, to provide a measure of confidence in their transactions, even more so that the company brand or other descriptive measures.

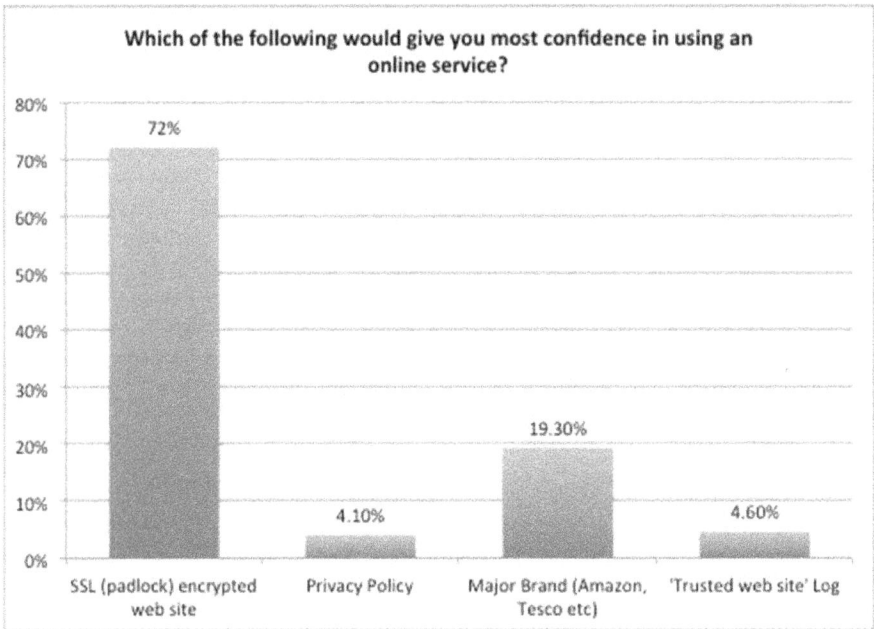

Figure 3: Technologies that give Confidence in Services (*N*=218)

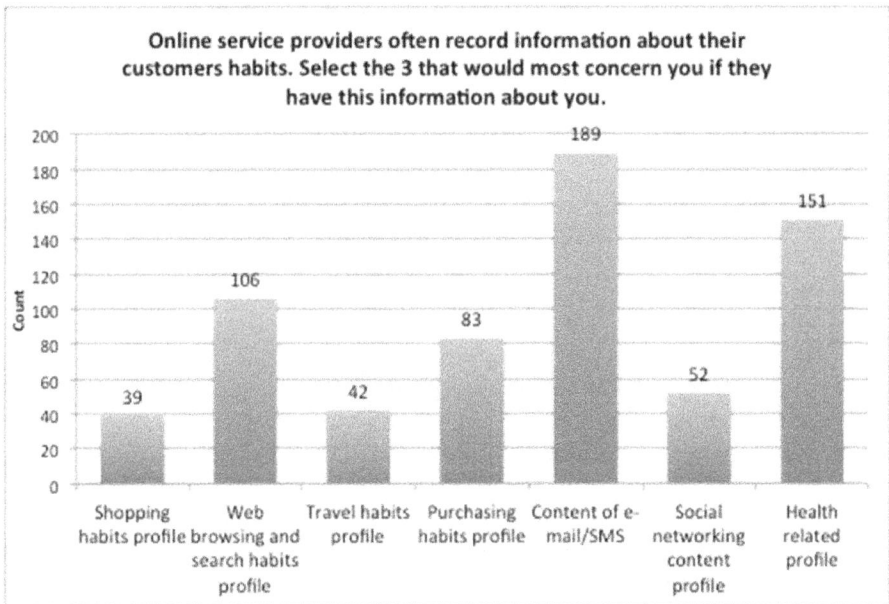

Figure 4: Most Sensitive Online Information (*N*=218)

Finally, participants were surveyed to determine the type of information that they perceived to be the most sensitive and wished for third parties to not have access to. The results of this investigation are shown in Figure 4, participants were asked to select the three most sensitive types of information.

Perhaps unsurprisingly, the contents of personal communications, email and SMS messaging, are in a significant majority, χ^2 (6, N=662)=211.79 p<0.01. More interestingly, is that this information appears to be slightly more sensitive to users than their medical or health data. The more open and generic information that might be disclosed in web browsing and online searching is considered more critical than more focused online purposes, such as shopping, travel and social networking. This suggests that users may have more of an awareness that their data is tracked in these more structured and enclosed interactions, but less so in general purpose Internet use. It is also possible that users regard data already in these systems to be 'available' as they have provided it knowingly and with a degree of informed consent.

4.   Technical Measures for Privacy

Using Transport Layer Security (TLS) removes the need for the end user to configure encryption and simplifies adding this layer of security. The mail system administrator must configure and enable the TLS encryption at the mail server level. This system also relies on the receiving server being correctly configured to receive the encrypted TLS communications. When correctly configured at both ends of the communication TLS provides encrypted transport between the e-mail server across the Internet to the point of the receiving e-mail server. This prevents eavesdropping at any point in between including on a local LAN or the Internet. This system does not protect the end user from interception within the mail system be a mail administrator. To this end, we seek to answer the following question: *how widespread is TLS encryption implemented and is it correctly configured?*

4.1. Pilot Study: Methodology

Item	Description
MX count	The number of mail exchange servers that were advertised in the DNS record for the e-mail address domain
Connected	That the e-mail server could be contacted during the test
TLS Available	Test that TLS is advertised as available on the e-mail server
Cert OK	Check that the digital certificate is valid, had not expired, not been revoked and is designated for this domain
Negotiated TLS	Test if the TLS negotiation completes successfully

Table 1: TLS Analysis Points

As pilot exercise a sample that used 1736 MX points was conducted to investigate this question. Using a number of e-mail address harvesting tools to collect e-mail addresses from web pages and a number of consenting individuals' mailboxes a TLS test engine was used to connect to the mail server for each of the e-mail addresses and conduct the TLS protocol setup procedure. The test engine recorded which stages of the TLS protocol where initiated correctly for e-mail mail server and if the server mandated TLS and required a trusted digital certificate or would allow for an untrusted digital certificate to be used. The original set of e-mail addresses contained many duplicates of domain names and these were removed so only one e-mail address for each domain name was tested. The testing collected data, described in Table 1, related to each email address

4.2. Pilot Study: Results

It was found that just over half of the domains tested (54%) had mail servers with TLS enabled. This does not mean, however, that half of the mail communicated between these servers will be encrypted using TLS as both end points are required to have TLS for the protocol to take effect. Assuming that there was an even distribution of communication between domains, this would show less than a quarter of the traffic between these servers would be using TLS.

The average number of MX points per domain name was 2 and it was seen that where the domain name had decided to implement TLS, the TLS was enabled across all of the MX points it operated. In terms of the percentage of servers within domains utilising TLS, the break down is shown Figure 5. The three domains identified in this graph .nz .ie .fi had low sample sizes that contribute to the high percentage with TLS enabled. Further work with a larger sample size may show different results.

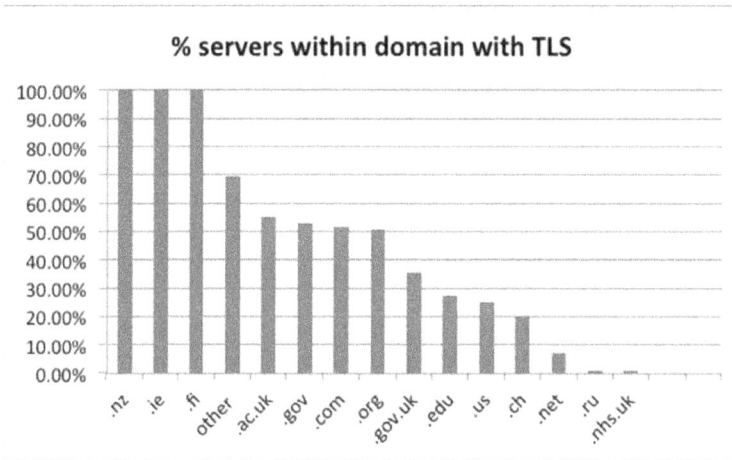

Figure 5: Percentage of Severs using TLS, by domain (Pilot Study)

On average, 37% of servers utilised TLS. It is quite clear from this sample that implementation of TLS is limited. The .ac.uk .gov and .org domains showed the highest implementations of TLS at around 50% of the sample with the other domains trailing off. What was is initially unexpected is the .nhs.uk domain space with 153 samples but only one with a TLS implementations. This is probably due to the addresses being harvested coming from web site general enquiry addresses with the majority of secure UK National Health Service (NHS) e-mail (NHSmail) traffic being routed internally via a separate private e-mail system that the NHS operate.

4.3. Larger-Scale Study: Results

Following on from the pilot sample, a larger survey of 17,148 MX points was undertaken using the same methods. It was discovered that 61% of domains surveyed had TLS enabled, compared with 54% in the pilot. The results show a higher overall percentage with TLS 47% of those surveyed by domain, compared to a figure of 37% in the pilot study; the results are illustrated in Figure 6.

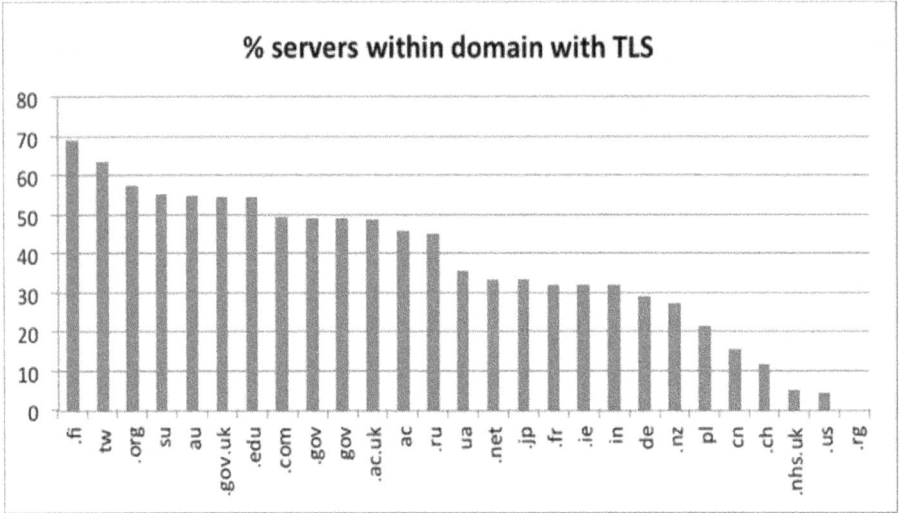

Figure 6: Percentage of Servers using TLS, by domain (Larger-Scale Study)

5. Discussion & Future Work

Our results provide a useful initial insight into the user perceptions of privacy in the online world and the implementation of technologies to support online privacy. Privacy cannot be guaranteed by a one-stop, single solution. Interventions range from policies and government legislation to technical solutions, such as encryption and protection from online attackers. As such, ensuring privacy is vast and coarse. Our future work focuses on developing a more detailed picture of the online privacy landscape by triangulating users experiences and perceptions with technical information, as exemplified in the work of this paper, to form taxonomy of recommended best practice for ensuring user privacy in today's online world.

To follow the initial user survey, a series of focus groups are planned. These are intended to gain an understanding of perceptions and practices related to individuals' use of computer systems in relation to issues of privacy.

Whilst a time consuming exercise, TLS surveying of a fuller sample of domains will provide a much more reliable analysis of the TLS implementation on the global Interet. In addition, it is intended that further work will look to address adoption of other technical security measures that might ensure privacy, such as the usage of encryption, authentication and nonrepudication technologies.

6. References

Colombo, P.; Ferrari, E., "Towards a Modeling and Analysis Framework for Privacy-Aware Systems," Privacy, Security, Risk and Trust (PASSAT), 2012 International Conference on and 2012 International Conference on Social Computing (SocialCom) , vol., no., pp.81,90, 3-5 Sept. 2012

Farrell, S. (2009). Why Don't We Encrypt Our Email?. IEEE Internet Computing Society , Volume 09 , pp. 1089-7801.

Goldberg, I., Wagner, D., & Brewer, E. (1997). *Privacy-enhancing technologies for the Internet*. CALIFORNIA UNIV BERKELEY.

Kemp, R. and Moore, A.D. (2007), "Privacy", Library Hi Tech, Vol. 25 Iss: 1, pp.58 – 78.

Kosa, T. A. (2010, August). Vampire Bats: Trust in Privacy. In Privacy Security and Trust (PST), 2010 Eighth Annual International Conference on (pp. 96-102). IEEE.

Robison, C.; Ruoti, S.; van der Horst, T.W.; Seamons, K.E., "Private Facebook Chat," Privacy, Security, Risk and Trust (PASSAT), 2012 International Conference on and 2012 International Confernece on Social Computing (SocialCom) , vol., no., pp.451,460, 3-5 Sept. 2012

Solove, D.J. (2002), "Conceptualizing privacy", California Law Review, Vol. 90.

Warren. A. (2002), "Right to privacy? The protection of personal data in UK public organizations". New Library World, p. Volume: 103 Issue:11.

Weissa, S. (2009). Privacy threat model for data portability in social network applications. International Journal of Information Management, Volume 01, 2009.

Yee, G. (2006), "Measuring Privacy Protection in Web Services," *Web Services, 2006. ICWS '06. International Conference on* , vol., no., pp.647,654, 18-22, doi: 10.1109/ICWS.2006.87

Chapter 2

WDFIA Papers

Retrieval and Analysis of Web Search Narratives for Digital Investigations

J.Haggerty[1] and M.J.Taylor[2]

[1]School of Science & Technology, Nottingham Trent University, Clifton Campus, Nottingham, NG11 8NS
[2]School of Computing & Mathematical Sciences, Liverpool John Moores University, Liverpool, L3 3AF
e-mail: john.haggerty@ntu.ac.uk; M.J.Taylor@ljmu.ac.uk

Abstract

Our reliance on accessing information on the Web ensures that it provides a wealth of information to a forensics examiner. Current tools for the analysis of a suspect's Web activity return evidence ranging from cached data to URLs visited. However, these tools are not without their limitations, such as textual presentation of results, issues related to private browsing, and links between Web searches and subsequent behaviour. This paper presents a novel approach that visualises search strings in Web browser log files to present a narrative of a suspect's interests, motives and actions over time. The aim of this methodology is to triage and analyse potentially large data sets from a suspect's daily interaction with the Internet and to demonstrate intent during the activity under investigation. In order to demonstrate the applicability of the approach, data from a Web browser history file is parsed for search terms and the results visualised.

Keywords

Digital forensics, Web clients, narrative, data visualization

1. Introduction

The World Wide Web (or Web) and the Internet is pervasive and provides many ways for a user to access the information that they require. The Office of National Statistics (ONS, 2014) suggests that in the UK alone, 73 per cent of the adult population accessed the Internet every day. Moreover, Internet access from mobile devices more than doubled between 2010 and 2013 to 53 per cent. All a user requires to access this information is a Web browser, an application that resides on the host computer and interprets information from Web servers. Information in this software is by default logged, primarily to aid the user experience. However, the reliance on this technology ensures that it provides a wealth of information to a forensics examiner during an investigation regarding a suspect's access and use of the Internet.

The importance of Web log information for an investigation has been known for some time and many forensics tools make use of this data. For example, *Pasco v1.0* (Jones, n.d.) is a forensics application that parses the Internet Explorer *index.dat* file to retrieve evidence of Web sites that a suspect has visited. The data is returned as CSV files providing information such as URLs and times of access. However, the volume of data that such software returns may be considerable with many redundant entries, i.e. entries not related to the event(s) under investigation. Moreover, whilst it extracts Web browser evidence, it does not provide a qualitative analysis of a suspect's activity over time, merely a list of Web sites visited. In order to meet these and other shortcomings, data visualisation tools and techniques can be employed to aid the investigation process and triage evidence returned. As Thomson et al (2013) suggest, data visualization may be used by analysts to alleviate the overheads of interpreting data sets and improve the ability of users to make sense of activity patterns in event logs.

This paper presents a novel approach that visualises search strings in Web browser logs to present a narrative of a suspect's interests, motives and actions over time. In this way, it reduces ambiguity in links between search terms and subsequent Web interaction, as well as providing temporal and textual analysis to demonstrate relational information to the forensics examiner. The aim of this approach is to triage potentially large data sets from a suspect's daily interaction with the Internet to provide further sources of evidence or to support hypotheses during the investigatory process. Moreover, it may be used to prove or disprove the 'Trojan defence', whereby a suspect claims to have inadvertently followed a Web link; Web searches are an active, rather than passive, interaction and may be used to demonstrate intent.

This paper is organised as follows. Section 2 discusses related work in Web log analysis and data visualisation for security and forensics investigations. Section 3 presents an overview of forensic analysis of Web browser logs and posits our approach. Section 4 presents the results of a case study of using the approach on a Web browser history file to demonstrate the applicability of the methodology. Finally, we make our conclusions and discuss further work.

2.   Related work

Web log analysis provides a wealth of information to the forensics investigator and the recording of user activity may take place on either the server or the client. Server-side Web logs record information about users that visit the Web site to improve the user experience and their log analysis may focus on content mining, usage mining or structure mining (Hadzic and Hecker, 2011). For example, Hernandez et al (2010) propose a model for the structuring of data to aid the log mining process across formats. Chowdhury et al (2010) propose an approach for mining Web access sequences, mainly focused on online databases. Nithya and Sumathi (2012) propose an approach for pre-processing data prior to analysis to remove usage noise and the recorded presence of Web robots. Whilst these, and other, approaches mine information available from servers, they are limited in their use for forensics investigations as the examiner would have to have prior knowledge of a suspect's use of the Web site.

Therefore, research in digital forensics has focused on client-side log mining and analysis to identify evidence. For example, Accorsi et al (2011) propose RECIF, an approach that utilises business process logs to identify illegal data flows. Al Mutawa et al (2011) propose an approach for the retrieval and analysis of Facebook Instant Messaging artefacts and identify issues surrounding the recovery of Arabic text. Alternatively, Hai-Cheng Chu et al (2011) focus on the live acquisition of previous

Facebook session evidence utilising the way in which data is written to a computer. Other approaches focus on Web browser logs and in particular the issue of a suspect attempting to disrupt potential evidence about their activities being recorded. For example, Said et al (2011), Ohana and Shashidhar (2013) and Satvat et al (2013) demonstrate the evidence that may be retrieved from a hard drive even when a Web browser is set to private browsing or when portable devices are used by a suspect. However, these approaches often focus on the extraction rather than triage and analysis of potential evidence relevant to the investigation.

The benefits of data visualization and interaction for large data sets have ensured that such approaches have been adopted within the security and forensics domains. Visualization enables an analyst to gain an overview of data during an investigation (Schrenk and Poisel, 2011). For example, Haggerty et al (2014) propose *TagSNet*, an approach for the quantitative and qualitative analysis of email data to enable a forensics examiner to analyze not only actor relationships but also visualize discourse between those actors. Koniaris et al (2013) present visualizations of their results of detecting attackers utilizing SSH vulnerabilities to attack honeypot systems. Giacobe and Xen Su (2011) propose an approach to visually represent security data in a geographical sphere based on IP address rather than physical location. Thomson et al (2013) posit *Pianola*, a system for visualizing and understanding the contents of intrusion detection logs.

Whilst these approaches provide visualisations of evidence, they do not demonstrate intent in committing a crime or taking part in a malicious event(s). The aim of this approach is to triage potentially large data sets from a suspect's daily interaction with the Internet. Moreover, the approach posited in this paper may be used to prove or disprove the 'Trojan defence'. The next section outlines the proposed methodology.

3. Methodology overview

A Web browser is software that enables a host to retrieve data from a Web server that resides on user's device. Web browsers come in several levels of functionality, from text-based applications to software that is able to interpret a variety of information, such as multimedia, images and executable code. The browser market is dominated by four major products; Internet Explorer, Chrome, Firefox and Safari. This software has in common the ability to record information by default about a user's actions when accessing information on the Web, primarily aimed at improving the user's experience. This activity occurs often without the knowledge of the user. They therefore provide a useful resource for a forensics examiner during an investigation as they provide a wealth of information about a suspect's online activity.

The way in which these four applications record, or log, user data differs between software. For example, Internet Explorer uses binary format log files to record a range of information, from cache data to Uniform Resource Locators (URLs) that a user accesses whilst on the Internet. This information is stored in a single file; *index.dat*. The other three applications use a SQLite database format to record information. This information may be both persistent and volatile. For example, Chrome stores historic information in persistent files. However, information on the current session is stored in text format that is replaced when the application is closed and then re-opened.

It should be noted that whilst Web browsers record a wide range of information about a suspect's activity by default, they could circumvent this by utilising the software in 'private browsing' mode. In an attempt to protect users' privacy, many of the main software providers have introduced this feature. The aim of this feature is to allow users to access the Internet without storing data related to the Internet session locally. Such features are useful when accessing the Internet from publicly-used computers, such as in libraries and Internet cafes. However, they may be used by a suspect to disrupt a forensic investigation by reducing the amount of evidence available to the examiner.

The amount of evidence that may be retrieved from private browsing sessions is dependent on the Web browser used by the suspect. For example, as Said et al (2011) and Satvat et al (2013) demonstrate, forensic examiners are able to retrieve data written locally to storage media with varying levels of success. For example, if a suspect were to use a Chrome browser, very little data may be retrieved; if they use Internet Explorer, a wide range of data will have been written to local storage and therefore may be retrieved. This is due to the different schemes used by each application to provide user privacy. Browsers such as Chrome do not write data locally whilst a user accesses the Web whereas Internet Explorer records data and then deletes the data associated with a private browsing session. As demonstrated by Said et al (2011), much of this deleted data may then be retrieved by the forensics examiner using tools and techniques associated with deleted file recovery. Whilst this may not retrieve a coherent list of Web site information that could be viewed in applications such as *Pasco v1.0*, it will result in strings that may be utilised by the methodology outlined in this paper.

The methodology posited by this paper aims to use search terms recorded in Web browser logs or elsewhere in local storage to provide a qualitative narrative of a suspect's activity and interests over time. This approach aims to overcome issues with tools such as *Pasco v1.0*. For example, if private browsing is used by the suspect, little evidence will be recorded that could be retrieved. However, as discussed above, strings containing search terms may be stored elsewhere. Search terms provide a qualitative view of a suspect's activity, motives or intentions. With the wide range of devices that a suspect has at their disposal, a search may be performed on one computer but the access of the Web server made from another. The analysis of search terms can be used to reduce the ambiguity of Web access and subsequent actions by a suspect. For example, a suspect may search for, "possible sentence for stabbing a person randomly on a bus", which may result in subsequent interactions with legal Web sites, perhaps not indicating the link between the search and the resulting behaviour. Finally, search terms may be used to provide a temporal and textual analysis to demonstrate the *intention* to engage in criminal or malicious activity.

As discussed above, Web logs come in a variety of formats and this affects both the location of information that is recorded and the techniques to retrieve the data. For example, Chrome utilises a number of files in SQL format that record a user's Web activity, such as 'History' and 'Archived History' whilst Internet Explorer uses the *index.dat* file to record a wide range of data and Web preferences (for a detailed discussion on *index.dat* file format and artefacts, see Jones (2003)). Information that may be retrieved ranges from URLs visited by the user to auto-complete information. The Chrome databases are located in `%systemdir%\Users\%username%\ AppData\Local\Google\Chrome` (Windows 7) and `/home/$USER/ .config/google-chrome/` (Linux) folders. The *index.dat* file is located in `%systemdir%\Users\%username%\AppData\Local\Microsoft\Wind ows\History\History.IE5\` (Windows 7) and it may also store historic information in daily, weekly, and monthly history logs.

As illustrated in figure 1, the methodology posited in this paper has three main areas of functionality: evidence retrieval, Web log mining and analysis, and data visualisation.

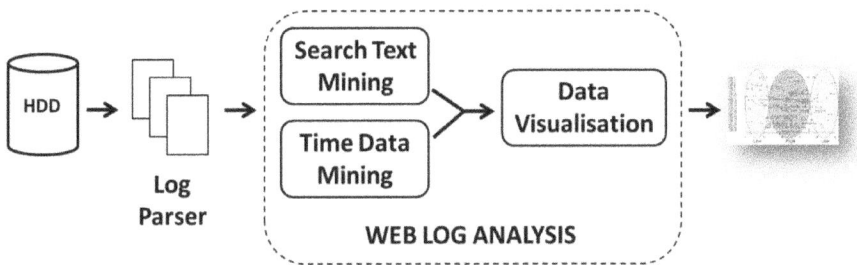

Figure 1: Overview of the Web log mining methodology.

As with any investigation, the data must be acquired in a robust manner, ensuring that the evidence maintains its integrity. Therefore, an image of the original hard disk drive (HDD) or storage media is made. The Web log files are accessed on this image and are pre-processed to provide a textual format for further analysis through text mining. The log parsers depend on the Web browser that is used by the suspect. For example, *SQLite3* can be used to view the Web logs of Chrome or Chromium browsers whereas the *Pasco v1.0* utility (Jones, n.d.) may be used to access Internet Explorer *index.dat* files. Information is written to local storage in binary format, thus the log parsers provides a means to read the data. The log parser returns information from the Web browser file format into text providing information such as Web sites visited and time of access. Amongst these results are records of search engine accesses and search terms used.

The pre-processed log files are passed into the program for textual and temporal analysis prior to visualisation. Textual analysis accesses URL descriptors associated with search strings to extract the search term used by the suspect. The Search Text mining function searches the URLs returned by the Log parser for strings associated with searches, such as "?q=" and "#q=" and strips the search terms from the URLs. The advantage of using this short search text rather than a search engine URL is that it can be used to identify searches made in a range of Web-based databases, such as streaming multimedia repositories and Web-based map sites. The data is also searched for dates and times of access. In this way, the forensics examiner is able to not only gain an overview of what the person searched for, but also the times that they made those searches. This can then be related back to the investigation to place the suspect's activity in context of the event(s) under investigation.

The initial URL prior to parsing is illustrated below. The search string inputted by the user is inserted into the URL within a search engine. The format of the recorded search is; <search engine URL> <query> <additional parameters>. As illustrated below, the search is indicated by the "?q=" string and the words used in the query are separated by "+". In the case below, the search term is repeated indicating an OR query. The additional parameters include information on the Web browser being used to access the site as well as input encoding. The text mining function extracts the search term used by the suspect by extracting the information following the "?q=" string. This therefore produces a string, "abc+xyz", from the example below.

```
https://www.google.co.uk/search?q=abc+xyz&oq=abc+xyz&aqs=
chrome..69i57j0l5.5985j0j8&sourceid=chrome&espv=210&es_sm
=122&ie=UTF-8
```

Data is passed to the visualisation function for temporal (timeline) and text visualisation. The temporal visualisation in the case study shows the forensics examiner the date of last access for the search term. It is recognised that users will repeat search terms to recall Web sites rather than bookmark their results but this information is not recorded in Chrome. Visualisation of the text is in two forms; whole search terms and individual words. The whole term visualisation places the search in context and shows the forensics examiner the intention of the suspect; it provides contextual narrative. This is visualised as a 'network of searches', similar to a mind map and relationships between searches made on the same day are highlighted by clicking the network node. Visualisation of individual words demonstrates common themes in the overall search narrative of a suspect by quantifying those words.

This section has provided an overview to the search term analysis approach that provides both textual and temporal visualisations of a suspect's online activities. In the next section, we demonstrate the applicability of the proposed approach by applying it to a Chrome history file.

4.   Case study and results

The History file of a Chrome browser is accessed to show user activity over a period of ten days. Log parsing outlined above is achieved using *sqlite3*. As discussed in the previous section, Chrome records a wealth of information about a users' online activities and stores this data in a number of database tables, such as downloads, URLs, keyword search terms, and meta(-data). Data is exported to text format from the URL table within the database to be passed to the application discussed above for temporal and text mining. Information recorded in the URL table includes the URL itself, number of visits and time of last visit. Therefore, in the temporal analysis, only the last date that the user visited a Web site is recorded and this is extracted by the temporal mining function.

Over the ten-day period, a total of 149 URLs were accessed, of which 41 contained search terms used in Google searches. Figure 2 provides a temporal view of the searches extracted from the Chrome History database. As discussed above, Chrome only records the last access (and number of times the URL was visited) and therefore, only one entry per search term is available. However, certain patterns of activity are clearly discernible. For example, searches around the 'Heartbleed' bug are followed by searches related to OpenSSL itself. Searches related to wireless security are followed by searches for downloads and tutorials related to exploitation of such networks. The temporal analysis therefore suggests a search narrative associated with malicious activity related to the security of networks. The extent to which the suspect has engaged in such activity could be ascertained by further analysis of all URLs visited, for example using *SQLite3*, and searches of the hard drive for software associated with security exploitation.

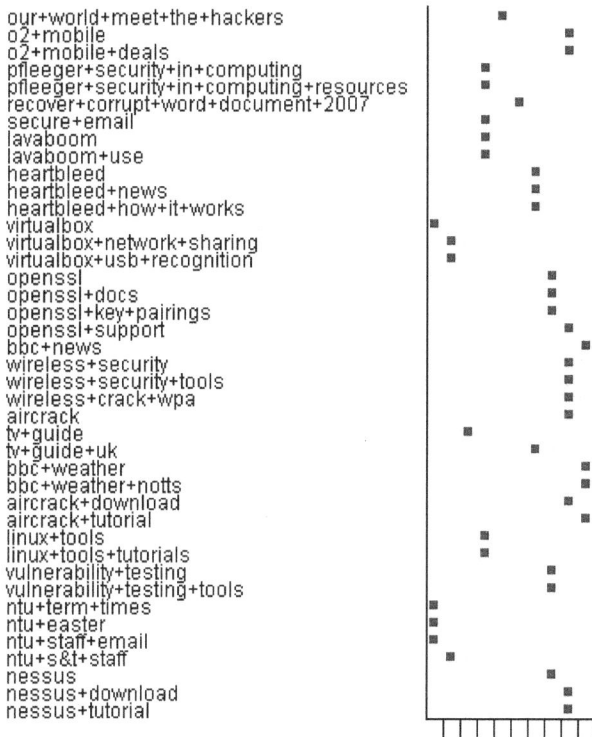

Figure 2: Temporal view of Web searches.

Figure 3 illustrates two network views which can be used by the forensics examiner to explore relationships between search terms used by a suspect. Search terms are arranged around the user to show their association. In addition, the examiner can select a node to show other search terms used on the same day. In this way, temporal information can be discerned and potentially follow the intentions of the suspect during a particular time period. In the figures below, the search term of interest is selected and the related searches are highlighted in red. In the figure on the left, the term "wireless+security+terms" is selected and on the same day, "o2+mobile", "o2+mobile+deals", "openssl+support", "wireless+crack+wpa", "aircrack+ download", and "nessus+download" are terms also searched. In the figure on the right, "openssl+docs" is selected and other searches were made on the same day for "openssl", "openssl+key+pairings", "vulnerability+testing+tools", and "nessus". In this way, we are able to determine that the suspect has been actively searching for network security issues and tools that may be used to exploit systems, depending on the context of the investigation.

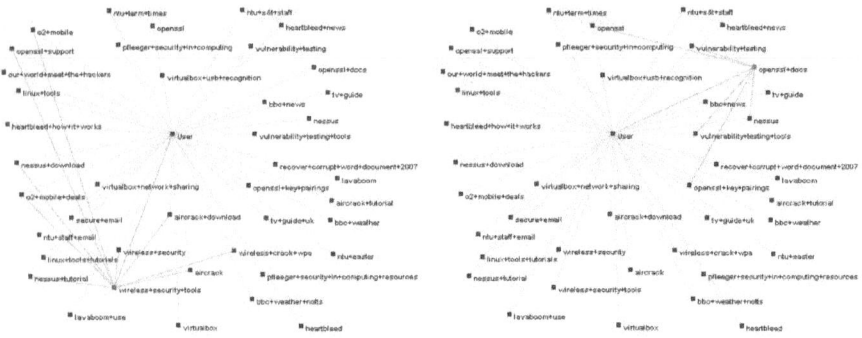

Figure 3: Network view of Web searches.

Figure 4 illustrates the key themes across the data set and the search narrative of the suspect. The visualisation in this figure is a tag cloud of all words whereby the font is sized by frequency of occurrence. Clearly discernible in this view is the prominence of "openssl" as a search term and its relationship with "heartbleed" could be explored using the visualisations above. In addition, the suspect also makes searches related to "security" and "tools". If this were an investigation into suspected computer and network misuse, these terms would identify intention and suggest forensic analysis of the hard drive for tools associated with such activity.

Figure 4: Overview of Web search words.

As demonstrated by the case study, search narratives provide a wealth of information to the forensics examiner. The methodology posited above may be used to triage potentially large data sets from a suspect's daily interaction with the Internet to provide further sources of evidence or to support hypotheses during the investigatory process. Moreover, as Web searches are active rather than passive in that a user must enter the terms of the search, it can be used to identify intention during an event(s) of interest and potentially prove or disprove a Trojan defence.

5. Conclusions and further work

Our reliance on accessing information on the Web ensures that it provides a wealth of information to a forensics examiner during an investigation regarding a suspect's access and use of the Internet. Current tools for Web browser log analysis may result in considerable evidence with many redundant entries and do not provide a qualitative analysis of a suspect's activity over time, merely a list of Web sites visited in textual form.

Data visualisation may be used forensics examiners to alleviate the overheads of interpreting evidence and to make sense of patterns in system logs. Therefore, this paper has presented a methodology to visualise search strings in Web browser logs to present a narrative of a suspect's interests, motives and actions over time. The aim of this approach is to triage potentially large data sets from a suspect's daily interaction with the Internet to identify Web search narratives. As Web searches are an active, rather than passive, interaction they may be used to demonstrate intent in criminal or malicious activity. In order to demonstrate the applicability of the approach, data from a Chrome history file is parsed for Web search terms and the results visualised. The case study demonstrates that visualisation of the temporal and relational information of search narratives can aid a digital investigation. Further work aims to extend the proposed approach to larger data sets, explore further visualisation techniques, and identify other Web interactions such as database queries.

6. References

Accorsi, R., Wonnemann, C. and Stocker, T. (2011), "Towards Forensic Data Flow Analysis of Business Process Logs", *Proceedings of the Sixth International Conference on IT Security Incident Management and IT Forensics*, Stuttgart, Germany, 2011, pp. 3 - 20.

Al Mutawa, N., Al Awadhi, I., Baggili, I. and Marrington, A. (2011), "Forensic artifacts of Facebook's instant messaging service", *Proceedings of the International Conference on Internet Technology and Secured Transactions*, Abu Dhabi, United Arab Emirates, 2011, pp. 771 - 776.

Chowdhury Farhan Ahmed, Syed Khairuzzaman Tanbeer and Byeong-Soo Jeong (2010), "Mining High Utility Web Access Sequences in Dynamic Web Log Data", *Proceedings of the 11th ACIS International Conference on Software Engineering, Artificial Intelligence, Networking and Parallel/Distributed Computing*, London, UK, 2010, pp. 76 - 81.

Giacobe, N.A. and Sen Xu (2011), "Geovisual analytics for cyber security: Adopting the GeoViz Toolkit", *Proceedings of the IEEE Conference on Visual Analytics Science and Technology*, Providence, RI, USA, 2011, pp. 315 - 316.

Hadzic, F. and Hecker, M. (2011), "Alternative Approach to Tree-Structured Web Log Representation and Mining", *Proceedings of the IEEE/WIC/ACM International Conferences on Web Intelligence and Intelligent Agent Technology*, Lyon, France, 2011, pp. 235 -242.

Haggerty, J., Haggerty, S. and Taylor, M. (2014), "Forensic Triage of Email Network Narratives through Visualisation", *Journal of Information Management and Computer Security*, forthcoming.

Hernandez, P., Garrigos, I. and Mazon, J-N (2010), "Modeling Web logs to enhance the analysis of Web usage data", *Proceedings of Workshops on Database and Expert Systems Applications*, Toulouse, France, 2011, pp. 297 - 301.

Koniaris, I., Papadimitriou, G. and Nicopolitidis, P. (2013), "Analysis and Visualization of SSH Attacks Using Honeypots", *Proceedings of EuroCon*, Zagreb, Croatia, 2013, pp. 65 - 72.

Jones, K.J. (2003), "Forensic Analysis of Internet Explorer Activity Files", Technical Report, available from http://www.foundstone.com/us/pdf/wp_index_dat.pdf, accessed 26 Mar 2014.

Jones, K.J. (n.d.), "Pasco v1.0", available from http://www.mcafee.com/uk/downloads/free-tools/pasco.aspx, accessed 26 March 2014.

Nithya, P. and Sumathi, P. (2012), "Novel Pre-Processing Technique for Web Log Mining by Removing Global Noise and Web Robots", *Proceedings of the National Conference on Computing and Communication Systems*, West Bengal, India, 2012, pp. 1 - 5.

Office of National Statistics (ONS) (2013), "Internet Access - Households and Individuals, 2013", Government Report, http://www.ons.gov.uk/ons/rel/rdit2/internet-access---households-and-individuals/2013/stb-ia-2013.html, accessed 26 March 2014.

Ohana, D.J. and Shashidhar, N. (2013), "Do Private and Portable Web Browsers Leave

Incriminating Evidence?", *Proceedings of IEEE Security and Privacy Workshops*, San Fransisco, CA, USA, 2013, pp. 135 - 142.

Said, H., Al Mutawa, N., Al Awadhi, I. and Guimaraes, M. (2011), "Forensic Analysis of Private Browsing Artifacts", *Proceedings of the International Conference on Innovations in Information Technology*, Abu Dhabi, United Arab Emirates, 2011, pp. 197 - 202.

Satvat, K., Forshaw, M., Hao, F. and Toreini, E. (2013), "On the Privacy of Private Browsing – A Forensic Approach", *Proceedings of the International Workshop on Data Privacy Management*, London, UK, 2013.

Schrenk, G. and Poisel, R. (2011), "A Discussion of Visualization Techniques for the Analysis of Digital Evidence", *Proceedings of the Sixth International Conference on Availability, Reliability and Security*, Vienna, Austria, 2013, pp. 758 - 763.

Thomson, A., Graham, M. and Kennedy, J. (2013), "Pianola - Visualization of Multiva-riate Time-Series Security Event Data", *Proceedings of the 17th International Conference on Information Visualisation*, London, UK, 2013, pp. 123 -131.

Digital Evidence Challenges in the Internet of Things

R.C.Hegarty[1], D.J.Lamb[2] and A.Attwood[3]

[1]School of Computing, Mathematics and Digital Technology, Manchester
Metropolitan University, John Dalton Building, Chester Street, Manchester, UK
[2]School of Computing & Mathematical Sciences, [3]School of Engineering,
Technology and Maritime Operations, Liverpool John Moores University James
Parsons Building, Byrom Street, Liverpool, UK
e-mail: R.Hegarty@mmu.ac.uk; {D.J.Lamb;A.J.Attwood}@ljmu.ac.uk

Abstract

The implementation of the Internet of Things will result in the connection of tens of billions of wireless devices to the Internet. These devices will form an intelligent substrate pervading all aspects of life. From intelligent home control to advanced city management systems, devices will sense their environment as well as interconnect and communicate with each other to form intelligent smart spaces. Individually and collectively, these devices produce and consume large amounts of personally sensitive data. This new environment provides a rich set of data sources; when used in conjunction with one another, they can greatly inform a historical situation that may have occurred with little or no reliable human witness evidence. However, this deeply pervasive environment will provide challenges to the various agencies that will need to interact with this new technology. This paper establishes the fundamental overarching challenges the IoT poses to digital forensics, and identifies the key areas that solutions should target.

Keywords

Internet of Things, Digital Investigations, Cloud Computing, Digital Forensics

1. Introduction: The Internet of Things

The Internet of Things (IoT), in the context of this paper, describes a world where many otherwise ordinary devices are uniquely identifiable, addressable and contactable via the Internet. Such *things* may be little more than a sensor or actuator augmented with basic transceiver electronics to manage connectivity requirements. Alternatively, these *things* may be sophisticated and comparable to typical consumer electronics devices, providing local computational functionality – such as a set-top Digital Video Recorder, or the headline-grabbing intelligent fridges commandeered in the infamous "Spam Fridge" attacks (Chirgwin, 2014).

As such, some *things* may have a degree of server functionality and respond readily to incoming requests and queries, whereas less sophisticated devices may simply generate and transmit their output data on certain triggers. They may take their power from a mains, self-generating or sustainable supply, or may be tightly constrained low-power battery operated devices with a limited power lifespan.

Additionally, their connectivity state – and therefore participation in the IoT – may be temporary or sporadic; based on the availability or status of power supply, the presence of a compatible *thing*-to-Internet gateway, or only triggered by *thing*-specific stimuli. The devices may therefore spend much of their time in a very low power state; idle or disconnected.

However, regardless of their appearance and power source, their placement – and looking to the future, their ubiquity – will allow them to collect and potentially store and process tremendous amounts of data. This data may not in itself be directly or deliberately personally identifying. Its combination and correlation with other datasets, both virtual and real, can provide significant insight into personal activity and environmental conditions.

This paper identifies the challenges IoT poses to established digital forensic procedures, and the areas in which solutions should be targeted. Section 2 provides an overview of the general digital forensics literature to illustrate where the challenges posed by the IoT interact with existing digital forensics models. In addition to this, recent works on the challenges posed by the IoT to digital forensics are reviewed to establish the state of the art research in this area. Section 3 describes the challenges posed by the IoT and some approaches to overcoming them. Section 4 identifies the key issues and emerging requirements of IoT investigations. Section 5 describes the future research directions and work required to develop solutions to the challenges posed to IoT investigations.

2. Related Work

2.1. Digital Forensics

Law enforcement agencies, private organisations and even individuals are familiar with the combination of digital and physical evidence resulting from forensic investigations. As electronic devices become pervasive this trend looks set to continue. For example it is commonplace for the police to check with mobile network operators, whether drivers were using a mobile telephone, when investigating road traffic incidents (GM Casualty Reduction Partnership, 2014) (Haines, 2007). Internet of Things devices augment today's digital data environment with potentially significant personal and context-setting data feeds. We identify the requirements for investigations in the IoT by first considering the seminal work of McKemmish (McKemmish, 1999) that describes Digital Forensics as:

> *"The process of identifying, preserving, analysing and presenting digital evidence in a manner that is legally acceptable"*

The application of this definition to investigation in the IoT raises a number of challenges. To develop an understanding of these challenges and their place in the digital forensic process we consider the two predominant models for digital forensic investigations. Table provides an overview of the models proposed by McKemmish (McKemmish, 1999) and NIST (Kent, Chevalier, Grance, Dang, & Kent, 2006).

Stage	McKemmish	Kent
1	**Identification**, in this stage the location and format of evidence is identified to enable an appropriate mechanism to be determined for the purpose of recovering evidence. Digital evidence can be found in a myriad of places; computers, mobile phones, smart cards, set top boxes etc.	**Collection**, encompasses identification, preservation and acquisition of relevant evidence
2	**Preservation**, it is imperative that evidence is preserved as in many cases it will be the subject of judicial scrutiny. In some circumstances changes to data are unavoidable. In these cases change should be minimised and the process causing the change documented along with an explanation/justification of why the change was required.	**Examination**, uses automated and manual tools to extract data of interest.
3	**Analysis,** consists of the extraction, processing and interpretation of digital evidence. It forms the main element of forensic computing. Following extraction, processing is often required to make data human readable. Processing of extracted data may be part of the extraction stage or a separate stage in its own right.	**Analysis**, the derivation of useful information from the results of the examination stage.
4	**Presentation**, the final stage of the process involves a presentation of both the evidence and the process by which the evidence was gathered along with the presenter's qualifications.	**Reporting**, is concerned with the preparation and presentation of the evidence and forensic analysis process.

Table 1: Digital Forensics Process Models

In the following section, we survey the literature relating to IoT forensics. We then revisit the investigatory stages detailed in Table , to consider the challenges specific to each stage of the investigatory process.

2.2. IoT Forensics

The identification and preservation of evidence in digital forensic investigations in emerging environments has always presented a challenge. Taylor et al (Taylor, Haggerty, Gresty, & Hegarty, 2010) suggested that the standards by which evidence is judged in digital forensic investigations may have to be altered to accommodate the changing nature of digital evidence from a cloud computing environment. We believe the same proposition holds true for IoT investigations.

Oriwoh et al (Oriwoh, Jazani, Epiphaniou, & Sant, 2013) identified preservation as a challenge, and suggested that devices undergoing investigation should not be turned off to preserve the modified, created and accessed times of files. Their assertion is likely drawn from conventional digital forensic investigations; however, the situation is much more complex in IoT investigations. Thought must be given to the limited resources available on devices, leaving the devices running at the scene of an incident will use power, and more importantly may result in overwriting of stored data due to constrained storage capabilities. Therefore, consideration is required to determine whether devices should be powered off or left running. We study this challenge in further detail in section 3.

The extraction and preservation of data from devices and services running in the IoT will present challenges. Proprietary data formats, protocols, and physical interfaces all complicate the process of evidence extraction (Miorandi, Sicari, De Pellegrini, & Chlamtac, 2012). Some schemes distribute information to adjacent nodes within the same topology or to external cloud services. In these scenarios, investigators need to be able to identify the benefit to the investigation in extracting data from other nodes, base stations, or cloud services (Attwood, Merabti, & Abuelmaatti, 2011). This approach could be viable and may overcome some of the challenges associated with extracting data from devices with limited storage. The data stored and processed in the IoT can be of a sensitive nature. We posit that the way in which large corporations aggregate and process data, may be the subject of future digital forensic investigations.

Oriwoh et al (Oriwoh et al., 2013) identify the challenge posed by devices crossing the boundaries of jurisdictions; while we agree this is a challenge. It is highly likely that data in transit between IoT devices and globally distributed cloud computing platforms cross these boundaries on a far more frequent basis. In Section 3 we question whether the emphasis of investigations should be on devices or data, and whether devices may be viewed as a metadata aspect of the data or if the reverse is true.

3. IoT Forensic Challenges & Approaches

The IoT will undoubtedly provide a richer source of evidence from the physical world than conventional computer systems. The way in which IoT is realising Zelkha et al's vision of ambient intelligence (Zelkha, Epstein, Birrell, & Dodswoth, 1998) means that environments are beginning to react to the user's requirements, without the need for conscious interaction by the user. As a result, IoT environments are likely to contain contextual evidence of which the perpetrators are simply oblivious. This paradigm shift means that digital investigations will increasingly encounter evidence from events taking place in the physical world.

The four main phases of digital forensics investigation from Table 1 face a number of challenges from the IoT. We discuss the implications of the IoT for each phase under the headings below and identify areas in which solutions should be targeted

3.1. Identification

Detecting the presence of IoT systems poses challenges to digital forensic investigations, as does the identification of a particular user's data. This raises the question of how to carry out what law enforcement term "search & seizure" when it is not apparent where the data being investigated is being stored, or where the data came from.

A potential solution to identification of data may be the integration of IoT device data into Building Information Modelling ("National BIM Standards," 2013);

Building Information Modelling (BIM) is a digital representation of physical and functional characteristics of a facility. A BIM is a shared knowledge resource for information about a facility forming a reliable basis for decisions during its life-cycle; defined as existing from earliest conception to demolition.

By combining the information about the IoT capabilities of a building or structure, it may be possible to answer the questions of; where has the information come from? Where is the information stored? It is also crucial to identify in what format the data is stored or encoded. This would narrow the scope of the investigation, and enable the selection of features or data that identifies an individual user from a much smaller data set. A composite picture of the data gathered about an individual user could be constructed from the data stored or forwarded by the buildings they have inhabited.

3.2. Preservation

There are established procedures in place to capture volatile evidence before it becomes unavailable, for example first responders can create memory dumps prior to a machine being shut down (Thomas, Sherly, & Dija, 2013). Evidence volatility in the IoT is much more complex; data may be stored locally by a *thing*, in which case the lifespan of the data before it is overwritten or compressed using a lossy technique is finite. The data from a *thing* may be transferred and consumed by another thing or a local ad-hoc network of *things*, alternatively it may transferred to the cloud for aggregation and processing.

The transfer and aggregation of data/evidence presents a challenge when securing the chain of evidence. In order to overcome this challenge and leverage the resilient nature of data in IoT in digital investigations, techniques are required to track and filter the transit of data across an IoT environment. Such techniques will facilitate the identification and extraction of data assumed to have been modified or deleted due to the constraints of IoT devices.

Preservation of the scene is a contentious issue in digital forensics. IoT investigations will complicate matters further due to the nature of the devices undergoing analysis. It is possible that data at a crime scene will be overwritten/compressed if the devices cannot interact with a cloud service provider to store their data, and they collect more data than they can store. This presents a problem for first responders, who must decide whether to preserve the evidence on the devices by allowing data transfer from the scene and then face the challenges of an inter-jurisdiction evidence collection process. Alternatively, they may sever the connection between the devices and the cloud and attempt local extraction of evidence from devices that may be of a proprietary nature. However, the physical placement, power availability or connectivity of each device may render this approach impractical. This also raises the question of whether – and how – a first responder or investigator should prevent devices recording information once a scene has been secured. Principle two of the ACPO guide indicates that a person may access the original data during in an investigation if they are capable of explaining the relevance and implications of doing so (7safe, 2011). Further research is required to determine what the implications are under a variety of circumstances. Ideally, a mechanism should be in place to enable an investigator to serve a "digital warrant" that prevents evidence being compromised.

We consider the interplay between the legal and technical challenges associated with gathering evidence from an IoT environment. A warrant is served during conventional investigations as the first part of the evidence preservation process. The warrant details the scope of evidence to be seized and examined. In the case of the IoT service providers, they often store data on behalf of their users. This means that individuals may not have direct access to their own data, or it may be presented to them in a different format than that in which it is stored. This complicates the preservation process, as the warrant may have to be served to individuals and their service providers.

3.3. Analysis

Analysis of data from an IoT environment will have to consider the provenance of evidence in order to demonstrate the evidence is reliable and authentic. Data provenance in the IoT differs from conventional digital forensic investigations in which the temporal dimension is often the main consideration e.g. file modified, accessed, and created time, email time lines (Inglot, Liu, & Antonopoulos, 2012).

The interaction between IoT and cloud computing facilitates the aggregation and processing of data from the IoT. The vast quantities of data generated by IoT and stored in large-scale distributed cloud environments (Osborne & Slay, 2011) is likely to be the subject of a cloud investigation. From a technical perspective the image, analyse present paradigm of current digital forensics practice (Allen, Whittaker, & Howard, 2005), (Grobler, Louwrens, & von Solms, 2010) does not map well onto the IoT domain. This is aside from the ethical issues of imaging these devices in multi-tenancy cloud environments (Naqvi, Dallons, & Ponsard, 2010), (Burd, Jones, & Seazzu, 2011). There are a number of technical barriers; IoT data is either stored on proprietary devices that are difficult to interface with or in cloud computing platforms where the scale, distribution and remote nature of the data preclude imaging as a viable extraction process. Distributed analysis techniques are required to analyse the data stored in cloud computing platforms. Some work has already been carried out in this area to tackle the challenges posed by cloud computing investigations (Hegarty, Merabti, Shi, & Askwith, 2012), (Garfinkel, 2007).

3.4. Presentation

Presenting the findings of IoT investigations poses a new challenge; data will often have undergone aggregation and processing using analytic functions that can alter the structure and meaning of data. At the device level, lossy compression techniques may reduce the granularity of the data order in to preserve limited resources such as memory, battery life, network bandwidth, etc. The granularity and semantics of evidence from the IoT will create challenges to digital forensic investigations. For example, one system may store temperature ranging from 0-5 as cold, 6-10 as average, 11-16 as warm and 16+ as hot. Another system may use different figures and describe the same temperature readings using different terminology resulting in a semantic gap. Ontological descriptors and standardisation of metadata has limited adoption, with a view to moving IoT devices towards a semantic sensor web (Sheth, Henson, & Sahoo, 2008). However, from a forensics perspective, the issue is that devices may adopt differing descriptor formats or may retain a proprietary format. Presentation poses a challenge regardless of the underlying format of the data, as the conflicting grammar describing data from IoT systems has the potential to be misleading.

4. Key Issues and Emerging Requirements

The emergence of the IoT will present new opportunities for data to be misused and lead to an expansion and development of new digital forensic techniques. We identify new approaches that may emerge out of the necessity to analyse the IoT.

4.1. Preservation Issues

Firstly we consider the preservation of evidence, forensic readiness is an area that is relatively well understood in conventional computing environments (Pangalos, Ilioudis, & Pagkalos, 2010). We agree with (Trček, Abie, Skomedal, & Starc, 2010) who state that an alternative approach is required to enable IoT forensic environments to achieve the same. As we suggested in Section 3 a digital warrant would assist in the gathering of evidence. This approach could be extended to "digital preservation orders" that prevent evidence from be contaminated or overwritten by reducing the resolution at which data is captured by devices, or freezing the data stored by service providers. The warrant would be digitally signed by the serving authority to enable the providers or devices to check the authenticity of the warrant. The providers or devices would them submit the requested information to the authority over a standard set of interfaces.

4.2. Aggregation Issues

The financial motivation behind many IoT systems is the value that comes from the data aggregated in the providers' systems. Such data sets are valuable marketing commodities. Future investigations may benefit from such data to provide or substantiate evidence about an individual or sequence of events.

However, to consider briefly an opposing standpoint; aggregated data may breach data privacy legislation, with the holders of data inferring information about individuals that breaches legislation. New techniques are required to reason over data and determine what can be inferred from large data sets, likewise techniques are required to investigate cases where "aggregation offences" are alleged to have taken place. Similarly, investigatory techniques are required to analyse cases where anonymisation techniques were inadequate, or rendered so by joint analysis of many data sets. Legal frameworks must be updated alongside the development of these techniques to ensure that the data gathered by the IoT is not misused.

While the aggregation of data provides the possibility of inferring useful information about an individual, it also introduces some challenges such as the semantic gap discussed in Section 3. One approach to tackling this challenge is the development of digital forensic tools that can bridge the semantic gap. These tools would enable calculation and comparison of the granularity of data from different sources. This approach would be particularly useful when conflicting evidence emerges from different IoT devices or service providers. It may be possible to resolve semantic conflicts and even use characteristics of the measurements taken by different systems to provide evidence that is more accurate.

5. Conclusion and Further Work

The IoT presents a large-scale source of potential evidence. However due to the heterogeneous nature of the IoT devices, the ways in which data is distributed, aggregated, and processed presents challenges to digital forensics investigations. New techniques are required to overcome these challenges and leverage the architectures and processes employed in IoT to in order to gain access to this rich source of potential evidence.

In order to realise the approaches proposed in this paper, a test bed is required for implementation, deployment, analysis and evaluation. The Contiki open source OS for the IoT ("Contiki OS," 2013) will be used to a test bed. To enable the deployment of techniques on a variety of different devices and network topologies. Experiments will be conducted to evaluate the resource overhead of issuing the digital warranty and preservation orders proposed in this paper. To analyse the trade-off between resource utilisation and evidence gathering, and compare the impact of a variety of certification techniques, that could employed to authenticate the warrants/preservation orders. The test bed will also enable experiments on evidence extraction and the development of standard interfaces for evidence extraction from current and future IoT systems

The development of guidance for investigators on how to carry out investigations in the IoT will be a major output from the development of the test bed. Experimental investigations will enable the identification of considerations that investigators must take into account when investigating the IoT. Along with the development of metrics to determine whether it is better to shutdown devices or leave them running in situ.

Our analysis of IoT forensics has prompted us to consider how we view and deal with data and devices in the broader digital forensics field. Is data a by-product of human-device or device-device interaction, or should the devices be considered as attributes of the data? What are the implications of these two viewpoints for the wider field?

6. References

Allen, W. H., Whittaker, E. J. A., & Howard, M. (2005). Computer forensics. *Security & Privacy Magazine, IEEE, 3*(4), 59–62. doi:10.1108/09565690610677463

Attwood, A., Merabti, M., & Abuelmaatti, O. (2011). IoMANETs: Mobility architecture for wireless M2M networks. In *2011 IEEE GLOBECOM Workshops (GC Wkshps)* (pp. 399–404). IEEE. doi:10.1109/GLOCOMW.2011.6162479

Burd, S. D., Jones, D. E., & Seazzu, a F. (2011). Bridging Differences in Digital Forensics for Law Enforcement and National Security. In *2011 44th Hawaii International Conference on System Sciences* (pp. 1–6). Manoa: Ieee. doi:10.1109/HICSS.2011.87

Chirgwin, R. (2014). SPAM supposedly spotted leaving the fridge. *The Register*. Retrieved from http://www.theregister.co.uk/2014/01/20/spam_spotted_leaving_the_fridge/

Contiki OS. (2013).

Garfinkel, S. S. (2007). Commodity grid computing with Amazon's S3 and EC2. *Usenix*, 7–13.

GM Casualty Reduction Partnership. (2014). Mobile Phones | Greater Manchester Casualty Reduction Partnership.

Grobler, C. P., Louwrens, C. P., & von Solms, S. H. (2010). A Multi-component View of Digital Forensics. In *2010 International Conference on Availability, Reliability and Security* (pp. 647–652). IEEE. doi:10.1109/ARES.2010.61

Haines, L. (2007). Cops may check crash drivers' mobile records • The Register. *The Register*. Retrieved from http://www.theregister.co.uk/2007/02/27/mobile_phone_proposal/

Hegarty, R., Merabti, M., Shi, Q., & Askwith, R. (2012). Scalable Distributed Signature Detection. In *Proceedings of the 7th International Workshop on Digital Forensics & Incident Analysis* (pp. 27 – 37). Heraklion, Greece.

Kent, A. K., Chevalier, S., Grance, T., Dang, H., & Kent, K. (2006). Guide to integrating forensic techniques into incident response. *NIST Special Publication*, (August).

McKemmish, R. (1999). What is forensic computing. *Trends and Issues in Crime and Criminal Justice*, (118).

Miorandi, D., Sicari, S., De Pellegrini, F., & Chlamtac, I. (2012). Internet of things: Vision, applications and research challenges. *Ad Hoc Networks*, *10*(7), 1497–1516. doi:10.1016/j.adhoc.2012.02.016

Naqvi, S., Dallons, G., & Ponsard, C. (2010). Applying Digital Forensics in the Future Internet Enterprise Systems - European SME's Perspective. In *2010 Fifth IEEE International Workshop on Systematic Approaches to Digital Forensic Engineering* (pp. 89–93). IEEE. doi:10.1109/SADFE.2010.28

National BIM Standards. (2013). Retrieved from http://www.nationalbimstandard.org/faq.php#faq1

Oriwoh, E., Jazani, D., Epiphaniou, G., & Sant, P. (2013). Internet of Things Forensics: Challenges and Approaches. *Proceedings of the 9th IEEE International Conference on Collaborative Computing: Networking, Applications and Worksharing*. doi:10.4108/icst.collaboratecom.2013.254159

Osborne, G., & Slay, J. (2011). Digital Forensics Infovis: An Implementation of a Process for Visualisation of Digital Evidence. *2011 Sixth International Conference on Availability, Reliability and Security*, 196–201. doi:10.1109/ARES.2011.36

Pangalos, G., Ilioudis, C., & Pagkalos, I. (2010). The Importance of Corporate Forensic Readiness in the Information Security Framework. In *2010 19th IEEE International Workshops on Enabling Technologies: Infrastructures for Collaborative Enterprises* (pp. 12–16). IEEE. doi:10.1109/WETICE.2010.57

Sheth, A., Henson, C., & Sahoo, S. S. (2008). Semantic Sensor Web. *IEEE Internet Computing, 12*(4), 78–83. doi:10.1109/MIC.2008.87

Taylor, M., Haggerty, J., Gresty, D., & Hegarty, R. (2010). Digital evidence in cloud computing systems. *Elsevier Computer Law & Security Review, 26*(3), 304–308. doi:10.1016/j.clsr.2010.03.002

Thomas, S., Sherly, K. K., & Dija, S. (2013). Extraction of memory forensic artifacts from windows 7 RAM image. In *2013 IEEE CONFERENCE ON INFORMATION AND COMMUNICATION TECHNOLOGIES* (pp. 937–942). IEEE. doi:10.1109/CICT.2013.6558230

Trček, D., Abie, H., Skomedal, A., & Starc, I. (2010). Advanced framework for digital forensic technologies and procedures. *Journal of Forensic Sciences, 55*(6), 1471–80. doi:10.1111/j.1556-4029.2010.01528.x

Zelkha, E., Epstein, B., Birrell, S., & Dodswoth, C. (1998). From Devices to "Ambient Intelligence." In *Digital Living Room Conference.*

Towards a Model for Acquiring Digital Evidence using Mobile Devices

S.Omeleze[1] and H.S.Venter[2]

[1,2]Information and Computer Security Architecture (ICSA) Research Group
Department of Computer Science, Information Technology Building
University of Pretoria, Private Bag X20 Hatfield 0002 Pretoria, South Africa
e-mail: staceyaomeleze@gmail.com; hventer@cs.up.ac.za

Abstract

In recent years, many criminal activities have gone unsolved due to lack of sufficient evidence to convict the perpetrators. However, with the evolution in mobile technology, mobile devices can now be used to provide such evidence. The advanced features of mobile devices such as photo, video and voice recording options have the ability to transform such devices into real-time potential digital forensic evidence-capturing devices. This paper therefore proposes a model that enables the use of mobile and portable devices to capture potential digital evidence and preserve the integrity of such evidence. This model therefore, takes into consideration the privacy policies, laws and ethics that may apply due to the devices' generated metadata, especially during a digital evidence presentation in a court of law or in civil proceedings.

Keywords

Digital evidence, SHA-2, Cryptographic Hash Function, privacy, Online Neighbourhood Watch (ONW) Model, Mobile devices, Crime and Law.

1. Introduction

In 2012, a survey conducted by Tsirulnik (2012) placed mobile devices as one of the most purchased items of electronic equipment in the world. This is attributed to the popularity of mobile applications (popularly known as apps) that are available for almost all activities, from health monitoring, news update alerts to real-time online gaming. The influence of digital forensic technology on crime management, especially with the exploding trend of mobile technology in society, can be explored in very beneficial ways. Over the years, many criminal activities have gone unsolved due to the lack of sufficient evidence to convict the perpetrators. The advanced functionality of mobile devices and portable devices can be used as a tool in the fight against crime. Cameras, voice recording and image capturing functions can become real-time digital evidence-capturing options for potential digital forensic evidence acquisition.

This paper attempts to aid the fight against crime by creating an online neighbourhood watch (ONW) model to acquire potential digital evidence using mobile and portable devices in South African neighbourhoods. The ONW model generates and stores potential digital evidence of criminal acts, which is then available to law enforcement agents and digital forensic investigators. The goal of the ONW model is to increase the volume of available digital evidence in order to enhance success in trials and to help secure conviction of the actual culprits. The ONW model can be applied in scenarios such as road traffic offences, domestic violence, robberies and other incidents that require concrete evidence as proof in a court of law or in a civil proceeding. For the purpose of admissibility of potential evidence acquired using the ONW model, digital data integrity checks are employed using the SHA-2 cryptographic hash function, digital watermarking, time stamps, geo location and digital signatures. According to Saleem et al. (2011), these are the appropriate methods to use when the integrity of data is paramount.

It is important to note that this work is part of an ongoing project to develop a tool/application that enables the integrity validation of potential evidence acquired using mobile /portable devices, to be used for further investigative analysis of a case. This potential evidence can be used to obtain a court warrant, or could be employed as potential evidence in a trial-within-a-trial, or gauge evidential weight for admissibility in civil or criminal proceedings.

This paper is structured as follows: Section 2 contains an introduction to the background on digital forensics, digital evidence and the legal issues involved. Section 3 presents the online neighbourhood watch (ONW) model with a detailed discussion of the use cases and how the integrity of acquired evidence is upheld. Section 4 evaluates and critiques the ONW model, while section 5 discusses the related research works. Finally section 6 concludes this paper with recommendations for future work.

2. Background

This background section is devoted to the discussion of a review of digital forensic science, digital evidence from a legal perspective, and its application to this research.

2.1. Digital Forensic Science

Digital forensics is a young science drawn from the traditional science of forensics that has been developed in conjunction with the biological sciences. Digital forensics is used in the identification of digital evidence by employing mathematically derived methods in proving consistency of bits in a digital forensic investigative scenario (Bunge, 1998);(Valjarevic & Venter, 2011); (Karie & Venter, 2013). Digital forensic field requires exploring, especially with the rapid developmental growth in technological advancement, the generation of big data and connectivity of the Internet of things. In defining digital forensics, Cohen (2009) considers digital forensics as a subject that started between art and craft, and contains a scientific body of knowledge with an underlying scientific methodology, which consists of four basic elements. These elements are the study of previous and current theories, methods and experimental bases, the identification of inconsistencies between current theories and experimental repeatability. Digital forensics could be viewed in terms of Bunge's (Bunge, 1998) classification of scientific problems, namely that digital forensics is a young science at its conceptual level of scientific development. Therefore, in digital forensics, the use of scientifically derived and proven mathematical methods is adhered to in the acquisition, preservation, collection, validation, identification, analysis, interpretation and documentation of digital evidence (Barske et al., 2010);(Cohen, 2009). In the verification of the integrity of digital evidence, numerous mathematical techniques are employed such as, the cryptographic hash function, the time stamp, bit stream, digital signature, chain of evidence, the chain of custody and geo-location (Dang, 2012); (Hargreaves, 2009). Since digital evidence consists entirely of sequences of bit binary values, it provides a means to aid the preclusion of criminal-related offences involving data messages.

2.2. Legal perspective

In dealing with digital evidence acquired using the ONW model, there is a need to explore the aspect of legal standards and what is acceptable in terms of privacy and human rights in South Africa.

In the Privacy of Personal Information (PPI) Act, Act 4 of 2013, Section 6 (c) (i) and (ii) and Section 37 (2) (a) and (b), the exclusions and exemptions to an individual's privacy rights are outlined. These exemptions apply when the interests of national security are at stake and when they involve the prevention, detection and prosecution of criminal behavior (Mujinga, 2013). Furthermore, the Electronic Communication and Transaction (ECT) Act, Act 25 of 2002, section 15(1), (2) and (3) defines the digital data that is admissible, the evidential weight of data information and the best evidence rule to be allowed in the usage of digital evidence in a South African court of law (Gazette, 2002). The ECT Act also states that data evidence must not be dismissed merely because it originates from a digital data message.

2.3. Integrity of digital evidence

One of the major roles of digital investigators is to ensure and provide proof that digital evidence has not only been acquired, retrieved and stored in a forensically sound process, but can also stand up to scrutiny in a court of law. The integrity of digital evidence is proven to render acquired digital evidence admissible. The integrity of digital evidence is elaborated on in section 14(1) (a) of the ECT Act, Act 25 of 2002 which states that digital data must maintain its integrity from the time of data generation to when it is analysed (Gazette, 2002).

The way that integrity is employed in the ONW model includes the use of cryptographic hash algorithms, digital watermarking, digital signatures and public key infrastructure (PKI) cryptography. These concepts are elaborated on in the next paragraphs.

A cryptographic hash function is used to prove the integrity of a message. The cryptographic hash function generates a hash value that can be used to put a seal on a message. It can be implemented using a hashed message authentication code (HMAC), secure hash algorithm (SHA) that generates 160-bit hash value and a SHA-2 that generates a unique 256-bit (32-byte) signature for every piece of digital data (evidence) received (Dang, 2012); (Pfleeger & Pfleeger, 2006). Furthermore, a digital signature is used to demonstrate the non-repudiation, authenticity and the integrity of a message.

Digital watermarking is a method that applies tamper detection, traitor tracing and integrity maintenance of digital data. This is achieved by using steganography techniques (i.e. information hiding) to embed unique data in a noisy signal to identify when an alteration occurs on the data file (Halder & Cortesi, 2010).

A PKI cryptography system utilizes a key pair to encrypt and decrypt data respectively. PKI is used in conjunction with hash values, i.e. by encrypting the hash value of a message in order to add a unique 'stamp', so that only the intended recipient of the message can decrypt the message with a public key, proving non-repudiation.

A Password management policy is a recommendation of the ISO/IEC 27002 (Calder & Watkins, 2008) (ISO27001, 2012) with a guideline for managing the security of a system effectively. According to ISO/IEC 27002, password selection must meet certain requirements such as, minimum length and strength of a password, maintenance of previous password records to avoid repeatability and the storage of user's password must be encrypted using a one-way algorithm. This is in order to achieve and ensure confidentiality and integrity of a system.

3. Online Neighbourhood Watch Model (ONW)

This section proposes a contribution of how potential digital evidence can be acquired using mobile devices through the ONW model.

The (ONW) model is an application model accessible via mobile devices or computers over the Internet. It enables users to upload digital evidence such as audio, video and digital photographs of a potential crime scene or incident to the ONW repository. It also allows an investigator to access the uploaded evidence whenever it is required, especially during criminal investigations.

Figure 1 illustrates the high-level view of the two main aspects of the ONW model. Part A is concerned with the activities of the user (uploader) and maintaining the digital evidence integrity which is achieved using the SHA-2 hash algorithm, digital signature, timestamp and geographical location of the user (uploader). Part B depicts the role of the Forensic Investigator/Law Enforcement Agent (the downloader) and the measures employed in maintaining the integrity of the potential evidence and the access control of the ONW repository. The repository employs sound access control measures, such as the role and attribute based access control policies, to manage the users' uploads to the repository. These policies include the concept of need to know so that the number of law enforcement agents accessing any particular piece of evidence is strictly limited and monitored. This paper, however, focuses on Part A of Figure 1 while Part B will be dealt with in further work.

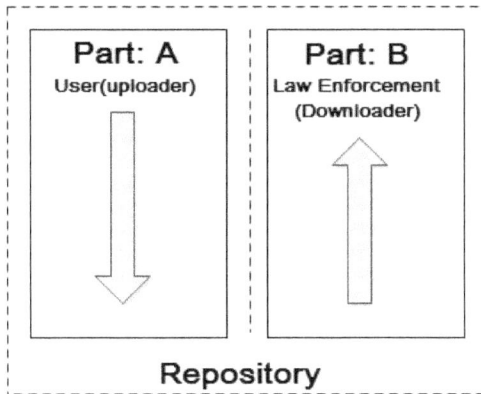

Figure 1: View of the ONW Model indicating Parts A and B

The (ONW) model as shown in Figure 2 consists of a process involving seven steps. The users' (i.e. uploader and downloader) operations in the ONW model are permitted based on their roles and access rights. The user (uploader) is enabled to upload potential data evidence into the repository, while the law enforcement agent or digital forensic examiner (downloader) is entitled to download and view the potential digital evidence stored in the repository during criminal or digital forensic investigations. The interactive processes of the ONW model are described in the following paragraphs and are based on the diagram in Figure 2.

3.1. ONW application

The ONW model application being developed is to accept potential digital evidence via a mobile application or web application. This application ensures the integrity of the potential evidence through the use of the geo-location, timestamp and the SHA 2 algorithm, which is embedded in the system. The potential captured evidence is then uploaded to the ONW repository following the processes shown in Figure 2. This can be done directly from the user's (uploader) mobile device or using a computer system where the ONW application installed.

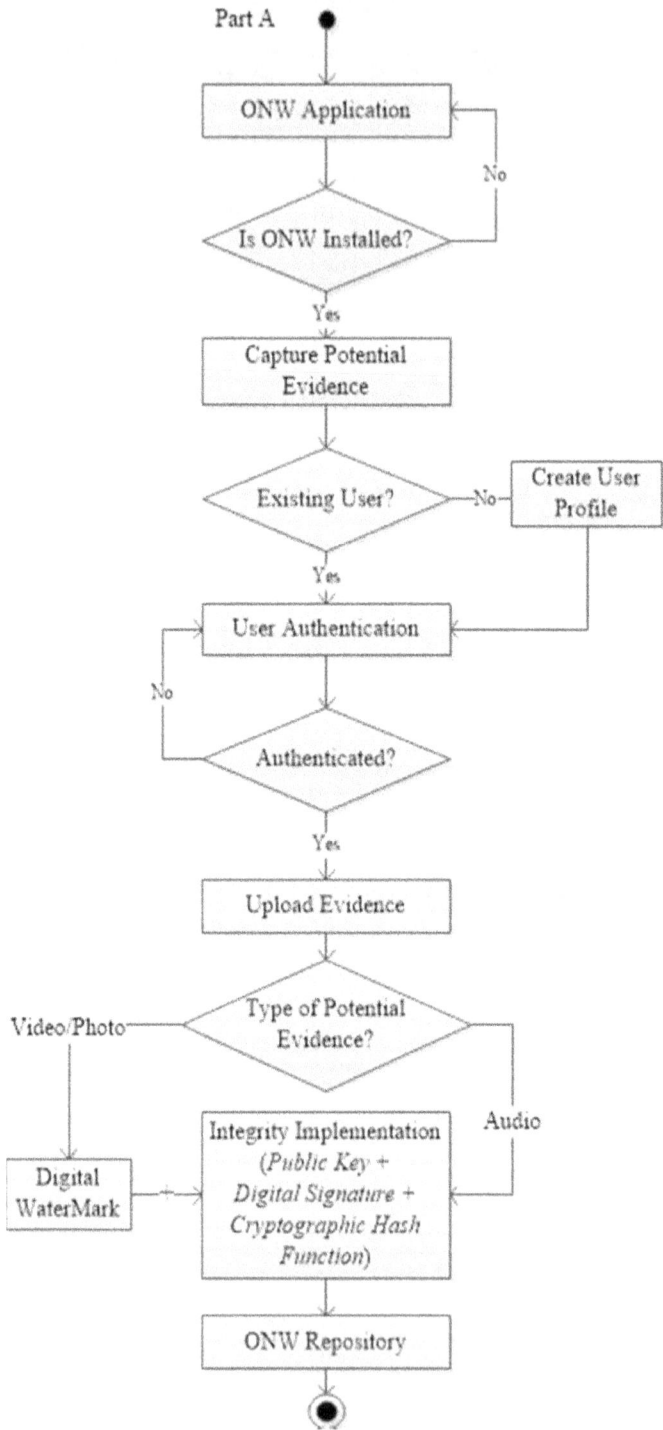

Figure 2: Flow Diagram of the ONW Model

3.2. Capture potential evidence

Potential evidence is obtained when the user notices an incident that could be viewed as a crime. The user may capture evidence in the form of a digital photo, video, or an audio recording of the criminal activity. The potential evidence must be captured in the domain of ONW in order to maintain and preserve the integrity of the potential digital evidence. This is to assure the applicability of the potential evidence in solving the cases and ensuring the admissibility of the evidence in a court of law. Digital evidence captured outside the ONW application domain is rejected when an upload is attempted.

3.3. Create a user profile

This step enables the user to create a profile for authenticating into the system and to allow for upload of the acquired potential evidence. An existing user need not create a profile on subsequent use of the system. However, a new user must create a profile to allow interaction between the user and the ONW model. On the creation of this profile, the user is authenticated to log in. User profile creation is compulsory to allow access to the ONW system.

3.4. User authentication

User authentication is to ensure that the user is who he/she claims to be. The registering of the device in the system and the gathering of the audit trail commence at this stage of the user's interaction with the system. An existing user has to login when evidence is captured, but a first-time user must create a user profile, as discussed in step 3 above, in order to gain access to the system. Authentication at this stage of the model design involves the use of a username and password retaining the password requirement policy of the ISO/IEC 27002 (ISO27001, 2012) (Calder & Watkins, 2008). Subsequently, however, other forms of authentication such as biometric and the implementation of authorization, i.e access control is employed. This authentication aspect of the model also helps in the system's audit trails, in terms of who does what in the system.

3.5. Uploading evidence

Once potential digital evidence of a crime is acquired, it is then uploaded to the ONW repository (as shown in Figure 2). The uploaded potential evidence is secured using encryption and access control mechanisms embedded in the system. The acquisition of this evidence must be done in the domain of the ONW application. This is to enable the inbuilt integrity checks in the application domain. The cryptographic hash algorithm seals the digital evidence in order to avoid/detect digital evidence alteration. The timestamp helps in determining the time that potential evidence was acquired and the geo-location shows where the potential evidence was acquired using cellular tower triangulation. The uploading of evidence is only possible if the user has created his/her profile and is logged into the system via the mobile or web application.

3.6. Integrity implementing

The ONW model implements and maintains the integrity of the acquired evidence by using mathematical techniques and an approved algorithm. These measures are employed to preserve the authenticity and integrity of evidence uploaded to the ONW repository, in order to corroborate the occurrence of a certain incident and further the admissibility of the potential digital evidence in a court of law (Gazette, 2002). Therefore to achieve the integrity of the acquired potential evidence the cryptographic hash function, digital signature, public key infrastructure (PKI) cryptography, time stamp and geographical location tag are employed. In this model, the hypothesis is based on the assumption that users can acquire three data formats, i.e. audio, video and digital photos, that can be used as potential digital evidence as shown in Figure 2.

In order to ensure the integrity of the potential evidence in the ONW model, a digital seal is placed on the digital evidence. The seal is a "tamper proof" feature placed on the acquired potential digital evidence that generates cryptographic hash values that can be compared during potential digital evidence download, to determine whether an alteration has been made to the digital evidence. For example, two digital images can be assured to be identical only if the hash values generated from each digital data item, using the same cryptographic hash function, are identical. When an alteration is detected, the message is discarded. In using a digital signature to ensure the integrity and authenticity of potential digital evidence, the use of a public/private key encryption system is employed to ascertain that data transmission between the mobile/portable device and the ONW repository is trusted and secure. For example, the integrity of potential video data evidence is achieved by using a digital signature within the cryptographic hash function and by encrypting the resulting cryptographic hash value with a private key (as shown in figure 2). The integrity of potential digital evidence obtained through digital photo image or video is achieved using a combination of methods. These methods include the cryptographic hash function, digital signature and PKI cryptography in conjunction with watermarking.

3.7. Storing evidence in the repository

The ONW repository stores the acquired potential digital evidence to be accessed by the user in part B of the ONW model (i.e. the investigator/law enforcement agent). In Part B of the ONW model (figure 1), digital forensic investigators and law enforcement agents will access the required potential digital evidence from the ONW repository. The data is then downloaded with the stored cryptographic hash value and digital signature with the matching half of the encrypted PKI. A re-computation of these functions is performed to verify potential digital evidence consistency and integrity.

Furthermore, a strict implementation of the chain of custody is adhered to so as to determine who accessed what, at what time and on what date. This process is followed in order to retain integrity and confidentiality of the acquired potential digital evidence and the ONW system. The law enforcement agent's access to the ONW model is based on role-based access control (RBAC) policies. Further discussion on RBAC is beyond the scope of this paper, as it will be covered in the

Part B of the model in future work.

4.   Appraisal of the ONW Model

The application of mobile devices as a means of generating potential digital evidence in a bid to minimize crime in a South African context is not without its difficulties. One of these difficulties may be the need to protect the privacy of individuals as outlined in the Privacy of Personal Information (PPI) Act, Act 4 of 2013 (Mujinga, 2013). However, in Section 6 (c) (i) and (ii) and particularly in Section 37 (2) (a) and (b) of this Act, there are numerous exclusions and exemptions to an individual's privacy rights when the interests of national security are at stake and when the prevention, detection and prosecution of criminal offences are involved.

The concept of the ONW model may be seen as infringing with law and ethics. However, in his analysis of the ECT Act 25 of 2002, Watney (2009) states that the Act sets out to facilitate digital data (evidence) generation and admissibility rather than inhibit it. With the ONW model in place, it becomes much easier to apprehend suspects involved in various nefarious activities in the community, thereby reducing crime and anti-social behaviour.

The digital evidence available in the repository of the ONW system can serve as the incident scene detection phase of an investigation. According to Valjarevic & Venter (2011) and Omeleze & Venter (2013), an incident scene conveys messages of what happened and how best to approach the investigation for both the law enforcement agents and the digital forensic investigators. The ONW evidence repository can also be employed during evidence front-loading (trial-within-a-trial) by the legal teams during pre-trial.   A trial-within-a-trial as stated in the Criminal Procedure Act, Act 51 of 1977, is an avenue which enables two legal teams in a trial to share the available potential evidence with the trial Judge, who then determines what is admissible based on the case and the digital evidence available, especially in criminal proceedings (Bellengere et al., 2013). Furthermore, section 15(1) (2) (3) of the ECT Act emphasized the need to explore electronic evidence and its admissibility based on the generation, handling, collection and integrity of evidence (Gazette, 2002); (Mujinga, 2013); (Papadopoulos & Snail, 2012); (Watney, 2009).   The possibility of creating the ONW system is based on the assumption that the majority of mobile phones/devices available are devices with features that can acquire video, audio and photo evidence at the scene of a crime.

Since the ONW model has no provision for a function that determines what a potential crime is or when a user (uploader) can commence potential evidence acquisition, the community member (user) must use his/her intuition and common sense to decide when/what is a potential crime.   For instance, in Gedanken experiments, human senses/thoughts tend to play a great role in determining the current state of its environment (Kuhn, 1977). That is, the observation of the behaviour of a subject triggers responses to stimuli. These responses to environmental stimuli could help the community members in their decision as to what constitutes potential evidence. It is left to the law enforcement agents and judiciary to decide what is actual evidence and whether a crime has been committed.

As a result, throughout this paper, the term potential digital evidence is used rather than digital evidence.

In the ONW model, the user authentication is implemented by means of a user name and password. However, the password must meet the password standard requirement policies (i.e. the user must use at least a upper case character, lower case characters, numbers and a special character) (ISO27001, 2012). With the ONW model's integrity and authenticity implemented, the South African legal system benefits. This is by making the best use of the increasingly dynamic and diverse forms of potential digital evidence acquisition, especially those acquired using mobile and portable devices for proof and fact-findings in legal and civil proceedings (Roberts & Redmayne, 2007).

With the incorporated integrity features of the ONW model, digital forensic investigators and law enforcement agencies are able to employ the ONW repository during digital investigations. This will yield faster results in identifying the culprits by establishing what happened during investigations (Karie &Venter, 2013). The success of the ONW model will not only reduce crime but also foster a better and closer cooperation between the ordinary person on the street and the government.

Furthermore, the philosophy of Ubuntu in South Africa that is, a community-based mind set where the welfare of the group is greater than that of an individual can be brought to service (Olinger et al., 2007). Moreover, with the provisions of the ECT Act, Act 25 of 2002 (an extension of the United Nations' Model Law), the international standards such as ISO/IEC 27043 and the cooperation of the South African judiciary, the ONW model can be extended to other countries and ultimately become a global crime-fighting tool. For example, in the development of ISO/IEC 27043 proposed by Valjarevic & Venter, (2011); (ISO27001, 2014) the International Criminal Police Organization (INTERPOL) is one of the main contributors in promoting a standard for digital forensic investigation that is identical in it's member countries and the world in general, thereby paving the way for the ISO/IEC 27043 model to become an international one (Valjarevic & Venter, 2012). The ONW model can similarly become a model adoptable for the acquisition of potential digital evidence using mobile devices worldwide, once this South African pilot project has been attested to work effectively in achieving faster prosecution and reduction of crime levels.

5. Related Work

This section discusses relevant research works that are related to the integrity of digital evidence and its admissibility in a court of law. Much research on evidence integrity has been conducted. However, none has focused on a model to capture potential digital evidence using mobile devices. Furthermore, the existing work focuses only on digital evidence statically stored and its integrity, as opposed to the ONW model, which focuses on capturing potential digital evidence in a dynamic and real-time fashion.

Richter et al (2010) mentions that using digital signatures and non-repudiation are not enough to ensure digital evidence integrity. They presented an embedded system that is able to collect admissible digital evidence through an automated process focusing on the non-repudiation of the digital evidence data by designing a secure environment and adding all relevant parameters to the measured data such as the location, identity of the device, timestamp, and the current status of the system.

Halder et al (2010) identified the challenges of using watermarking as a method for copyright identity protection, tamper detection and maintaining integrity due to issues such as usability, robustness, and interference. The ONW model employs digital watermarking as an added feature to digital signature, public key infrastructure (PKI) cryptography and cryptographic hash function to ensure the implementation of integrity. This is to support and manage the flaws that may otherwise occur when digital watermarking is solely used.

Furthermore, Ani et al (2013) analysed the threats to the integrity of digital evidence using the VMware hypervisors to strengthen the hash function and incorporate reliability rating factors, as a means of conceptualizing integrity levels of digital data. They further enumerated appropriate algorithms for the implementation of digital evidence integrity to include secured hash algorithm (SHAx), digital signature, PKI cryptography and message digest algorithm (MD5).

Casey (2011) listed five properties that digital evidence must retain in order to be admissible in any proceedings. These are authenticity, completeness, reliability, and believability and also, that potential digital evidence must be tied to an incident in order to prove that an incident occurred and is related to the incident in a relevant way. The ONW model satisfies these properties and requirements by implementing timestamp, geo-location and secure hash algorithm (SHA-2) of the acquired potential digital evidence at the point of upload to the ONW repository.

Watney (2009), Papadopoulos & Snail (2012) enumerated the Common Law requirements for digital evidence admissibility to include; production, meaning the digital evidence must be relevant; presentation, that is, the digital evidence must be in its original form and finally, the authenticity of the digital evidence must be provable.

In another research, Papadopoulos & Snail (2012) detailed a set of guidelines required by a South African court in the application and assessment of evidential weight. These are, the reliability of the manner by which the potential digital evidence was generated, stored, or communicated and also the manner in which the integrity of the potential digital evidence is maintained plus its originality. The ONW model also fulfils these requirements.

6. Conclusion

The ONW model concept is a project that involves a public drive to use mobile/portable device technology for the enforcement of neighbourhood security. This is achieved by developing a model that enables the uploading of potential digital evidence to the ONW repository. This will engage both the community members and the law enforcement agencies in crime reduction in South African neighbourhoods. It will assist not only the law enforcement agencies but also the digital forensic experts and the judiciary to conduct conclusive and decisive case investigations.

The ONW model demonstrates a means to acquire potential digital evidence and at the same time maintain the integrity of the various potential evidence formats acquired. The integrity of a photo image and video recording is upheld by using a private key, digital signature, cryptographic hash function and an additional option of digital watermarking. In order to further protect the integrity and confidentiality of the acquired potential digital evidence from unauthorized access, a password policy is used.

For future work, the authors will develop part B of the ONW model as depicted in Figure 1. Part B manages the access to the acquired potential digital evidence in the repository taking into account the privacy rights of the evidence generators considering the Privacy of Personal Information (PPI) Act, while at the same time making the evidence available to the intended stakeholders during criminal, civil and disciplinary proceedings. With the development and implementation of the ONW model as a fully-fledged system, the fight against crime in South Africa will be given a significant boost.

7. References

Ani, U. P. D., Epiphaniou, G., and French, T (2013). *A Novel Evidence Integrity Preservation Framework (EIPF) for Virtualized Environments: A Digital Forensic Approach*. In the Second International Conference on Cyber Security, Cyber Peace fare and Digital Forensic (CyberSec2013) (pp. 97-106). The Society of Digital Information and Wireless Communication.

Barske, D., Stander, A., and Jordan, J. (2010) A *Digital Forensic Readiness framework for South African SMEs*. In Information Security for South Africa (ISSA), 2010, pages 1–6. IEEE. ISBN: 9781424454938.

Bellengere, A., Palmer, R., Theophilopoulos, C., Whitcher, B., Roberts, L., and et al, (2013). *The Law of evidence in South African - Basic Principles-Procedural Law*. Oxford University Press, Southern Africa.

Bunge, M. (1998). *Philosophy of Science: From Problem to Theory*. Transaction Publishers, New Brunswick, revised edition ISBN: 9780765804136 (Vol. 1).

Casey, E. (2011). *Digital evidence and computer crime: forensic science, computers and the Internet*. Academic press.

Calder, A., & Watkins, S. (2008*). IT Governance A Manager's Guide to Data Security and ISO27001/ISO 27002* British Library Cataloguing-in-Publication. 4th edition. ISBN 978 0 7494 52711.
Cohen, F. A. (2009). *Digital Forensic Evidence Examination*, Fred Cohen and Associates out of Livermore, third edition. ISBN: 9781878109446.

Dang, Q (2012). *Recommendation for Applications using approved Hash Algorithms*. Computer Security Division Information Technology Laboratory. Accessed 19 November 2013.

Government Gazette (2002)*Electronic Communications and Transaction Act, Act 25 of 2002*. South Africa Government Printer. Accessed 02 February 2014.

Hargreaves, C. J. (2009). *Assessing the Reliability of Digital Evidence from Live Investigations involving Encryption*. Ph.D thesis, Department of Informatics and Sensors, Cranfield University,UK. Accessed 15 December 2013.

Halder, R., Pal, S., and Cortesi, A. (2010). *Watermarking Techniques for Relational Databases: Survey, Classification and Comparison. J. UCS, 16*(21), 3164-3190.

ISO27001security.com (2014). *ISO/IEC 27043 Information Technology Security Techniques for Incident Investigation Principles and Processes* (DRAFT). Accessed 02 February 2014

ISO27001security.com (2012). *ISO/IEC 27001 Information Technology Security Techniques for Incident Investigation Principles and Processes* . Accessed 18 May 2014.

Karie, N.M. and Venter, Hein. S (2013).*Towards a Framework for enhancing Potential Digital Evidence Presentation*. In: Information Security for South Africa, 2013, pages 1–8. IEEE.

Kuhn, T. (1977). *A function for thought experiments*.

Mujinga, M. (2013).   *Privacy and Legal Issues in Cloud Computing-the SMME position in South Africa*. SRI Security Research Institute, Edith Cowan University, Perth, Western Australia - Accessed 17 March 2014.

Omeleze, S. and Venter, H. S. (2013). *Testing the Harmonised Digital Investigation Process Model using an Android Mobile Phone*. In Information Security for South Africa, 2013, pages 1–8. IEEE.

Olinger, H. N., Britz, J. J., and Olivier, M. S. (2007). *Western privacy and/or Ubuntu? Some critical comments on the influences in the forthcoming data privacy bill in South Africa*. The International Information & Library Review, 39(1): 31–43.

Papadopoulos, S. and Snail, S. (2012). *Cyberlaw @South Africa III - The law of the Internet in South Africa*. Van Schaik Publishers, third edition. ISBN-10 (13): 9780627028076.

Pfleeger, P. C. andPfleeger, S. L. (2006). *Security in Computing*.Prentice Hall Publication, Upper Saddle Rivers, NJ, Boston, USA ISBN, fourth edition. ISBN-13: 978-0132390774 ISBN-100132390779

Richter, J., Kuntze, N., and Rudolph, C. (2010, May). *Security digital evidence*.In Systematic Approaches to Digital Forensic Engineering (SADFE), 2010 Fifth IEEE International Workshop on (pp. 119-130). IEEE.
Roberts, P., and Redmayne, M. (2007). *Innovations in evidence and proof: integrating theory, research and teaching*.

Saleem, S., Popov, O., and Dahman, R. (2011). *Evaluation of security methods for ensuring the integrity of digital evidence*. Institute of Electrical and Electronics Engineers (IEEE Xplore Digital Library).

Tsirulnik, B. G. (2012). *Mobile Phone ranked most used electronic device*: Forrester. Information Security.

Valjarevic, A. and Venter, Hein. S. (2011). *Towards a digital Forensic Readiness framework for Public Key Infrastructure Systems.* In Information Security for South Africa (ISSA), 2011, pages 1–10. IEEE.

Valjarevic, A and Venter, Hein S (2012) *Harmonized Digital Forensic Investigation Process Model.* Information Security For South Africa (ISSA), IEEE, 2012.

Watney, M. (2009) *Admissibility of Electronic Evidence in Criminal Proceedings: An outline of the South African Legal position.* 2009 (1). Journal of Information, Law & Technology (JILT), 2.

Author Index

www.ingramcontent.com/pod-product-compliance
Lightning Source LLC
Chambersburg PA
CBHW031933190326
41519CB00007B/507